THE EVERYTHING TAROT BOOK

Discover your past, present, and future:
It's in the cards!

M.J. Abadie

Adams Media Corporation
Holbrook, Massachusetts

Acknowledgments

Mary Orser and Richard Zarro kindly gave permission for the use of the Sun, Moon, and Mercury Attunements, from their book *Changing Your Destiny*.

An Everything Series Book.
The Everything Series is a trademark of Adams Media Corporation.

Published by Adams Media Corporation
260 Center Street, Holbrook, MA 02343

ISBN: 1-58062-191-0
Printed in the United States of America.

J I H G F E D C B A

Library of Congress Cataloging-in-Publication Data
Abadie, M.J.
The everything tarot book / by M.J. Abadie.
p. cm.
ISBN 1-58062-191-0
1. Tarot. II. Title.
BF1879.T2A27 1999
133.3'2424—dc21 99-40913
CIP

All other interior illustrations by Kathie Kelleher.

To Tarot Master Chris Santini of Tucson, Arizona
who shares his gift by reading and teaching in
honor of a deep lasting friendship.

Contents

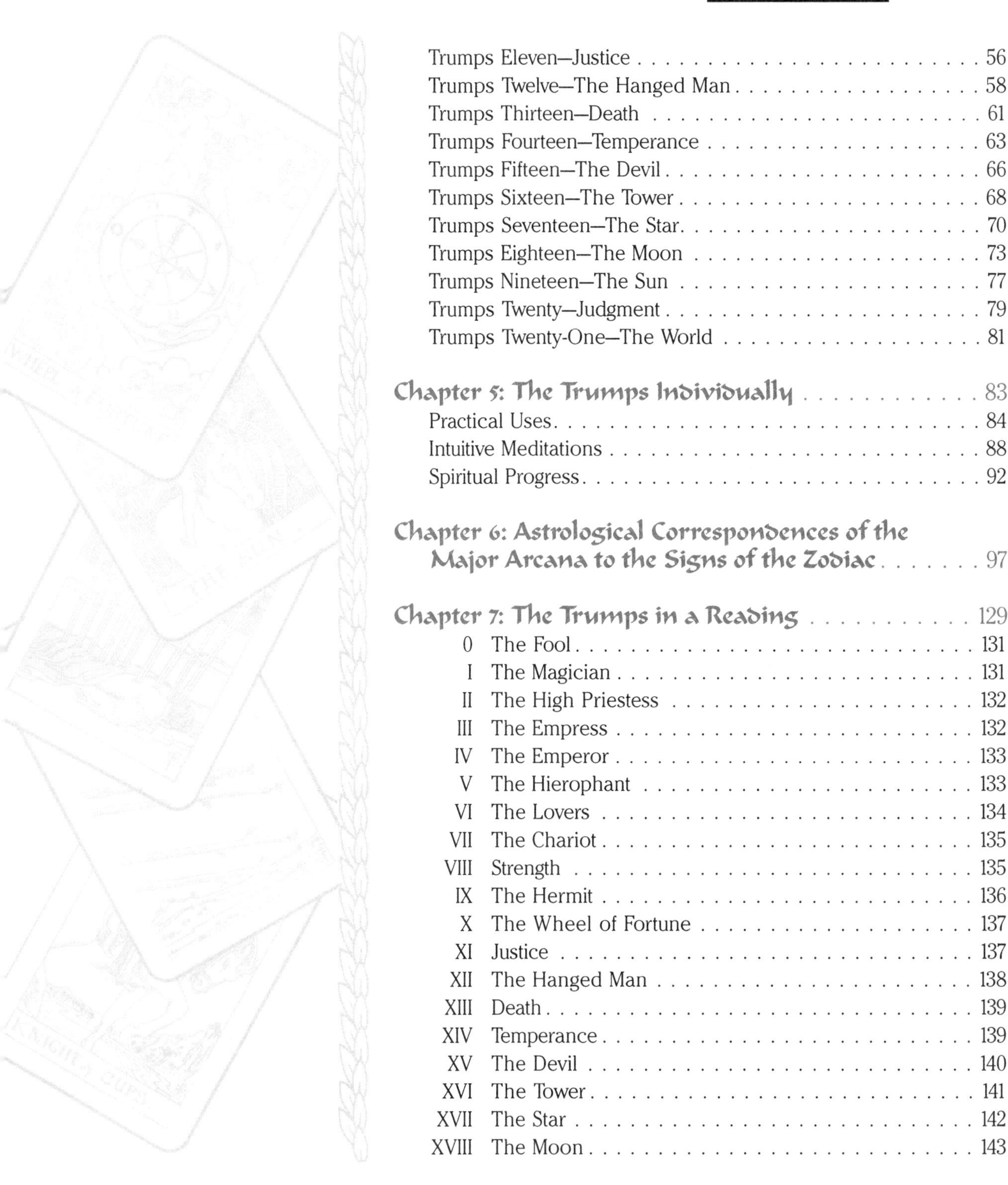

Part III:
The Minor Arcana: Symbolic Interpretation

Part IV: How to Do Readings

Introduction

The History and Mystery of Tarot

The Tarot has experienced a resurgence in the past two decades and has become especially popular recently, with newly minted modern Tarot decks coming out frequently. There are now dozens of decks from which to choose, representing themes from Egyptian and Celtic to Native American and Feminist.

Over time, the Tarot cards have had their ups and downs, falling from popular interest only to be once more resurrected by those in search of the deeper meanings behind their complex symbolism. As the saying goes, "Truth will always out."

The earliest known "book" of Tarot cards still in existence are those from 1840–42, of which seventeen remain. The first entire deck still in existence was painted by the Italian Bonifacio Bembo for the Duke of Milan.

Many theories exist about the origins of the Tarot. During different periods of history, occult (the word means "hidden") studies were either freely available to all or deeply secret, depending upon the prevailing authorities of the culture's attitude toward occult knowledge.

One theory is that in the great library of Alexandria in Egypt, whose female librarian Hypatia was world-renowned for her wisdom and learning, there existed scrolls (which was how books were made in those days) containing all of the wisdom of the ancient world.

One of these "books" was supposedly based on the legendary *Book of Thoth*, derived from the mystery schools of Egypt. The allegorical illustrations on the Tarot cards are said to contain these secret teachings, which in the Major Arcana represent a course in personal development. The esoteric teachings were hidden in the seemingly innocent pictures.

Gypsies are said to have carried the cards to Europe and "gypsy" is considered a corrupt form of "Egyptian." Considered by the Church to be "the devil's picture book," the cards were quickly condemned by the Catholic Church as heretical. Just to possess them was a dangerous act.

There seems no doubt that the cards were a means for preservation of ancient knowledge that the Church considered dangerous,

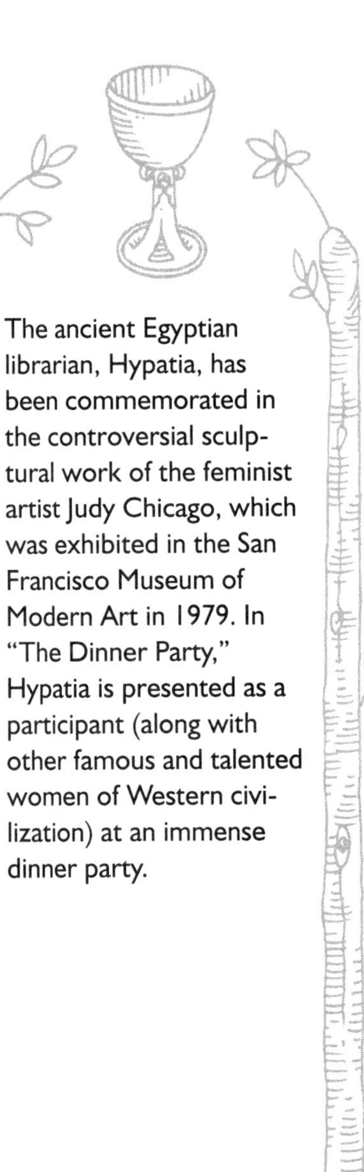

The ancient Egyptian librarian, Hypatia, has been commemorated in the controversial sculptural work of the feminist artist Judy Chicago, which was exhibited in the San Francisco Museum of Modern Art in 1979. In "The Dinner Party," Hypatia is presented as a participant (along with other famous and talented women of Western civilization) at an immense dinner party.

or heretical, at a time when it was literally a danger to your life to believe anything other than the established Church dogma.

Though we can only speculate on its origins, the Tarot images are inextricably linked to ancient beliefs, mythologies, and religious systems such as the Hebrew Cabala. Others, notably Pythagoras, believed that letters and numbers are in themselves divine beings possessing extraordinary powers; the Greek neo-Pythagorean school taught these ideas.

No matter the origin of the Tarot, it is clear that its motifs refer directly to fundamental human psychological and spiritual experiences. The more one studies them and practices their use, the deeper one's understanding becomes, and the more they resonate to the inner life, as well as to events in the outer life. They are primarily meant to be used for enlightenment, for discovery of the authentic *Self.*

ber cards) are believed to have been added at a later date, around the time of the first known deck in the fourteenth century. This theory suggests that they derive from an Italian card game known as *tarrochi.*

Though we will never know their true history, that needn't prevent us from using their wisdom, for the Tarot cards do indeed tell a powerful story: the story of the development of human life. It is an adventure story, like the hero's journey, filled with challenges, obstacles to be overcome, lessons to be learned, reconciliations to be achieved, honor to be protected, goals to be formulated and reached. In this universal story, each of us undertakes his or her own Way, following whatever symbolism speaks to us at the moment of a reading. It is this amazing flexibility that has allowed the Tarot and its marvelous symbols to endure through long and tumultuous centuries in order to come down to us today.

The Soul of the World

In the view of the alchemists and mystics, the universal significance of such symbols as the Tarot presents and preserves was thought to spring from the *anima mundi,* or soul of the world, which was seen as a vast repository of knowledge, like a universal library, that was filled with the memories and wisdom of the entire human race—past, present, and future. Sometimes called the "Akashic records," this source of knowledge could be accessed by anyone willing to make the effort of deep contemplation.

Within this collective pool are all the basic figures found in religions, myths, legends, and fairy tales. Taken together, these figures encapsulate a magical storehouse of profound esoteric knowledge. For example, The Empress symbolizes the essence of femininity as represented by the great mother Goddess of the world's most ancient religion. She can be seen as the representative of what Goethe called "the eternal feminine," in both myth and psychology.

Thus does each figure of the Tarot call forth from the individual's unconscious a deep resonance. Contact with these images in a conscious, intentional way allows their hidden counterparts—denizens of the deepest layer of human collectivity—to surface and become integrated into a person's life.

Properly conducted, a reading is a story—the images on the cards meld into a meaningful pattern that can clarify the issues confronting the person for whom the reading is held. In a profound sense, if taken rightly, a reading can act like a vivid, enlightening dream or a moment of the flash of inspiration—the "Ah-ha" experience. "So, that's how it goes!"

Tarot cards are wonderful for meditation, as well as for divination, or the answering of questions. They act to stimulate the intuition, which is the key to the gateway of the unconscious. They act to illuminate the hidden factors in a person's life that bear on the situation at hand. Often, the person him- or herself may be unaware of these inner issues that are secretly shaping the course of his or her life. The Tarot, by contacting what is inside the person, reveals them.

Search is an expression of the urge to discover what "holds the world together at its inmost core" (Goethe, *Faust)* to establish an order and meaning for our place in the cosmos . . . man's thrust into outer space is the counterpart of the quest into inner space in search of integration and fulfillment

—Edward C. Whitmont, M.D., *The Return of the Goddess*

Part 1

The Basics of Tarot

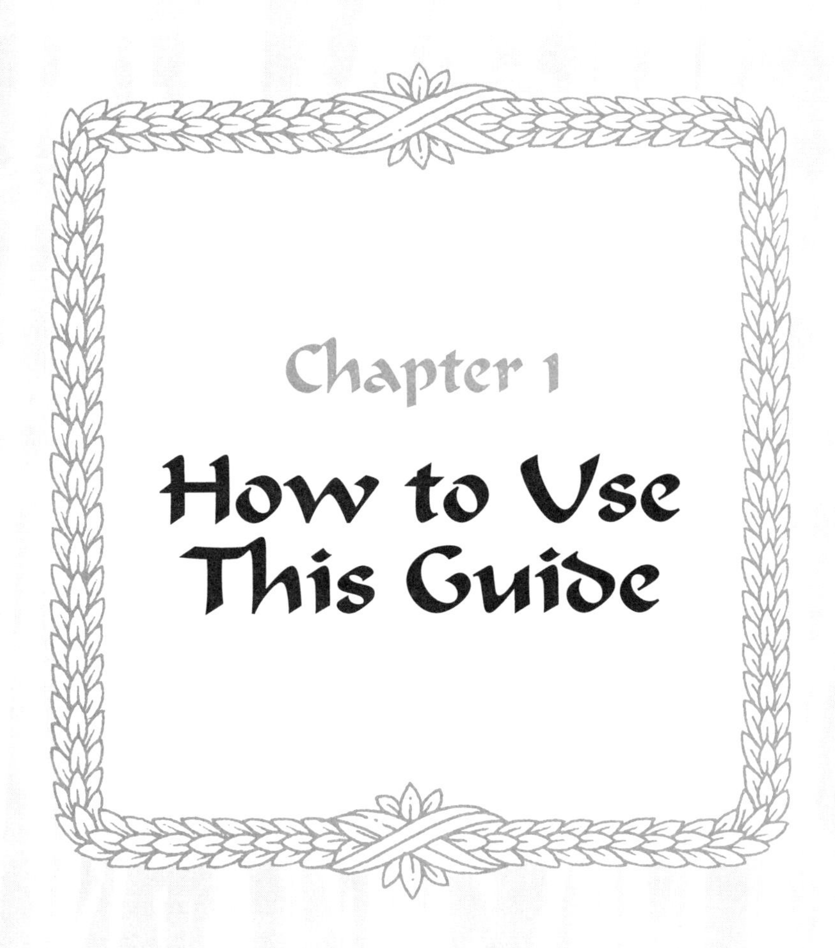

Chapter 1

How to Use This Guide

The Tarot is a powerful tool, but it must be used properly and with respect, not only for the knowledge it contains but for its ability to connect with the deepest reaches of the human psyche. Although the Tarot can be successfully used to answer mundane or practical questions, its highest value is as a guide to the development of our intuition, which in turn leads to spiritual development.

The word "psychic" evokes conflicting and sometimes negative emotions in people, reminiscent of the fear of the unknown and of those who supposedly can manipulate hidden, and therefore dangerous, forces. This is simply nonsense. Being psychic, or using psychic/intuitive methods is no more mysterious than computer language and programming, which to those of us who are nonscientific is about as mysterious as it gets. Unlike the ability to manipulate complex computer code, which must be learned just as a foreign language is learned, intuition is a basic component of the human being from the start. Children, in fact, often exhibit astonishing feats of intuition for the simple reason that no one has yet told them it is "wrong" or "weird" to be able to access direct knowing.

Therefore, the first requirement in using Tarot is to take it, and yourself, seriously, and to have an open mind. Fear will block results and a frivolous attitude will only produce a similar result.

Everyone is psychic, to one degree or another. Like musical aptitude, anyone can learn to play the piano or another instrument or to read music, even to compose. Naturally, as in all of the arts—and divination is an art—talent is a factor, and some people are naturally more talented than others. The beauty of the Tarot, however, is that the more you work with it, the more adept you become.

Imagine this scenario: You need information about the future ramifications of an impending decision regarding a major life change—it could involve your career, your marriage, a relocation, a pregnancy, or someone close to you. Instead of worrying and wondering and endlessly nagging yourself to come up with a right decision—or swinging back and forth between two alternatives—you simply take out your Tarot cards (or you consult a professional reader).

Preferably, you have a special private place where you can be quiet and alone. When you settle yourself before using your cards, you take a few moments to relax completely according to your preferred method, slowly allowing your conscious mind to sink to the deep level of your inner non-conscious mind. While holding your cards, or shuffling them, you formulate a succinct question about the situation for which you desire counsel. Calmly, you feel this question becoming a part of your entire being. Then you lay out your cards in a predetermined spread.

Believe it or not, you already have the innate ability to get the answers you want. Some of us can do that without a physical aid, such as Tarot or an astrology chart, but the use of Tarot, or any other physical tool, functions to focus the power of your intuition, which already knows the right answer. The Tarot cards are simply a convenient way to do this, to get at the inner truth of the situation.

Sound impossible? It isn't. Right now, today, you have this power. The problem is that you don't know you have it, *and* you don't know how to use it. But in fact your non-conscious mind is already programmed to give you the answers you want and need—you just don't know the correct keys to press to access the vast resources of information already in your mental software. That's where and why Tarot can help.

And the answers will amaze you. In my experience, the Tarot has the ability to reach right around surface problems and get to the real root of the situation. So often, we displace (to use a psychological term) what's really bothering us onto a simpler issue. For example, a woman once came to me for a reading saying she wanted advice about whether or not to go into business for herself. However, when I laid out the cards the references were all to the state of her marriage. At first I was puzzled, for her question had been clear and straightforward and I hadn't at the time been fully aware of the uncanny ability of the cards to get at the heart of the matter, no matter what the actual question.

As it turned out, when I asked about her marriage, she burst into tears and said that the only reason she was thinking of quitting her job and going into business for herself was as an escape route from a difficult marriage. She figured setting up her own business would require every minute of her time and every ounce of her energy, effectively removing her from participation in her marriage. After the reading, she understood that if she were really to make progress in her life she had to face and resolve her marriage issue.

This actually wasn't a surprise to her, for her non-conscious mind knew all along what the root of the problem was, and its promptings had directed her to come to me for a reading, which served to cut through her avoidance of the real problem.

The Golden Dawn

During the nineteenth and early twentieth centuries there occurred new interest in occult disciplines, including astrology, the Tarot, ritual magic, the Hebrew Cabala, Gnosticism, geomancy, etc. The group called "The Order of the Golden Dawn," of whom Arthur Edward Waite was an influential member, produced many writings. In 1910, Waite commissioned artist and dramatist Pamela Coleman Smith to illustrate a Tarot deck. It was published as *The Pictorial Key to the Tarot* and became famous in its own time. Symbolically, Waite's deck was influenced by a number of occult philosophies. Today, the Waite deck (sometimes called the Ryder-Waite deck) continues to be the most popular and influential Tarot deck of this era.

If the doors of perception were cleansed, everything would appear to man as it is, infinite. For man has closed himself up, till he see all things thro' narrow chinks in his cavern.

—William Blake, *The Marriage of Heaven and Hell*

We humans are only at the beginning stages of discovering our almost unlimited capacities. Scientists say that we use, at best, only ten percent of our brain's capacities, and that's when we are being especially productive. Most of us jog along in our daily lives using only about five percent, or even less. Can you imagine what would happen if we all used substantially more of our innate intuitive capacity? What problems we could solve, what progress we would make!

Today, many people are already aware that humans possess the potential to transform themselves and their environments. One of France's most eminent brain specialists, Dr. Frederic Tilney, puts it bluntly: "We will, by conscious command, evolve cerebral centers which will permit us to use powers that we now are not even capable of imagining." Not only New Age practitioners like Tarot card readers are aware of this, but scientists, educators, theologians, and psychologists as well know that the potential for the human race is, in the words of Dr. Richard Leakey, "almost infinite."

Releasing your psychic potential is a little like being the conductor of a great orchestra, except that you are also all the instruments. The conscious mind is the conductor, whose job it is to get all the parts going in concert, in harmony. Most of us have heard of "right-brain" and "left-brain" and we know that the so-called left brain rules our analytical, rational thinking while the right brain presides over nonverbal, imaginative thinking. The challenge is to learn to blend all our parts into one harmonious whole, to allow each one to interact with and enhance the others. In this endeavor, the Tarot is an excellent method of integration.

By focusing the conscious mind on the question and on the spread of cards, the intuitive self is engaged. In a sense, it provides directional clues to self-awareness, especially what you may have hidden from yourself. Because it is specific and detailed, it allows the left brain and the right brain to interact smoothly, the way the navigator directs the pilot, and once we understand that two sides of the brain are better than one, we are in a position to tap into the reserves of the mind for any purpose we wish. The power is yours to command, and the Tarot deck puts it right into your hands. Designed to draw on your own innate clairvoyance, it acts as a catalyst to produce information you need.

As you begin your study of the cards, let them speak directly to your inner self, tune into what *you feel* about each card. The interpretations given here are useful, but they are not carved in stone. You are free to be creative in how you use the cards. The more you practice, the better you will get at sensing which meaning is appropriate. For myself, after many years of study, practice, and doing professional readings, I find that the cards in a spread act as a *template*, or a field, through which information flows. You must, of course, first learn the standard meanings of each individual card before you can learn to see a whole, a *gestalt*, within a spread.

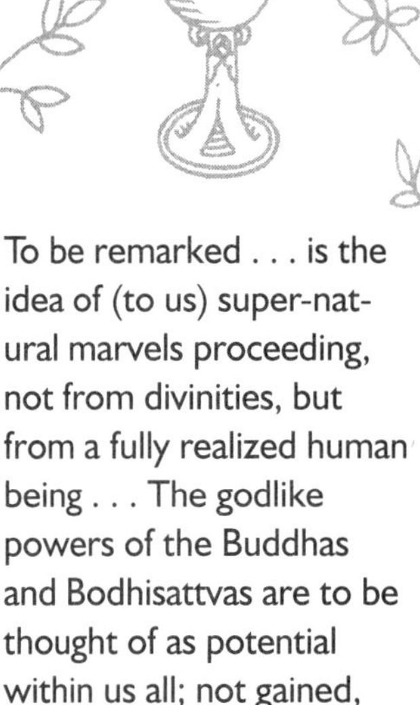

> To be remarked . . . is the idea of (to us) super-natural marvels proceeding, not from divinities, but from a fully realized human being . . . The godlike powers of the Buddhas and Bodhisattvas are to be thought of as potential within us all; not gained, but recovered, or in the Platonic sense "recollected," when the impediments of ignorance will have been either slowly purged away or suddenly transcended . . .
>
> —Joseph Campbell, *The Mythic Image*

The Structure of the Tarot Deck

A Tarot deck consists of seventy-eight cards. Of these, the first twenty-two are identified as the "Major Arcana." These "arcana," which means "mysteries" or "secrets," are held to represent the mysteries or secrets of the Universe that reflect Universal Law. As such, they are the most complex and, therefore, require more diligence to understand. Their importance is primary.

Each of the Major Arcana cards is illustrated with specific symbols, which are basically the same in all decks, even though they may differ thematically according to the philosophy of the designer. Some decks, for example, reflect nature themes, or are related to a particular tradition. Further, each of the Major Arcana has a title, such as "The Magician," "The Empress," "The Lovers," "The Moon," "The Tower," and so forth. Additionally, they are numbered from One to Twenty-One, with "the Fool" being Zero.

The fifty-six remaining cards are called the "Minor Arcana," presumably because they contain information that is of a less secretive nature, and therefore suitable for those with little training to easily use. It was considered safe for non-adepts to have access to it.

The Minor Arcana are divided into four suits, as is a deck of ordinary playing cards. These are the Wands, the Pentacles, the Swords, and the Cups. (Note: Different writers order the suits of Minor Arcana differently; I use the Wands, Pentacles, Swords, Cups order because it is the same as the order of the elements astrologically: Fire, Earth, Air, Water, to which each suit corresponds, respectively.) Within each suit of fourteen cards, there are four

Court cards—King, Queen, Knight, and Page. (In an ordinary playing deck, there are only three court cards, King, Queen, and Jack.) Each suit also has an Ace, which is considered to be the One card, and the following cards are numbered Two through Ten.

There is some dispute about the ordering of the Major Arcana. Some authors focus primarily on the order of the cards (0-22) contending that they form a system through which the development of an individual's life can be traced. Some interpreters have introjected psychological meanings into the Major Arcana, while others have seen them a representative of spiritual development and growth. Often, the ordering of the Major Arcana is a result of the authority's own personal point of view.

From my standpoint, I see no reason why all of the above could not apply separately or together, given the situation, the person being read for, the objective of the reading, and other life factors. Nor do I see any reason a person using the cards cannot interpret them according to his or her own lights, philosophically or spiritually, as others have done before them. Waite, for example, placed card Zero between cards Twenty and Twenty-One and interchanged cards Eight and Eleven.

One writer, Sally Gearhart, in *A Feminist Tarot*, asserts that the various systems of organizing the Major Arcana came into being as a result of the oral tradition, where people developed stories to help them remember the specific attributes of each card. In her opinion, it is easier to remember what the individual cards mean if we relate them to each other in groups.

For myself, having started out with Tarot as a part of my study of ancient symbolic art, it is the symbols themselves that is the most important factor. Clearly, once one has gone deeply into symbology—and the unique human ability to create symbols—it becomes apparent that the great mysteries, not only of the Universe, but of our human lives are larger and more complex than any system, however complete, can encompass.

Thus, I prefer to take them as a whole, the whole always being larger than the combination of its parts. That being said, do whatever works for you. Everybody is different, nobody's memory works exactly like anyone else's. If splitting them up into smaller groups helps you to get at the meaning and retain it, by all means do so.

My personal experience has taught me that the Major Arcana cards possess many different layers—and that as one works with

Symbolism: Personal, Collective, and Universal

In most traditional societies, symbolist ideas were applied on three levels: personal, collective, and universal.

At the personal level, symbolist thought was applied to the circumstances and needs of specific individuals [the level we are largely concerned with in this book]. Here, emphasis was on discerning personal fortunes through study of the omens or symbols of daily life, casting divinatory horoscopes for individuals [and the use of other forms such as runes and Tarot cards].

On the collective level, symbolist principles were applied to the subtle dynamics of entire societies or civilizations . . . with an eye to understanding how each reflected changes of fortune in the life of the community . . . at this level [divination was used] for the entire nation or for a mass event, such as a battle, in the hope of fathoming the deeper patterns governing the collective destiny.

At the universal level, the symbolist perspective was directed toward understanding and deciphering nature's patterns. Here, the universe in all its forms revealed itself as a great book encoding the truths of spiritual reality. Through a study of symbolic meaning . . . the symbolist hoped to glimpse the workings of the Divine Mind. Practitioners of this approach ranged from classical thinkers like Pythagoras to more recent mystic-scientists like Kepler or Newton, for whom discoveries into nature's laws held spiritual rather than strictly physical significance.

The important point here is that virtually every civilization in history actively subscribed to the essential tenets of the symbolist worldview, on one or more of these levels. And while most clearly apparent in . . . divination, superstition, and magic, such expressions reflected a more implicit, all-encompassing symbolic vision that extended to all aspects of experience, at varying levels of subtlety.

—Ray Grasse, *The Waking Dream*

them these layers reveal themselves, like digging into an archeological site. There is the strictly practical level–The Empress may be a direct reference to your mother or your desire to become a mother; there is the mundane, or worldly level–The Magician may refer to your desire to live a more creative life, to be more creative in your work; then there is the level of spiritual development–The Devil may be a statement that it is time for you to throw off the obstacles that are preventing your living more fully and deeply, that you need to tend to your soul needs rather than your material concerns.

Each person unfolds according to their own inner blueprint–there's no hurrying the process that insists on taking place on its own time schedule. There are cycles in life that show us the patterns we are following, and suggest new direction (these are most clearly shown in the astrological chart, which is an excellent adjunct to the Tarot). The cards of the Major Arcana can be a guide for us to explore universal concepts as they apply to where we are in our lives at the present moment.

The Minor Arcana may seem less important, but they serve to give off *immediate* information. Through study of the Minor Arcana, we can observe the ongoing process of how we grow and develop. We can also pinpoint the areas of life that are currently in need of our attention, for each of the suits represents a distinct realm of our activity and growth. These are:

WANDS–mental activity, the outer world, work or career
PENTACLES–money, security, the physical world
SWORDS–self, obstacles one is facing, spiritual issues
CUPS–emotions, love, romance, the unconscious

Teaching Yourself Tarot

The first order is, of course, to learn the cards and their meanings. The second is practice. My advice is to read through the entire book as a first step, marking any sections that particularly appeal to you. Using your own deck alongside the illustrations (here based upon the Waite deck) and comparing it, you will begin to get a "feel" for the cards.

The next step is *practice*. If you are serious about learning and using the Tarot, you must practice. There's an old New York joke about a tourist, late for a musical performance and lost, who rushes up to an old Jewish peddler, almost knocking him over, and demands: "Quick, tell me how do I get to Carnegie Hall!" The old man dusts himself off and intones, *Practice, practice, practice.*

When I first began the serious study of interpretation, I spent the first hour of every day working with the cards. Earlier, when I was studying them as part of my work with symbolic art, with no intention of using them for readings, either for myself or others, I concentrated on learning the specifics of the symbolism only. This was a good base, but you can also learn the symbols and their meanings bit by bit as you practice laying out cards and interpreting them.

If you do not have the leisure to spend your first hour of the day with your cards, then at least set aside some specific time, preferably daily, or as often as you can manage. Obviously, the more time you spend in practice, as with a musical instrument, the more proficient you will become. Much will depend on your aims. If you want merely to do fortune-telling, or predictions into the future, you can concentrate on the interpretations and the sections related to the spreads and readings. However, I do not recommend concentrating only on predictions; there are too many variables in the psychic world to make major life decisions based on them. The Tarot is best used to access psychological states and for spiritual development. But the choice is yours to make.

If, as I hope, you want to make a serious study of the Tarot in order to access its wisdom, then concentrate on each of the Major Arcana in turn. Read the description and the interpretation, compare it to its counterpart in your deck (unless you are using the deck) and focus entirely on each card until you feel you "know" it intimately and have a "feel" for its energy. You can take one card a day, or however often you are able to schedule your sessions with the cards.

After you have familiarized yourself with the Major Arcana, which is the heart of the Tarot, turn to the Minor Arcana. Study the meanings of the four suits (Chapter 8), for the entire suit covers a single area of life.

Next, move on to the Court cards, which often are used to represent people–King, Queen, Knight, Page (Chapter 8)–and become familiar with those images. Then review the number cards of the Minor Arcana until you have a sense of them. This process will enable you to do practice readings.

Earlier decks were fairly simple, mostly based on medieval images. Under Waite's direction, Smith's illustrations enlarged upon the older images in the Major Arcana, and she created new illustrations for the Minor Arcana, to which Waite ascribed fixed meanings. As a result, the Waite deck became the standard for many years. As Tarot decks have proliferated in recent times, many have been based upon it both in terms of illustrations and interpretations.

Obviously, your proficiency in using the Tarot—whether you are giving readings for yourself or others, or if you are primarily using it as a means of self-development—will be a direct result of the amount of time and effort you put into studying and doing your own interpretations, as it is with any new skill you may want to master. Regular practice for a short time can be combined with occasional longer practice sessions; however, as you study the cards and begin to use them in a methodical way, you will find yourself gaining a fine appreciation of the breadth and depth of this wisdom source—a fascinating subject for anyone interested in the way the human psyche functions.

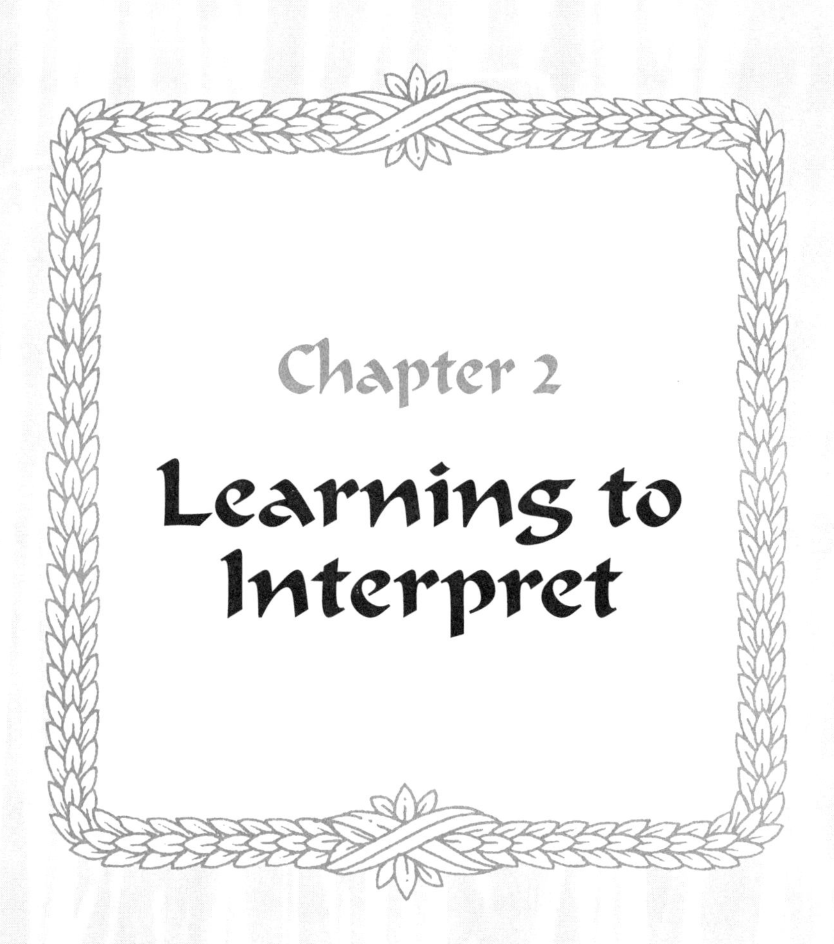

Chapter 2

Learning to Interpret

The first step in learning to interpret is to familiarize yourself with your own deck of cards, comparing it with the illustrations in this book, noting similarities and differences.

You may find that your own first impressions of the cards differ from the interpretations found here, or in any other book. This does not mean you are wrong. This book is only a guideline, not a dogmatic text. The illustrations on the cards will resonate differently with different people, and will depend upon individual temperament as well as what purpose you intend in learning and using the Tarot.

Bear in mind as you study your cards that they have been derived from multiple cultures, that behind them stands a mystery. Each person's reaction to the cards is unique, as is your thumbprint. However, at first it is best to learn the standard interpretations. You can take off from there once you have learned and practiced with them. The rule of thumb is: do what makes sense to you.

Another factor in interpretation, again depending on the deck you choose, is that overall the individual decks follow a theme—some use obviously Christian symbology; others are frankly pagan; some are Feminist; others are Native American or shamanistic. Therefore, it is important that you are both aware of and comfortable with the symbols on your personal deck of cards. If you are "put off" by the symbols, or if the art does not seem meaningful to you, get another deck. It's important that you feel in sympathy with the cards you are using in order for them to reach into your unconscious depths.

During the course of my study of and professional practice reading Tarot, I have used many decks, for different purposes. (We will discuss using more than one deck in Chapter 14.) Though I have found other decks useful—and some are quite beautiful from a purely aesthetic viewpoint—I have always returned to the Waite deck; it seems to "speak" to me. Yet I know other readers for whom it does not work at all. So, the first step in learning to interpret is to make friends with your own cards, or to find a deck with which you feel compatible. (We will also discuss choosing a deck in Chapter 14.)

Examining the Cards in Detail

This is the most important first step. Every detail on each card, especially of the Major Arcana, is a meaningful symbol. Remember that symbols can act on different levels of the psyche. There are many ways to discover your own inner dimensions. One of the best of these is the contemplation and meditation upon symbols that are meaningful to *you*. Experience has shown that the use of symbols to which we do not readily relate is less effective than those to which we do relate. The symbols produced by your unconscious mind are truly yours. Like dream symbols, they are unique to you and can reveal you to yourself. Therefore, there are as many interpretations of the symbols of the Tarot cards as there are readers. How the card speaks to you and how you feel about the symbols it presents is what is important.

Remember, in interpreting Tarot you are using your *intuition*, and intuition is not a logical/rational activity. If you are accustomed to being mostly left-brained (as most of us are), it may at first seem a bit strange. You may experience odd sensations, such as a mild pulsing in the forehead, or a lightness, or the sense of being pulled inward. Do not let this frighten you. Your intuition cannot hurt you. However, if at any time you are studying the symbols on your cards you feel uncomfortable, stop and try again later. If you encounter any negative feelings, pay attention to them and make notes of which cards, or which symbols, produce anxiety or discomfort. Negative information is only that—*information*. Psychic information is like a weather forecast: if we know the weather is going to be stormy, we can take sensible precautions.

The thing about intuition is that it uses *all* of you. It is precisely the holistic nature of intuition that gives it its power. In your unconscious, you have a huge data bank of experiences upon which to draw, most of which you are not even aware of. You know much more than you think you know, and your intuition has the ability to come up with new and creative combinations of knowledge to correctly interpret the cards *for you*, and to produce solutions to any problems about which you are consulting the cards. In short, your unconscious is an innovator with great creative ability. As you examine each card carefully, paying attention to the details no matter how small, you will begin to "get a feel" of what each card means.

Keeping a Record

As you study each illustration, make notes of your impressions—of the card as a whole, and of each of its individual symbols. Accustom yourself to noticing every detail that each illustration contains. Try to relate to the details on a personal level, saying, "What

The highest purpose of the Tarot is as a system of self-initiation or enlightenment. It is a map into the realms of spiritual bliss. It is a record of man's relationship with the cosmos. In short, it is a textbook of occult teachings. The Hermetic Order of the Golden Dawn equates each Tarot trump with a path on the Qabalistic Tree of Life. In this way the Major Arcana is a symbolic map of inner space, describing the highways of consciousness, from the lofty spiritual heights of divinity, down to the material world of human beings and matter. . . . Although the "pathways" [of different card systems] are slightly different, they take consciousness over the same terrain and allow the user to reach the same states and stages of consciousness.

—Gerald and Betty Schueler, *The Enochian Tarot*

does this mean to me?" For example, the Fool carries a rose. The rose has a generally accepted universal meaning–but maybe you don't particularly care for roses as flowers. Maybe you think of the thorns instead of the fragrance. You can accept the standard interpretation, or substitute one of your own.

When examining the cards of the Major Arcana (by far the most important and most complex as they are considered to contain disguised knowledge), carefully note each of the main figures on the cards–whether they are sitting, standing, their postures, positions of their hands and limbs (what today is called "body language") for its significance. Pay attention to any accessories–human, animal, or inanimate–that appear with them. Notice also the background and the foreground, for each detail on each card is a meaningful symbol. Even something so minor as a flower or some greenery is a factor in the overall interpretation of the card as a whole.

Start your own book of impressions. Use a notebook, or looseleaf pages, with the title of the card at the top. Each time you study the card, date your entry. Over time, you will find that your impressions change and expand. You may find, after some time, that going back to a card will give you a different slant on it. This means that the illustration has reached further into your unconscious. Remember that the cards are multilayered in meaning. What you derive from your own free examination of the pictures at the beginning will be an important factor in how you both understand and use the Tarot.

Expect change over time. The natural inclination, for a beginner, is to interpret each card individually in a reading, and then to try to put together a whole from the individual cards. But once you have implanted the meanings into your own unique unconscious, you will find that a glance at an entire layout of cards will give you an impression of totality. But this only comes with much study and practice. By keeping a detailed record, to which you can return just as you might reread a diary, you will be creating the building blocks for a complete overall "take" on the reading before going into its details.

Make no attempt to be analytical about your responses to the cards–just write down what comes to you spontaneously. If a question arises, write it down but don't try to answer it at once. Return to it later. Once you complete an intensive study of the Tarot, you will be amazed at how significant your first impressions were to your entire process of learning to interpret.

Keeping a Tarot Journal

All travelers are advised to keep a record of their journey. A Tarot journey is no exception. In fact, keeping a Tarot notebook can in and of itself be a spiritual practice. A journal not only will tell you where you have been, it will show you the form of where you are going. It can a serve as a channel into your higher self.

The spiritual quest can seem like a lonely trek through an unknown and unpopulated wilderness. A journal is a wonderful companion for it is truly a friend.

Make a covenant with your Tarot journal. Think for a few minutes about why you are doing this and why you are willing to make a commitment to writing your experiences—and copying your layouts indicating what cards appear in which positions—regularly in your journal. Then put this into words. Study what you have written for a few minutes and see if you are satisfied with your purpose. You may want to make changes. Your statement of purpose might go something like this:

> *I'm keeping my Tarot Journal for the purpose of getting in touch with my Higher Self, my intuition, and with the aim of generating more consciousness. My goal is to become more aware of messages from my sacred mind and to act on this information for my spiritual growth and development. I believe that keeping this journal will aid this process by providing me with a framework in which I can record and reflect upon my experiences and wherein I can chart my progress.*

When you are satisfied with your written statement of purpose, write out a contract that you are making with yourself. It might go something like this:

> *[Statement of purpose.] Therefore, I make a covenant with myself to pursue this effort on a regular basis. I promise to record my Tarot work faithfully* ______________________

You fill in the blank. You might say, " . . . every day for fifteen minutes," or " . . . every day," or " . . . at least twice a week for half an hour," or " . . . for no less than one hour per week," or " . . . a total of X hours per month."

You are making this agreement with yourself, and it is up to you to keep to the terms you make. Trust your inner Self to keep up its half of the bargain.

Let your Tarot journal be a gift you give yourself. Rereading what you have written is a way to show yourself of how much progress you have made, and it makes a wonderful learning tool. Reviewing it regularly is like having a teacher at your elbow.

Consider the time you spend with it as time spent with your Higher Self, or the Source, or God, whichever term fits your personal belief system.

Chapter 3

Handling Your Deck

How should you handle your Tarot deck? *With utmost care.* Treat it as you would any precious possession of great value. *Never* leave it lying about unattended. *Always* return it to its special place immediately after you have finished using it, either for practice, meditation, or a reading.

Methods of Shuffling

Most Tarot decks are oversize, that is, larger than a deck of ordinary playing cards. A new deck will be stiff and usually slick as the cards are impregnated with a protective lacquer-type coating. You will need to "break in" a new deck just as you must break in a new pair of shoes. This can be done by ruffling the cards at the edges a few times, to give flexibility. In time, as you handle each card separately, they will become softer.

Shuffling is an individual matter. Whether you allow anyone else to shuffle or touch your deck is also a matter for you to decide. I know readers, like myself, who have the person being read for handle the cards (whether they simply hold them, shuffle them, or mix them in another manner), but I also know readers who are adamant that only *they* will shuffle (or handle) their decks. If you decide that you want no one else to handle your deck, that is fine, but if you feel, as I do, that the person being read for needs to put his or her vibrations into the deck, then I give below some methods for clearing out vibrations and "purifying" the deck in between uses.

I have a special method that I use before a reading, as do most readers. As you work with your cards, you will develop your own initiatory procedure. The main point is to put the vibrations of the moment—your own if you are practicing or reading for yourself, the other person's if you are reading for someone else—into the cards, and clear them afterward.

Since oversize decks are difficult to shuffle in the overhand manner of an ordinary playing deck (like a professional card dealer shuffles), one alternative is to hold the pack in one hand and with the other slide out small sections and reposition them, doing this several times until you feel the cards are well mixed. Another method is to spread them out, like in the children's game of Go Fish, and stir them around with both hands. A third possibility is to cut the cards into several stacks, restack them, cut into more stacks, restack, and so on until you feel "right" about the amount of mixing you have done.

In my readings, I allow my clients the choice of how they will handle the cards. Some people are shy, reluctant, or feel unsure—these people I tell to simply hold the entire deck in both hands while they formulate clearly in their mind what they want the reading to achieve for them. This method works fine, and then I do the shuffling.

One reader I know well shuffles the deck overhand (if you are a man or have large, strong hands the overhand shuffle is easier, as it is with a worn deck) precisely seven times. He does not permit the client to touch the cards.

These methods of shuffling, or mixing the cards, are a personal matter much related to temperament. You may be a person who wants to maintain complete control (if so, you are probably a fixed astrological sign), or you may be a person who wants to "share" (in which case, the chance is you are a mutable sign). If you want to start the process but allow the other person to participate at some point, you are probably a cardinal sign. Any or all of these methods are valid, and you don't have to stick with just one way. As you evolve in your use of the Tarot, you will find that how you handle your deck will evolve also.

Blessing the Cards

It is a good idea to bless your deck each time before you use it, and with a new deck to have a short blessing ceremony before you use it for the first time. This need not be complicated. If you already use blessing as part of your usual activities, that will be sufficient. If you do not already have blessing rituals, simply place the cards in front of you, hold your hands palm-down over them, and say, silently or out loud, "I call upon the divine powers to bless and protect these cards, for my intention is to use them for good only. I declare that only good shall come from their use and that all negativity shall be turned away from them."

Clearing Vibrations

It is important to clear the vibrations from your deck each time you use it, especially if another person is involved. However, if you use a totally *separate* deck only for your own spiritual practice it is not necessary to clear out your own vibrations; in fact, you want the deck to be impregnated with your vibrations. But, if you do readings with that same deck (which I do not advise) even if only for yourself, then you should clear it after each reading so that there is no residue that might affect the next reading.

There are four methods of clearing, or purification. I will give these in the same order that I use for ordering the Minor Arcana: Fire, Earth, Air, and Water.

Fire Purification

Fire is excellent to use for clearing. Fire has been used for ceremonial procedures since the beginning of time, and many

divinities are associated with the divine fire. The use of fire for clearing is associated with Spirit, with the primal spark of life, and is of course necessary to our existence. Fire is pure energy: it comes from a material source (such as wood or coal) but fire itself is immaterial. Thus it has the capacity to mediate between the visible and the invisible worlds—it transcends form into formlessness.

To clear with fire, you can place your deck of cards, unwrapped but protected, in bright sunlight for an hour or more. Or, you can light a candle on the table (or on the rug or floor) where you consistently work with your cards and allow the candle to burn beside them (being careful, of course, to watch over the process) while you silently invoke the Spirit of Fire asking it to clear out the old vibrations. One nice way of using this procedure is to get a long-burning candle and dedicate it to the purpose of clearing your deck. Do not use the candle for any other purpose. If possible, put it in a glass receptacle such as a heavy glass vase that will enclose it entirely. When you finish clearing, thank the Fire Spirit for its help.

Earth Purification

Of all the four elements, none is as revered as the earth, for it is our home and our source of all sustenance. As far back as we have artifacts for prehistoric cultures, we find earth goddesses. No one, I think, does not feel a deep, sometimes mystical, connection with the earth. Just a pot of soil with a plant in it reminds us that we are fundamentally connected to our mother earth, from which all life springs. Earth is grounding—in fact, we call the soil under our feet "ground." It is stable, serene, enduring.

To clear with earth, use salt—preferably coarse sea salt (available in health food stores). Salt, the essence of earth (we speak of people who are "the salt of the earth") was once one of the most valuable commodities available to humans. Indeed, we cannot live without it. The Cabalistic tradition considers salt a sacred word because its numerical value is the same as God's name of power, YAHWEH, multiplied by three. Salt is also a crystal, which makes it useful for realigning energies.

For a salt-clearing, put your unwrapped deck into a small bowl and lay a sheet of clean white paper over it to avoid getting salt on the cards themselves. Make sure the cards are completely covered. Then, while silently invoking the Spirit of Earth, pour a layer of salt over the cards on top of the paper and leave for at least twenty

A Note on Tarot Rituals

In her book *Choice Centered Tarot*, Gail Fairfield makes this comment:

> "The purpose of rituals is to help us focus on the issue or task at hand. Over the years, various people have discovered that certain action patterns help them to focus on the Tarot cards. They have systemized those patterns into rituals. Some of the most common rituals are:
>
> - Keep your cards in a pine box
> - Wrap your cards in silk (or cotton)
> - Sleep with your cards under your pillow
> - Never let anyone else touch your cards
> - Lay all your readings out on a pine board
> - Always face East when doing a reading
> - Light a candle (or incense) for a reading
> - Always face your readee
> - Shuffle and cut three times to the left
> - Shuffle once and cut three times
> - Don't shuffle, cut once to the right
> - Have only the readee shuffle
> - Have only the reader shuffle

. . . I feel that these rituals are very personal . . . If you like rituals, use them. If you have developed a habit, like holding the remaining cards in your hand after dealing out the layout, and that habit seems to help you focus, use it. No ritual is especially sacred. Its value is that it helps you to focus on the reading. The most powerful rituals are often those we invent ourselves. Use whatever rituals feel right for you when working with the Tarot."

minutes. Afterwards, pick up the paper with the salt on it and dissolve the salt in water. Pour the salt water down the sink drain (*not* the toilet) and run clear water after it. Give thanks to the Earth Spirit.

Another earth-clearing method is to use quartz crystals. To do this, place a large crystal on top of your unwrapped deck for an hour, preferably in a sunny location. It is best to reserve a crystal for this purpose alone. If you use a crystal, you must also periodically cleanse the crystal by the salt method. To do this, simply make a solution of your salt with water, one-half cup salt to one cup water, and let your crystal soak in the solution for twenty-four hours. Depending on the frequency with which you use your cards, and need to clear them, cleanse your crystal more or less frequently.

Air Purification

Of all the methods of purification and cleansing, perhaps air is the most intimate to us as we experience it constantly with the in-and-out flow of our breath. Through our breathing, we are in constant communication with the element of air, though we are mostly unaware of this unless we get a cold or become short of breath. Not only that, but we share this element in common with all other humans—indeed with most other living creatures on the earth, plants as well as animal. The power of air as a cleansing method is unique, as it air itself—invisible, but with great power. “Who has seen the wind?” but we all know what wind is and what it can do.

To clear with air we can use the Native American traditional way of using smoke, called *smudging*. With this technique, which is incidentally the quickest of the clearing techniques mentioned here, the ascending smoke serves as a channel connecting us to the Great Spirit. Smudging consists simply of lighting a bunch of herbs and wafting the smoke over or in what is to be cleared.

Although different herbs are used for different purposes, sage is the most common (and most commonly available—you can get it in the supermarket). To clear your deck by smudging, simply put a few sage leaves (or a heaping tablespoon of the ground herb) into a fireproof dish or vessel (I use a large shell) and set fire to it. When the smoke begins to form, gently move the dish over your unwrapped deck of cards while invoking the Spirit of Air. Do this for a few minutes until the smoke begins to dissipate. Whole leaves burn better than ground, and you can purchase “smudge bundles” of dried leaves with the stems still on them from stores specializing in natural foods and herbs, from some alternative bookstores, or from organic producers of herbs (who often sell by mail).

If you are a gardener/cook, you may already grow your own herbs. If so, simply gather a bundle and tie the stalks and leaves tightly together with string and hang them upside down in a cool, dry place to dry.

As always, when using fire in the home, be cautious. If you are using a bundle, hold a fireproof bowl under it to catch any sparks. Never leave the burning herb unattended, and when finished make doubly sure that all smoldering remains have been put completely out. You can stir the smoking herbs with a metal fork until the smoke dies out and then leave the bowl in the kitchen sink until it is thoroughly cold.

The beauty of the smudging technique is that not only do you clear your deck, you clear yourself and your room as well. You can also use this technique to clear your room after a client leaves, if you do readings for others.

Water Purification

Water—just the word evokes cleanliness and freshness. Water has been used in spiritual ceremonies in all cultures since the beginning of time. We all know how water can make us feel clean and fresh, how a long, cold drink of spring water on a hot day can refresh, how a bath or shower can literally change our outlook. Using water to cleanse your deck is an excellent way of clearing out any negative emotions that may have been provoked by your reading.

The power of the Spirit of Water relates to intuition, to renewal and rebirth. It is central to the Christian tradition of baptism. Clearly you cannot soak your deck of cards in water—but you can create a water atmosphere with a mister. Simply fill the mister with pure water (distilled or from a spring), invoke the Spirit of Water asking it to cleanse and renew your cards, and spray-mist the air above. When doing a reading, I always place a container of water on the table to "catch" any negative vibrations that may be coming from my client's emotional reaction to whatever problems are being investigated through the cards.

Another method is to take a sprig from a plant—a pine sprig is especially good—dip it into a bowl of pure water and sprinkle it

Some Tarot enthusiasts insist that the cards should be kept in a pine box (as well as wrapped in silk) in order to keep "bad vibrations" from contaminating them. As I don't believe in bad vibrations and consider the cards to be a tool for enabling me to tap into my own intuitive level of consciousness, I agree with Gail Fairfield that any ritual is strictly personal. I like silk for its softness and luxury, and because it is natural. Caring for your cards as the treasure they are will create an optimal atmosphere for their use, but there's no need to get caught up in any rigid superstition about them. Treat them as you would any other valuable object you own and use.

around the area where you work with your cards. Some cut flowers in water will serve the same purpose.

If you like, you can make "charged" water by leaving a bottle of water in sunlight, or moonlight; or by putting water in differently colored bottles. Misting produces negative ions which literally change the energy in a room. When misting, use the finest spray you can, sending light puffs of mist into the air above your cards. Be careful not to get them wet. Misting is also a good way to clear the energy field between clients, if you read for others.

Care and Storage

There are many methods and rituals for storage and handling of Tarot decks. You can wrap your deck in a beautiful piece of silk, which may have symbols printed on it. You can use a silk scarf (which is what I do) that has special meaning to you (mine was a gift from a dear friend who succumbed to AIDS while still in his thirties). Some people like to find a silk remnant that was part of an older tradition, like a tapestry or a piece of cherished clothing such as a grandmother's or mother's wedding gown. You can use a simple square to enfold your deck, or you can make a pouch like an envelope or with a drawstring. You don't even have to sew to do this as you can use fabric glue or an iron-on hem adhesive to stick the parts together. I do not recommend keeping cards in a leather pouch (such as jewelry sometimes comes in) because leather is the product of a slaughtered animal. Silk is a natural extrusion of the silkworm. Plus, silk has calm and soothing characteristics as well as the unique property of keeping cool in summer and warm in winter.

Before you handle your deck, be sure to wash your hands thoroughly in warm water, preferably with a sweet-smelling, pure soap. Glycerin is the best because it contains no animal products, but any pure soap, such as castile, will suffice. Dry your hands on a soft towel and lightly apply some neutral greaseless lotion to them. Treat your hands with care and respect, for they are the direct physical conduit for your vibrations to affect the cards.

Part II

The Major Arcana: Symbolic Interpretation

Chapter 4

Description and Meaning of the Trumps

Trumps Zero—The Fool

Description

The Fool is a fascinating figure, yet he can be an ambiguous symbol. Related to the jester or the joker of the ordinary playing deck, which is usually used as the "wild card," he seems beyond ordinary cares and concerns.

He is a male figure standing on the edge of a cliff, as if about to step off into thin air. Yet, his gaze is brightly upward as if he expects the heavens to support him as his next step will take him over the edge of the cliff. In some decks, he is looking back over his shoulder, but he is always unconcerned—or unaware—of any danger lying ahead. Usually he is youthful, but sometimes he is an older figure who has obviously been on the road a long time.

Like a hobo, he carries all his worldly possessions tied in a small bag on a stick over his shoulder. Behind him, the Sun, symbol of the source of all life, is shining on his enterprise. He may carry a rose, symbol of love, or a traveler's staff. Often he is dressed in bright colors and the general impression of the colors is cheerful and sunny. Sometimes he is wearing the parti-colored costume and cap and bells of a medieval court jester; or, he is dressed in the plain garb of a wanderer.

Often he is accompanied by a dog, which is a symbol of the instinctual nature, for a dog has the uncanny ability to follow an invisible trail, using his nose and other senses. The little dog gambols about him, sometimes pulling him back from the danger ahead. It is a protective symbolic figure as our instincts, if followed, do provide us with guidance on our life journeys.

Ordinarily, the Fool is shown as a person full of confidence—often the confidence of youth—and trust in the beneficence of the Universe. He symbolizes that blind leap of faith that we all must take upon entering the journey of life itself, especially if that journey is spiritual.

Interpretation

When the Fool appears in a reading, depending on its position in the layout, it is an indication of someone who is about to embark on a new way of life. This may involve a physical journey, such as changing where one lives, starting a new job, or getting married or divorced. Often, the appearance of the Fool indicates one who is ready to start on a spiritual path, who has made peace with the need to experience absolute faith and trust in the Universe. In such a case, the person has no sense of worry or fear and feels that protection is in play and that everything will turn out well. The person may be consciously in touch with the intuitive realm of his or her being, or he or she may simply be enjoying a state of naiveté and innocence about what the future will bring. The Fool represents a state of openness and is relying on his inner truth to support his adventure.

Mythologically, the Fool is linked to Dionysos, the early Greek god of sacred revels in honor of the Great Goddess. In medieval courts, the king's fool, or jester, was given great license to make fun of everything and everybody with no threat of punishment or recrimination. His was a special role in a time when simpletons, or fools, were thought to possess "divine madness," and irrational behavior was thought to be the result of possession by a god or spirit. "Silly" meant to be blessed. The Fool is also associated with Parsifal, the Authurian knight known for his innocence, and with the Green Man of the Celt tradition, a god of new life and fertility and Nature's ability to restore itself.

Also known as "Le Mat," the Fool corresponds to the number Zero and to the Hebrew letter Shin.

Trumps One—The Magician

Description

The Magician is powerful, representing as he does worldly wisdom and the control of unseen forces that operate in human lives, which serious practitioners today call "magick," so spelled to differentiate it from the parlor tricks we call magic. The Magician is a deeply complex symbol. Almost always a male figure, he stands alone before an array of the traditional magician's tools. In most decks, these are the symbols of the Minor Arcana suits, each of which applies to an element: a pentacle for Earth, a sword for Air, a cup for Water, and a wand for Fire. To possess knowledge of these "elementals" is to gain power in the world. Usually holding a wand, a phallic symbol, he holds one hand aloft, to the heavens, or the upper world of divine power, while the other hand points downward to the Earth, the base of life. Above his head floats the symbol for Infinity. He knows how to use his tools in order to connect the two worlds of spirituality, or metaphysics, and reality, or the mundane plane of existence.

In the Waite deck, above him are trailing vines, like grapes, symbol of wine, a sacred drink in many cultures, while at his feet is a garden of roses, lilies, and greenery. These represent the vegetable kingdom in general; roses refer to desire and the five senses; lilies, to purity and proper use of arcane knowledge.

The totality of these symbols tell us that the Magician is in possession of knowledge that enables him to manipulate the material world through aligning it with the spiritual plane, in order to create the desired circumstances.

The Magician's costume varies with different decks–from Egyptian to Greek to Medieval–but he always wears a belt. In the Waite deck, this is a coiled snake, the *ourobouros*, or snake biting

his tail, an alchemical symbol for wholeness. He can therefore be connected to the power of healing through connecting the two worlds within one's self.

Interpretation

The appearance of the Magician in a reading indicates latent powers, yet to be taken up and brought into manifestation. Also known as the "Juggler," this card suggests that everything in the universe is spread out before us for us to learn to use correctly to manifest the results we desire. These are literally the basic materials of creation and it is the task of the Magician to handle them well, to manipulate and control them for beneficent purposes. This is mental work that affects the material realm.

Thus, the Magician shows us that what we consider to be illusion is another form of reality, and what we consider to be reality can be mere illusion. This is not trickery but a deep understanding of how we must learn to use our intellects, our intuitive abilities, our personal talents, and our practical skills in order to mediate between the two worlds, both of which affect us simultaneously.

The Magician is a card of power, for just as a mage, or true magician, stands at the center of the universe with the tools and ability to manipulate it for his purposes, so does each of us create, or recreate, our own universes within ourselves, first in our minds, and then in our manifest realities. This card tells us that our nature is one with the nature of the universe. It suggests that we have the ability to control our own lives, that we can manipulate people, things, and events–so long as we go about it the right way and for the right ends.

This card is primarily about *self-development*; as Tarot Arcanum One, it is the *beginning* of the road to spiritual enlightenment, the starting point. It does not say that we are already able to control our universes, but that we must learn what mode to use in order to gain our ends and reach our goals, whether they are strictly mundane or whether they are intended to stretch us spiritually.

Mythologically, the Magician corresponds to great Hermes-Trismigistus, messenger of the gods, and guide of souls in the underworld. As messenger of the gods, he has the ability to communicate between the celestial and earthly realms and a guide figure, on the inner level, where he mediates between our conscious daylight world and the unconscious, hidden recesses of the psyche, often in dreams. The Magician suggests the use of higher intuitive forces, which may appear as a flash of insight. The Magician can serve as an inner guide who, if we listen carefully, will prompt us to develop and fulfill our potential—from within.

Also known as "Le Bateleur," the Magician corresponds to the number One and to the Hebrew letter Aleph.

Trumps Two—The High Priestess

Description

The High Priestess is a card most mysterious, representing that which has yet to be revealed, secret knowledge, the duality of life on Earth. She symbolizes feminine spiritual power, or the Goddess from whom all life comes and to whom all returns in the ever-cycling round that is life.

She is always a serene-faced female figure, usually seated with a book on her lap. In the Waite deck, this book bears the word "Torah," but in other decks it is merely an open book suggesting the divine law that underlies the manifest Universe. The scroll or book in her lap represents the "Akashic records," the divine repository of our lives past, present, and future. Sometimes, she is found standing, holding a staff and pointing toward an unseen object in the distance, another indication of something yet to be revealed.

In most decks, she sits or stands between two pillars, which represents the opposites of the dual nature of our world: good and evil; light and dark; truth and deception; positive and negative. In her person, she promises reconciliation of these opposites to those willing to follow the spiritual path of understanding universal law. In the Waite deck, the High Priestess sits at the doorway to the temple, which represents the body, as if welcoming students to enter and learn her secrets. However, the crescent moon at her feet warns of the danger of releasing higher knowledge to those unprepared to handle it.

In the Waite deck, the pillars are marked "B" and "J," for Boaz and Jachin; in other decks, the pillars are unmarked and can be read as portals of a doorway to the interior of life's mysteries, with the High Priestess as the guardian of the entryway. Also in the Waite deck, she sits against a background of pomegranates, a reference to Persephone,

Coming into Silence

Silence is the royal road to the center of the Self. The proverb tells us that "Silence is golden," yet it seems as if we experience silence as terrifying. An increasing amount of human-made sound saturates our world. Once we were awakened by the cock's crow or birdsong. Today, we wake to the BUZZ of an alarm clock or a radio so that even the first few minutes of our day are filled with mechanically delivered sound. The TV fills our ears while we dress and eat breakfast; driving to work, we play the radio or a tape.

Why is silence so hard to bear? Do we fear that in silence we will hear what we do not want to hear? Does the prospect of our own inner voice strike dread in us? Are we afraid of discovering that life can be lived at different levels? Pierre Lacout in *God Is Silence* says:

> Daily silence experienced in humility and fervour as an indispensable exercise in spiritual nourishment gradually creates within us a permanent state of silence. The soul discovers in such a silence unsuspected possibilities. It realizes that life can be lived at different levels.

A major component of the spiritual journey is reflection. Without silence one cannot reflect. As the popular culture does not value silence, it clearly denigrates reflection, which is seen as a threat to the established order of work and community involvement. Reflection leads to questioning—and questioning leads to independent thought, which in turn leads to weakening of social, political, and religious authority.

In order to experience the sacred in yourself, you must *dare to turn off the sound*. Try turning off all the electronic sound conveyors and listening instead to the simpler sounds around you—you might hear a baby bird peeping, a child babbling, a cat's footfall, rain dripping, or your own breathing. You might become aware of the natural silences that fall in the interstices of the flow of sound.

The sacred is everywhere around us, but it speaks with a still, small voice that is drowned out by the level of noise we permit and even encourage in our lives. Contact with the sacred occurs in the quiet stillness, when mind and heart are at rest. This point of silence is comparable to "the still point at the center of the turning wheel." This still center is the gateway between the striving ego and the Self, which seeks wholeness and unity. To find our center, we must become quiet and still. Only then can we thread our way through the usual untidy jumble of our colliding thoughts to that place within where spirit dwells.

—M.J. Abadie,
Awaken to Your Spiritual Self

Mythologically, the High Priestess is linked to the Egyptian goddess Isis, queen of the intellect, in her veiled form. Isis is the goddess who understands fully the workings of the Universe and is familiar with both the upper world and the underworld, where her husband Osiris reigns. Her essence is divine wisdom and a deep understanding of the laws that underlie and unite both realms. She knows the secrets of regeneration after death, of the transformative powers inherent in secret knowledge.

Also called "La Papesse," the High Priestess corresponds to the number Two and to the Hebrew letter Beth.

daughter of Demeter, who leaves the daylight, or upper world, to tend to the dead in the underworld, where she eats pomegranate seeds. In some decks, she carries flowers or is seen against a background of vegetables and vegetation, another reference to the Goddess, or Grain Mother.

On her breast, the High Priestess wears a cross, symbolic of the four elements—Fire, Earth, Air, and Water—held in balance. She always wears a crown, usually a crescent, the "horns of the moon," or a variant of it. In the Waite deck, between the horns sits a sphere, representative of the full moon. This particular card is reminiscent of the Egyptian mother goddess Hathor, who wears a similar headdress. Hathor can be considered a forerunner of Demeter/Persephone, as one who gives life and takes it back in due course.

Interpretation

When the High Priestess appears, she indicates that something hidden, or interior, is preparing to come forth. Or, that the person needs to pay more attention to his or her inner world of dreams, imagination, and intuition. She calls attention to the need to develop awareness of the totality of the person, the night side, so to speak, as well as the daylight personality and activities. Usually, the person is ready to accept the importance of developing this part of his or her life, but may have been holding back out of fear or inertia.

Her appearance can indicate that the person is attempting to hide something that needs to be revealed, or it can mean that the person is too much involved in an isolated inner world and needs to reconcile the inner life with the outer one.

Psychologically, the underworld refers to the unconscious, or what is in the process of coming into being. In this twilight realm, of which dreams are a component, we encounter our inner selves through intuition and fantasy. The High Priestess is an image representing our potentials that have yet to be discovered and brought forth—our secret selves longing to be recognized.

Trumps Three—The Empress

Description

The Empress is a card of beauty and nurturance, the matriarch incarnate, symbolic of the Universal Mother as monarch. She represents the *social* concept of the feminine in the maternal role: procreation, nurturing, the security and comforts of home and domestic harmony. A positive card.

The Empress is always a mature female figure, usually seated on a throne. Though in some decks she is standing in a field, she is always surrounded by flowers and vegetation representative of the bounty of Mother Nature and her harvest. Full-breasted and pregnant, she symbolizes fruitfulness and earthly abundance. As such, she is related to all of the fertile mother goddesses from Demeter and Ceres of the pagan religions to the Virgin Mary of the Christian tradition.

As a symbol of her royal position, she holds a scepter and wears an imperial crown of great magnificence. In many decks, a shield or coat of arms leans against her throne, at her feet. In the Waite deck, this is heart-shaped and bears the astrological symbol for Venus, which is also seen depicted somewhere on cards for the Empress from other decks. Venus, of course, is the planet of love, beauty, desires, and pleasure. It is the quintessential traditional feminine symbol.

Mythologically, the Empress is linked to all of the mother goddesses of antiquity, but especially to Greek Hera, the wife of Zeus and the quintessential matriarchal maternal figure. She is called Juno by the Romans and has an asteroid named after her. As a primary symbol for feminine fertility, she is associated not only with all of the great fertile mother-goddesses of the pagan religion but also with the Virgin Mary of the Christian tradition.

Also called "L'Imperatrice," the Empress corresponds to the number Three and to the Hebrew letter Gimel.

Interpretation

When the Empress appears, there is a strong feminine element at work. As a mother figure and representative of the traditional female role, the Empress is a creative force that works for harmony. She brings disparate things together, reconciling differences, like a mother running a household must do. This is a card of emotional control and making things work together toward a common social goal.

As a female authority, her appearance may signify, depending on its place in the spread, the person's need to *become* that female authority, especially if the person is a woman. If a man, the indication is that he needs to recognize the feminine component of himself and acknowledge its power to harmonize.

The Empress also refers to the person's emotional and physical resources—for nurturing, healing, feeding, and supporting other people. Often, there is a situation in the person's life where deep and total love and nurturing are required—sometimes by the person him or herself, sometimes by others in the environment. This card is related to the caretaking process and may refer to the way the person was mothered and how he or she feels about that, for the first and most significant relationship we form is with our mother, and this relationship has a direct bearing on all subsequent relationships we form. Sometimes this card indicates that the person either had an overbearing "smother mother," or is acting out that role. It is an excellent card to use for meditation upon issues of nurturance, of marriage commitment, or of abundance.

Trumps Four—The Emperor

Description

The Emperor is a figure of supreme authority, as his title suggests. He is usually seated on a throne, flanked by animals. In the Waite deck, these are ram's heads, symbolic of traditional masculine power. He wears robes over a full suit of armor, holds a scepter in the shape of the Egyptian ankh, and is crowned elaborately. In some decks, his shield, bearing the symbol of the imperial eagle, leans against the throne. He is clearly a figure to be reckoned with. Often he is shown outdoors, against a backdrop of mountains, another reference to worldly power. His age and position of authority speak of experience and wisdom gained. Although he is depicted as a warrior, his attitude is one of passive kindness as the beneficient ruler of his empire.

Yet, while passive, his attitude is one of being willing to fight for what is right and what is his duty to protect. He is depicted as the executive, or leader, who has reached the summit of authority because of his willingness to exert all his energy to achieve his high position. This is a positive card in terms of worldly power.

Thus, he is a father figure, as the Empress is a mother figure. As in families with traditional values, the father is the one who lays down the ideals, morals, and aspirations for the entire family to follow. He is the builder of the material world who strives to make his constructions of lasting value and importance. He emphasizes solidarity.

Interpretation

When the Emperor appears, look for issues related to authority. Although the Emperor represents worldly power and wisdom, he is not simply a figure who gives commands to others. His achievement is to understand that the maintenance of peace and security requires

Mythologically, the Emperor is related to Zeus, the father-god of the Greek pantheon. The Romans called him Jupiter; the Scandinavians, Thor. All were known for throwing thunderbolts, or lightning. In some decks the Emperor carries thunderbolts instead of the ankh.

From a pagan perspective, because the Emperor *follows* the Empress, he represents the horned god who always accompanied the Great Mother Goddess, of which Pan is the most common figure. As consort to the Empress, he represents parenthood and masculine creativity.

Also known as "L'Empereur," The Emperor corresponds to the number Four and to the Hebrew letter Daleth.

the willingness and ability to defend it. "The price of freedom is eternal vigilance."

The Emperor is a teacher figure, and what he teaches is the meaning and use of power in this world of the here and now. Though not overtly aggressive, he tells us that it is necessary sometimes to take up arms against negative or evil forces. With the Emperor, there is no compromising with one's knowledge of what is right and good, no rationalizing that the ends justify the means. As a protective male force, especially of the home and of domestic harmony, he personifies the ideal that what is worth having is worth fighting for.

The Emperor in a reading can also indicate issues relating to one's relationship with one's personal father, or to authority figures in general. He can mean that the time has arrived to *become* the authority figure rather than depending on others to wield the sword in one's behalf. In my experience, the Emperor often appears when the person is struggling to achieve personal independence, to overcome the inner parent tapes, to become his or her own person.

The Emperor says that one must, often at a late date in life, come to terms with what "father" means in his or her life, and face and reconcile issues related to this issue. Whether the personal father relationship has been positive or negative, it is important to realize that at some point an adult must in fact become his or her own father.

When the Emperor appears, he can be an indication that the real father of the person has either recently died or may die soon, a situation which can bring up feelings of being abandoned by a protective father figure. If this is the case, then the person must face up to responsibility for his or her own life. Even if the personal father was a negative factor, there is always a yearning for someone else to take care of us, protect us, advise us. Yet, in the final analysis, separation from the parents is a crucial stage in human development and must be accomplished.

Another interpretation is that there may be someone in the person's life who is *acting* as a father figure, a boss or a husband. Whether this is positive or negative will be indicated by the placement of the card in the layout.

Meeting Your Guide

Here is a method for making contact with a guide/teacher. There is no right or wrong way to contact a guide; some appear spontaneously without your asking, others respond to your call. In this meditation, you are going to meet a guide whom you can trust and rely on. To prepare yourself, do the following:

1. Articulate a question you wish to ask your guide. State the question as clearly and succinctly as you can. Vague questions beget vague answers. State the subject about which you wish guidance.
2. Do not ask a question that can be answered by a simple *yes* or *no*.
3. Stick to the present situation; avoid generalities.
4. Do not ask a question requiring a prediction. Simply asking for guidance is always good.
5. Be willing to trust your guide; accept whatever comes to your mind. If you draw a blank, try later.
6. When a guide appears, pay attention to the appearance. Ask for a name or a symbol.

After you have prepared yourself for your encounter with your guide, find the time to be alone and undisturbed for half an hour. Relax yourself completely and let go of the day's tensions and cares.

Mentally take yourself to a place somewhere in nature—a forest, the seaside, a flower-filled meadow, a lake shore, a cove, a woods—whatever appeals to you. See in front of you in this pleasant place a veiled object, full of mystery. A puff of wind comes along and blows away the covering and your guide is revealed to you. Take whatever image comes and begin to dialogue with it. Ask your question and wait for an answer. If one doesn't come at once, be patient. The answer may come in words, through intuition or telepathically, as an image, even a snatch of song or an instruction to read a book or magazine article.

In these guided meditations, the specifics are not as important as making the contact. Whatever springs into your mind is the right answer, because you are using a process to contact your own inner wisdom. Your guides are within the realm of the deepest part of your being, which is connected to all reality everywhere at all times and places.

When you have met your guide, introduced yourself, and asked your question, notice the details of the place so that you can return here whenever you like. Fix it in your memory. When you get the answer to your question, thank your guide and say you will look forward to further dialogue in the future.

If you do not get an answer, or if the answer seems to make no sense, accept that also and try again later. Remember you are learning a new skill.

Before leaving, make an appointment to meet with your guide again at a set time in the future and follow through on this with another meditation.

Trumps Five—The Hierophant (or High Priest)

Description

The Hierophant is a figure of the same authority and power as the Emperor, with the difference that the Hierophant's power is of a spiritual nature while the Emperor's is temporal. Thus, he is considered to be a figure of a religious leader such as the Pope of Roman Catholicism. Some decks title him as "The Pope." He is seen seated on a throne, dressed in priestly raiment, crowned, and holding a scepter. His implements will vary according to the religious theme of the deck.

His scepter symbolizes the three worlds–physical, astral, and etheric. His free hand is held aloft in a position of blessing.

Standing before him are usually two or three acolytes who face him, either as participants or as supplicants or students, representing his wisdom and understanding as a representative of religious authority as it stems from organized religions.

Like the Emperor, he is a passive figure containing in himself the wisdom of a spiritual calling, and like the High Priestess, he sits or stands between two pillars, which (as in Trumps Two) stand for the duality of the world of matter and spirit. As a spiritual teacher whose task it is to connect the world of men with that of the gods, that is, to forge a link between the material and spiritual worlds, he is a *pontifex*, an ancient word that meant "maker of bridges," and which is used to designate a priest.

In this role, he can be seen as a teacher to those who seek the keys to the sacred Mysteries. Below him are two crossed keys representing the intellect and intuition and the need to use them in tandem, in a morally conscious context that includes the desire and responsibility both for making spiritual decisions for others and for blessing them. Unlike the High Priestess, whose world is primarily internal and ephemeral, the Hierophant's influence is of-this-world

and his spirituality can be achieved through conscious choices made on an intellectual basis.

Interpretation

When the Hierophant appears in a reading, there is the suggestion that the person has chosen a specific religion or a particular life philosophy with which to guide his or her life. In such a case, there is usually a great deal of loyalty to it, whatever the person's concept of "God" may be. There is also the possibility of disentangling one's self from such an association.

In some organized religions, the supreme deity does not speak to the individual directly, or to the general populace. Therefore, institutionalized religion makes use of human "interpreters" who preach or teach the "word of God" or the divine will to their followers.

The Hierophant symbolizes *any* organized institution, be it religious, philosophical, or educational, spiritual or temporal, that exerts authority over its followers or participants, a kind of "mind control." In such groups there is always a person, or a group of people, doing the controlling. They always insist that their way is the *only* way, that theirs is the ultimate truth: either you obey them or you will be damned to all eternity.

Therefore, when the Hierophant appears, the idea of *choice* is posited. At this stage of your spiritual development, you are challenged to remain a follower or to break out and find your own individual spiritual truth. This card suggests that you have the opportunity—and often the desire—to choose your own road to salvation, to interpret the "word of God" in your own way. The Hierophant presents this challenge: will you continue to depend on an outside authority, or will you learn to think for yourself? The answer is yours alone, and there may be considerable conflict concerning the issue, but what you decide will affect the rest of your life and how you live it spiritually. This is not always a positive card, for it can indicate those who wish to exercise authority over others for their own purposes.

Mythologically, the Hierophant is linked to the Centaur, or Chiron, teacher of Apollo, the sun god and healer. Half man, half horse, the Hierophant represents the quest for meaning in life. Related to the sign of Sagittarius, which represents higher learning and the dissemination of knowledge, he is a teacher figure who is there to guide the spiritual seeker find a connection or bridge between the two worlds—the inner and outer, the material and immaterial. His understanding goes beyond organized religion and is not based on any rigid dogma but on the truth of the unconscious inner world of the psyche.

Also known as "Le Pape," or "The Pope," the Hierophant corresponds to the number Five and to the Hebrew letter He.

Trumps Six—The Lovers

Description

There are two basic images for the Lovers: one shows a couple of young lovers either nude or clothed, standing apart or touching. Above them is an angel-like figure with its wings spread out over them and its hands held above their heads in a gesture of blessing. The Waite deck shows them as Adam and Eve, standing respectively before the Tree of Eternal Life and the Tree of the Knowledge of Good and Evil. Imagery in other decks suggests choice is involved as well as the possibility of union.

Other decks depict three people, as if the third party—who might be another young person or an older parental figure—were an influence on their relationship. In decks where three figures are shown, a winged, cupid-like figure on a cloud points an arrow in the direction of one of the women. Egyptian-style decks show one young man and two young women, the implication being that he must choose between them, another symbol that this card is about choice.

Interpretation

Although many readers interpret this card as basically about romantic love, it is allegorically a statement about *union*—of opposites, whether people, such as a man and woman, or inner conflict. The Lovers refers to discrimination in the making of choices, and the male and female figures are symbols not only of human love and marriage but also of the dual nature of ourselves. We all have opposite traits within ourselves that need to be reconciled and lived with, just as well as married couples, or any other sort of partners, experience conflict that requires making choices, sometimes tough ones, and effecting reconciliation.

When the Lovers appears, it is pointing to this need to heal an inner rift. Although it can herald a romantic involvement, it most often turns up when a critical life decision must be made, sometimes in connection with a love relationship. There are obstacles to be overcome, both within and without.

This card suggests that you are at a crossroads—you have to consider all of the ramifications of the situation and carefully make discriminating choices in order to further your own development and to accommodate the needs of others in the situation. There may be much activity in the form of short trips (one person may live in another place, for example), or you may be commuting to contact business partners.

Mythologically, the Lovers reflect Eros, the son of the great goddess of love and beauty, Aphrodite. Eros was named Cupid by the Romans, and it is his job to shoot the arrows of love, which was considered a form of madness, at unsuspecting youths. Thus, Eros/Cupid was often depicted blindfolded to represent that, as we are all told, "love is blind." But Eros has another role—to guide us toward our true destiny, which is to say "Do what you love and everything else will follow naturally."

Also called "L'Amoureux," the Lovers corresponds to the number Six and to the Hebrew Letter Vav.

Trumps Seven—The Chariot

Description

The Chariot is depicted as a strong male figure holding the reigns of two beasts, usually Sphinxlike, one black and one white. Sometimes the beasts are unicorns or other mythical beasts like Perseus, the winged horse. The charioteer is fully-armored and carries a scepter suggesting royalty or that he is in the service of royalty. He wears a belt and a skirt decorated with zodiacal glyphs, symbolic of Time. The wheels of the chariot signify the ever-changing life cycles, and on his shoulders are crescent moons suggesting emotional factors and unconscious habit patterns that need changing.

The animals are pulling in opposite directions, and he is manfully holding the reins taut to keep them in tandem, another symbolic statement of the need to master and reconcile conflicting needs, both inner and outer.

In some decks, such as Waite, the charioteer holds no reins, suggesting he is using sheer will power to keep his steeds going together in a forward direction. The beasts pulling the chariot signify the opposing forces, which were reconciled at the stage of the Lovers, and represent the person's mastery of these opposing forces and control over inner conflicts. This card suggests that before taking on outer enemies or obstacles it is essential to be in charge of the inner opposites so that they function in harmony. The Chariot is a symbol for the Self and its direction, as is any vehicle that appears in a dream, such as an automobile.

Astrological Reference for the Hanged Man

The Hanged Man's appearance in a layout often is a pointer to a transit of the planet Neptune against the person's natal chart. Neptune is associated with all that is diffuse, illusory, vague, otherworldly, imaginative, psychic; his transits can be especially difficult because of the vagueness of the effects. There is a breakdown of the ego-structure that can be accompanied by feelings of defeat, confusion, apathy, depression, or by addictive behaviors.

Depending upon the person's level of consciousness, a Neptune transit can also bring into play feelings of exhilaration and an opening up to a sense of being at one with all life, with the Universe. There can be a feeling of being "out of this world," because Neptune is outside time and space, symbolizing the "other," a dimensionless or multidimensioned universe.

The ego dissolves in Neptune's vapors. Under his influence, one comes to realize that the ego is not ultimately real. This realization, if encountered in the right spirit, is liberating for it promotes detachment from over-identification with the physical self and its concerns. With Neptune, we are in touch with the *ideal real*, which transcends physical reality, and lets us understand that, "I am not my body." We come to know that the essential Self is boundless and limitless.

Neptune is the planet of mystics, seers, visionaries, and the transcendent realm, which represents the level where individuality is merged into universality. Many people have had visionary, ecstatic, miracle cure, and near-death experiences under Neptune's influence.

Persons who are heavily dependent upon a prescribed structure to contain their lives will be most disturbed by a Neptune transit, for it can fog over everything and make the most solid-seeming of structures turn to ungraspable mist. Those with a somewhat weak ego structure may fare best because they are not bound up in the definitely structured format of someone with a strong ego. Thus, they are more sensitive to the transformative energies coming through them.

Often someone with a Neptune transit just wants to sleep and dream, which is a good idea because it puts the person in touch with extraordinary realities.

Neptune is a great teacher and bringer of higher consciousness and, though this can manifest merely as escapism (often through drugs and alcohol), his transits give us an opportunity to develop insight into our real needs. This often evolves from the desire to spend time alone to sort the confusion being experienced. With Neptune, we have the impetus to get to the root of what is amiss in our lives, both psychically and physically, and to seek out a positive therapy that suits our unique needs. Also, conditions can vanish as mysteriously as they presented, with no apparent cause either for the onset or the resolution.

Mythologically, the Chariot is related to many cultures. Helios, the Greek Sun god drove a chariot of fire across the heavens. In the Hindu culture, the Lord of the World drives his chariot along the road of Time. In ancient Rome, the god of war, Mars, was depicted triumphantly riding to victory in his chariot. These mythic images suggest that the charioteer has triumphed over all conflicting forces, found his or her true path in life, and is now being guided by intuition and a sense of clear and unambiguous purpose.

Also known as "Le Chariot," The Chariot corresponds to the number Seven, which is linked with the hidden rhythms of the universe, and to the Hebrew letter Zayin.

Interpretation

When the Chariot appears, there is a need to be in control of competing forces, whether these are inner conflicts or whether they represent people or a situation in your life that requires you to take command in order to reach your goals. Like the celebrated but seldom achieved "bipartisanship" of government, the solution to the problem at hand is to take the middle road between the conflicting elements.

You may feel unequal to the challenge of controlling the multiple factors of a given situation, but if you choose to just "go with the flow" and make the best of where it takes you, you will succeed. Once you have resolved within your own mind the conflict, even if that requires considerable struggle, you will be in a position to stay on course. To do this, you need firm resolve—*self-mastery*. With a strategy determined by clear-thinking and a sense of purpose, you will overcome all obstacles.

Receiving the Chariot in a reading, depending on its position in the spread, is generally favorable. It indicates you have the means to triumph over all obstacles and stay the course you have set for yourself. It can also mean that assistance is on the way as a result of your own strength and determination. It can also suggest you are in the process of transforming yourself and your ways of thinking and doing in order to create a firm foundation from which to go forward and achieve your desires. You are at this time keenly aware of how to use your past experience to reach a major goal and you are in touch with deep inner resources.

At a literal level, it relates to travel and transportation and could mean changing your mode of transport, such as buying a new car, or traveling by rail or some other form of wheeled vehicle.

Trumps Eight—Strength

[Note: The Waite and Grey decks show Strength as Number Eight; many other decks, however, show Justice as Eight and Strength as Eleven. This book follows Waite's ordering of the cards.]

Description

Most decks depict Strength as a woman in relationship to a lion. Some writers see this as a struggle, but in many decks there does not appear to be any conflict between the woman and the lion. In fact, she seems to be in total control of him, even affectionate with him.

A few decks do show a strong young man wrestling with the lion, perhaps a reference to Heracles or Sampson, in which case he is bare-handed, a suggestion that he needs no weapon. But, in most decks, Strength is a female figure.

In the Waite deck, the woman is bending over the lion in a gesture of gentleness, closing his jaws as if she expects no resistance to her touch. She is garbed in a flowing garment and wears a garland of flowers in her hair. Above her head is the symbol for infinity. In other decks, she is caressing the lion, riding atop him, or simply shown beside him.

Although many interpreters view this card as one of struggle with one's inner "animal" nature, I see it as symbolic of self-confidence and inner strength, of being in harmony with one's instinctive nature. The woman is taming or making friends with the powerful force represented by the animal nature in humans, one which we ignore or deny to our detriment, even peril. Though the lion is clearly the more physically powerful of the two, the woman represents human courage and will power that masters the instinctive realm not by force but by cooperation.

Mythologically, Strength relates to the original pagan goddess known as the "Lady of the Beasts," from an era when it was believed that women naturally possessed understanding of the ways of Nature, for they were not only planters but also healers. In ancient pagan times, this goddess reigned supreme. Later, she was personified by the Greeks as Artemis, goddess of the hunt.

Also known as "La Force," Strength corresponds to the number Eight and to the Hebrew letter Cheth.

Interpretation

When Strength appears in a reading, you are exhibiting moral courage and fortitude. You have learned to work in harmony with your own instinctive nature, to listen to it and hear its whisperings. As in tales of the hero's journey, the seeker often meets with animals, representative of the instinctive realm, who guide and help him on his way. Strength indicates that you have come through difficulties and learned to rely on inner strength to solve your problems.

This is a time when faith in yourself will pay off, when your position is strong because you have made yourself strong through suffering trials and tribulations without being defeated by them. It is a time to let people around you know who you are—especially anyone who has been dominating you.

The indication is that it is the feminine principle that does the work of reconciling the mental-rational facility with that of the intuitive-instinctive nature. The feminine is always in closer touch with nature than the masculine. Whether the reading is for a man or a woman, the same principle applies. The lesson is that we do not conquer our animal natures by brute force (which is the typical masculine mode of approach to obstacles) but by gentleness and feeling our way into rapport with the instinctive side of our nature.

Depending on the placement of the card in the spread and the question that is being asked, Strength is an indication that what is required in the situation is for spiritual strength to replace or overcome physical strength.

Trumps Nine—The Hermit

Description

The Hermit is a guide figure represented as an old man, often bearded, holding a lighted lantern aloft in one hand and a staff in the other. He is dressed in the long robes of an anchorite or monk, plain and unadorned except for, in some decks, a knotted or tasseled cord around the waist. He radiates the wisdom of the archetypal old man figure, the sage of myth and legend.

The Hermit is always standing, sometimes walking, looking ahead at what only he can see—your future. He is of sober mein, an ancient who is experienced on many levels and now functions as a teacher and guide. The background is usually of mountains in the distance, suggesting he has reached the heights and returned to our plane to assist us in our development. He is wise in the ways of all the worlds, visible and invisible, material and immaterial.

He travels alone, a seeker after truth, lighting the way ahead for those who follow after. He needs no trappings of rank or royalty, wears no adornment, and carries no baggage. His goal is to search and to show others their true direction. His wooden staff symbolizes his connection to the forces of nature and of the instinctual realm.

The Hermit's slightly bent posture and serious expression link him to Father Time, or Saturn—the planet that symbolizes boundaries and limitations, the obstacles that appear on everyone's life course. His solitude suggests the periodic need to withdraw from the hectic world of everyday in order to regain perspective through silent reflection.

Mythologically, the Hermit is linked to Uranus and Cronos, the god of Time. The myth of these two fathers—both disposed by their sons because they refused to face up to the facts of their inevitable ends—warns us to accept the reality that all must grow old and die in order for new life to emerge. The "death" may not be a physical one but the shedding of life-denying ideas that serve as limitations on the Spirit, in order that we may renew ourselves in rebirth.

Also known as "L'Hermite," the Hermit corresponds to the number Nine and to the Hebrew letter Teth.

Interpretation

When the Hermit appears in a reading, there are two separate possibilities of interpretation. One is that a guide figure is at hand, offering help. Depending on the card's position in the layout, the guide figure may be close at hand only waiting for the querent to make communication with him, or he may be at a distance and require the person to make an effort through meditation or consciously beginning a search.

A second interpretation is that the questioner must voluntarily withdraw from contact with the outer world for a time in order to search his or her soul for the meaning of his or her life. The implication is that the inner work needs to be done *now*, and that Spirit cannot speak to you if you are totally distracted by the hurly-burly and noise of everyday life. The need to search for Truth for the individual is urgent, and it can only be done alone.

Whichever interpretation seems to suit the readee, and the question being put to the Tarot cards, the overall meaning is that the time has come to reunite with the Source, whether for guidance or inner balance. Sometimes, the guide figure may represent a person, such as a counselor of some sort—a therapist or clergy person—but usually it refers to inner guidance, or the getting in touch with a guide from the other side.

The Hanged Man and the Mind

It is interesting to note that the Hanged Man bears two references to the *mind*. One is the connection to Mercury, the planet that rules mental processes; the other is to the sign Aquarius, the fixed Air sign of the mind. (Aquarius rules the ankles; he is suspended by one ankle). Because I am an astrologer, these indications seem to me especially significant when the Hanged Man appears in a reading, and I ask the client, *Who's in charge of your mind?*

The immediate response might be, "I am, of course!" But some thought may bring the surprise discovery that you aren't as much in charge of your mind—what and how you think—as you might want to believe. Many people base their thinking on "what Mother would think," or "What father would say," or even opinions of neighbors, teachers, doctors, colleagues, or friends.

Not being in charge of your mind produces an entire spectrum of difficulties, from minor ones like not being able to decide what to wear based on your own needs and preferences to major ones like choosing a life mate based on someone else's qualifications for the "right" person.

Or, you may have trained for a profession and been taught rigid methods of thinking. "Don't make waves," becomes the dictum of the day. The rude iconoclast, the breaker of rules, the questioner of things-as-they are, is branded unruly and undesirable, even made an outcast. If you secretly think there's a better or more innovative way of doing things or of thinking about them, but continue to slavishly follow the dicta of any system that bears an "-ism" after the name of its originator, you are not in charge of your mind.

And as long as you are not in charge of your mind, you are not in charge of your life!

Individually and globally, we all have problems. To find solutions, we need to learn to *see* in new ways. We must all become *seers*. The seer—one who sees—is the sage because he can see what others cannot see, and it is the development of this capacity that the Hanged Man represents.

As he demonstrates, the truth-seeker must find the way alone, often painfully and slowly, sifting and sorting about through various systems of thought to find the answers he or she seeks, and this process *must* start with the *individual*.

It takes persistence, self-control, and self-knowledge to stick to one's guns and find and hold to that inner reality which is one's true Self. It is this path to which the Hanged Man points, the path that will set us free—free to be who we are, free to think unfettered, free to "create our own reality."

Trumps Ten—The Wheel of Fortune

Description

The Wheel of Fortune is variously depicted according to the deck. Invariably there is a wheel–usually with eight spokes, a reference to ancient symbolism for the wholeness of the world as produced by the ever-turning cycles of life, death, and rebirth. The Wheel is also a symbol for the Sun's path across the sky. There are always figures attached to the wheel, sometimes human, sometimes mythical.

The Waite deck shows a sphinx holding a sword at the top of the wheel, calmly watching as the karmic wheel revolves. Around the wheel are letters that spell "Rota," a reference to the "Royal Road of the Tarot." The ascending figure on the right is a jackal-headed man, called Hermanubus, who is known for keen eyesight, while a serpent descending on the left side represents the earth and the sexual energy that arises from it. Above and below, at the four corners of the card, are winged creatures holding open books. These correspond to the Bull, the Lion, the Eagle, and the Man, which represent the fixed signs of the zodiac, Taurus, Leo, Scorpio, and Aquarius respectively. In the Christian tradition, these refer to Matthew, Mark, Luke, and John.

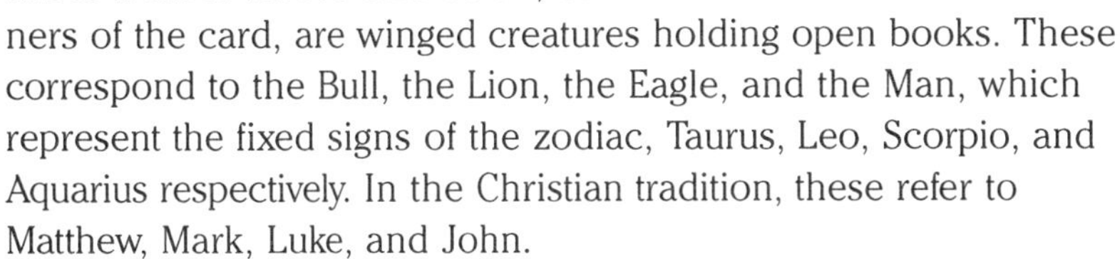

Other decks show monkey-like figures caught on the wheel, or people in flowing robes wearing garlands in their hair, or eight young women between the spokes wearing expressions that vary through the stages from joy to despair. The suggestion is that the figures are rising and falling through the various life cycles as the wheel turns. Occasionally, the wheel stands alone, obviously turning, or it is a disc decorated with symbols suspended in the sky. Sometimes a blindfolded woman is turning the wheel.

Interpretation

When the Wheel of Fortune appears in a reading, it means that something has been put in motion over which you now have little or no control. You are being forced to accept the action of the forces of destiny, to get in tune with them, and to align yourself with their aims. Generally, however, the outcome is considered favorable.

These forces already set in motion foretell of changing circumstances, usually for the better, beneficial changes that will promote your growth and advancement. Balance may be an issue if you are resisting change, but you now have no choice but to go along with whatever process is working in your life. Things will run their course, and "What goes up must come down." The Wheel of Fortune is a reminder that every period of intense activity must be followed by a fallow time of rest and inactivity. Where you are in your own personal cycle will be shown by the other cards in the spread.

This card almost always heralds good fortune coming as a result of what you yourself have put into motion, even if you aren't totally aware of what you have done to get the process going. You may have applied for a new job, met a new person, begun a romance, decided to take a college course, or had a chance encounter that got the ball rolling—or the wheel turning. It means a new phase, possibly the need to make an important decision, or even a totally unexpected circumstance developing that will literally change your life.

This card is a restatement of the famous line from *The Rubiat of Omar Kayhan*, "The moving finger, having writ, moves on, nor all your charm nor wit can cancel half a line of it."

Mythologically, the Wheel of Fortune is linked to the three Fates, collectively called the *Moiari:* one spins the thread of life, the second weaves it, and the third cuts it. Thus, the Wheel of Fortune is a reminder of the mysterious cycles of life, death, and rebirth and of the invisible forces that measure them out to each of us. This connection suggests that there is a greater force, that behind the seemingly random changes in one's life, there is an intelligent plan of order. The three spinners represent our own unconscious selves and they are an indication that, in some way, we create our own Fate and direct the course our life will take.

Also called "La Roue de Fortune," The Wheel of Fortune corresponds to the number Ten and to the Hebrew letter Yod.

Trumps Eleven—Justice

Description

The Justice card shows a female figure, as a rule robed, sometimes armored, and crowned. She holds an upright sword in one hand; in the other, perfectly balanced scales. In some modern decks, she is either a nude figure with arms outstretched in absolute even balance, or she is shown in Egyptian type decks as standing in between a large set of scales while holding a smaller set.

Unlike the modern image of Justice as blindfolded, this Justice is open-eyed, suggesting *divine* justice rather than the laws of man that have been carved in marble and otherwise codified. That she stares straight at the viewer suggests that divine justice is not bound by human limitations and tendency to error and bias.

Interpretation

When the Justice card appears in a reading, it can be an indication of an actual legal matter pending or being considered. Whatever the situation to which it refers, there is always the indication that you must weigh many factors in order to make a reasoned and factual assessment, i.e., judgment, of the matter at hand. The Justice card warns you to take guidance from your inner self, not to rely solely on human advisors. Also, it cautions prudence and care, the need to deliberate calmly and carefully before taking action or concluding an outcome.

If others are involved, you would be well advised to take their point of view into your considerations for issues of fairness are paramount now. You can expect legal matters, if a part of the circumstances, to proceed smoothly and fairly in a dispassionate manner, and be confident that Justice will prevail as a result of your own temperate behavior and rational thought. Depending on what other cards appear in the spread, there may be a third party coming to your aid who will assist you to get the fair outcome you deserve. This card can also represent anyone involved with the legal profession–a lawyer, a judge, witnesses, law enforcement officers, and the like.

Symbolically, Justice is related to a mythic lineage that stretches as far back as ancient Egypt. In Egyptian mythology, the goddess Maat—whose name means truth and justice—stood in the underworld with a pair of scales upon which she weighed the newly dead person's soul against "The Feather of Truth" to decide if the soul was worthy to pass into the realm of Osiris, god of the underworld.

Also known as "La Justice," Justice corresponds to the number Eleven and to the Hebrew letter Kaph.

Trumps Twelve—The Hanged Man

Description

The Hanged Man is a tantalizing figure. A male, hanging upside down, one leg crossed behind the other knee, his arms folded so that he clasps his hands behind his back, he would seem to be in supreme torture, but his expression is serene as if he is thoroughly enjoying his state. Suspended as he is by one foot, tied at the ankle, he seems to be engaged in a rather bizarre form of meditation or ritual.

In the Waite deck, he is hanging from a tree, its living roots in the ground, and the crosspiece which supports him is growing with leaves. Some authorities say this is the Tree of Life itself. Around his head is a golden halo, like the rays of the sun–yellow is the color of Mercury, planet of the mind. Other decks show only the horizontal beam, but it too has leaves on it, showing it is living wood.

There is no clue as to why he is in this odd predicament, except it is evident he chose it and that he is deriving some satisfaction from the position. If he is suffering, as one might assume, he doesn't show any signs of it. The suggestion is that he is seeking enlightenment.

Astrological Reference to the Death Card

When the Death card appears in a reading, it usually signifies that the person is experiencing a transit of the planet Pluto against the natal chart. Pluto is *the* planet of transformation. Ruler of Scorpio, under his influence hidden things are flushed out into the open to be dealt with.

Representative of the regenerative process, a Pluto transit marks the rebirth we experience when we finally say, "Nevermore" to past patterns of self-destructive behavior and negative thinking. Pluto is subtle—its evolutionary power works slowly and at great depth, permeating the psyche, replacing old aspects of the personality with new ones in a process of fundamental transformation.

Like the Death card, Pluto refers to a *metaphorical* death, something that must be allowed to die—things we hold onto from the past—hopes, dreams, memories, cherished ambitions. We can be held back from fully living our lives by these anchors to the past.

Often, a Pluto transit will bring events or conditions that act as a mirror of something that did not get handled in the past, at the appropriate time. It is only by confronting that past and resolving it that coping with the present is possible. A Pluto crisis is an opportunity to *transform old, unwanted problems* into new life energy.

A force beyond the ego, Pluto operates with extreme power—often manifesting as power struggles. It can cause a person to feel totally out of control. Pluto rules death and decay as well as regeneration, which means that Pluto transits can bring a sense that everything is disintegrating around one.

If those undergoing Pluto transits can accept the need for building a new reality, rather than desperately trying to maintain the old structure, the process is less upsetting. The time comes when the old structures no longer work. They cannot be repaired or patched up any longer. The only choice is to destroy them and rebuild, to let go of whatever must be let go in order to hasten the birth of the new.

Mythologically, the Hanged Man is related to all of the dying and resurrected gods of mythology, of which there are many. Odin was the Norse god who voluntarily hung for nine days from "the windy tree" called *Yggdrasil*, another form of the World Tree, in order to achieve knowledge of the runes and magic. Attis was a Greek who bled to death under a pine tree. The pagan world was filled with "corn gods" who were literally sacrificed annually so that their blood, sprinkled on the corn fields, would produce an abundant harvest. Later on this sacrifice became ritual not literal, to symbolize that we symbolically "die" in order to be reborn in Spirit.

Also known as "Le Pendu," the Hanged Man corresponds to the number Twelve and to the Hebrew letter Lamed.

Interpretation

Many if not most writers see the Hanged Man as a card of self-sacrifice and martyrdom, but I view this tantalizing card as voluntary surrender to the process of achieving enlightenment, doing whatever it takes to reach that goal. It may require giving up superficial pleasures and trivial pursuits, but that is hardly a major sacrifice for one who has chosen, or is choosing, a more spiritual way of life.

Granted that giving up adult "toys" in order to grow spiritually requires sacrifice in some sense—but remember that the word "sacrifice" derives from the Latin *sacra fice* which means "to make sacred." So, his is a sacred pursuit.

When this card appears in a reading, depending on its position in the layout, the person is usually already aware that a call to a less materialistic way of life has been received. The card indicates the person is ready for whatever personal sacrifice is needed, or is preparing to make such a gesture. In the latter case, the querent may need to pause in his or her life and suspend ordinary activities to better realize just where he or she is going spiritually. Often, The Hanged Man signifies someone going through a major transformation, perhaps caused by illness or some loss, the result of which has been to shake up the old way of life and make the person realize that there is more to life than money and material goods.

This card can indicate that a new commitment to the development of the querent's inner self is demanded. There may be an intense need to get off by one's self in order to re-evaluate just what is and what is not important to the querent. Sometimes he or she is finding it very difficult to let go of the old pattern, whether it is a relationship, a job, a world view, or a group of other people. Being called "selfish" for wanting to make changes may be a problem that needs to be overcome.

Trumps Thirteen—Death

Description

The Death card tends to frighten people who see it come up in a reading, but despite its grim depiction it symbolizes the transforming powers of life and death. Many decks picture a skeleton with a scythe grinning toothily and wearing a black hooded robe. The Waite deck pictures Death as a man in black armor riding a white charger, suggesting the perpetual movement of the cycles of life and death.

The knight carries a banner on which is embroidered the mystical white rose, symbol of pure and true love. The rose, with five petals, represents the five senses of material life combined with the immortality of the heart, or soul. Greeting the knight with hands outstretched in blessing or supplication, is a priest figure with a mitered cardinal's hat and two children looking on in awe. In the background, the sun is rising, a sign of resurrection, over a body of water representing the unconscious realm.

Other decks show backgrounds that are sparse and bare, sometimes there are severed body parts lying about randomly. One deck shows the four horses of the Apocalypse riding through a stormy sky. Another shows a black-robed and hooded faceless figure standing in a woods; he appears to be supporting with one outstretched arm a huge white rose that dominates the card visually.

Mythologically, Death is related to such figures as the Hindu goddess, Kali, who wears a necklace of skulls, and to the Greek Hades, god of the underworld, renamed Pluto by the Romans. Also called "La Mort," Death corresponds to the number Thirteen, which is associated with magic—it is the number of lunar months in a year and the traditional number of witches in a coven.

Interpretation

Receiving the Death card in a reading does *not* portend a physical death. What it means is the end, or death, of a cycle. Whenever a stage in one's life ends, there is need for mourning. Which of us, growing older, does not mourn for lost youth? But we grow up and find other satisfactions. It is only the refusal to accept that something is ending—trying desperately to hold on to what is clearly over—that causes trouble. Employing cosmetic means to stave off the approach of age that heralds eventual physical death is a useless effort to avoid the inevitable. What gives importance and meaning to this card is the querent's *acceptance* of the change that cannot be avoided.

Thus, in essence, the ultimate message of the Death card is the promise that new life follows disintegration.

Trumps Fourteen—Temperance

Description

Temperance is a lovely card featuring a winged angel standing in a stream with flowers growing up from the water and the rising sun shining in the background. The angel may be either male or female, or androgynous. The angel has a halo or a sort of disk banded around the forehead. In most decks, the figure is pouring liquid–the elixir of life–from a golden vessel into a silver one in a continuous stream, suggesting the interplay of the material and spiritual worlds and the eternal flow of the waters of life. The word "vessel" is related to the great Mother Goddesses of antiquity, and the body is often referred to as the "vessel of the soul." Thus, both the angelic figure and the cups are symbolic references to the feminine principle of cooperation, balance, harmony, receptivity, and creativity.

Mythologically, Temperance is linked to the Moon. Its number is fourteen and on the fourteenth day after the New Moon the lunar orb is at the exact midway point of its monthly cycle. In ancient times, there were special ritual ceremonies to honor this point of the lunar cycle, and the Moon Goddess. Another mythological reference is to Iris, the goddess of the rainbow, daughter of Zeus and messenger to the gods. Called "angel," which means messenger, Iris is a gentle, beneficent figure, equally at home in the sky, on earth, and in the sea. Her magical shimmering colored bows enchant us and remind us of the ephemeral nature of life.

Temperance corresponds to number Fourteen and the Hebrew letter Nun.

Interpretation

Temperance, as its name suggests, is about moderation in all things. The word is derived from the Latin *temperare*, which means to moderate, blend, or mix together harmoniously. When Temperance appears in a reading, depending on its position in the spread, the person is being cautioned to have *patience*, which may be difficult under the circumstances. However, the circumstances of his or her situation will serve to teach the difficult lesson of being able to wait calmly when it seems like nothing is happening.

Often, the querent is like the person in the back seat of a cab stuck in traffic, pushing his or her foot hard on the floor as if to connect with the accelerator and get things moving. But the only course is to sit and wait for things to move in their own time. Interestingly, this card was earlier named "Time," which is a key to its symbolic meaning.

The person who receives Temperance in a reading is not in a position to hurry matters along. It is just one of those times when there's nothing to do but wait. The trick is to make waiting constructive. This is one of the great lessons of the Zen masters. Learning to wait, when waiting is the only choice, is an art that has to be learned and mastered. Learning to do nothing *mindfully* is a milestone on the spiritual path—it's of vital importance to know that there are times when not only nothing *can* be done, nothing *needs* to be done. Therein lies the state of grace.

Astrological Reference to the Devil

When The Devil appears in a reading, it nearly always points to a transit of the planet Saturn, known as the Lord of Karma—of restrictions, limitations, lessons to be learned. These transits are indicative of lessons to be learned. They represent areas of your life that are being challenged and behavior patterns that require examination and change. Most people experience Saturn's energies as if an external force beyond their control overtakes them; however, this is not the case. The unconscious mind, in reaction to the conscious mind refusing to take the required action, programs the event that precipitates the reevaluation that is the prerequisite to change. A Saturn transit puts you in touch with your *real* needs. Often people who experience loss or illness under a Saturn transit "see the light," and are empowered to make alterations to their viewpoints and live more in accordance with who they really are.

Many of the major crises of adulthood are represented by the energy of Saturn—tough times when one has to make a decision to forego one path in favor of another. Saturn is *reality*—it is the need for duty and discipline, and she who does not learn these twin lessons is never fully adult. Reality is *structure*, and structure is Saturn's province. Reality means limitations—this, but not that; one thing, but not the other. To master Saturn is to master necessity.

Transits of Saturn urge one on toward maturity. They tend to focus one's concern on areas of life that need work, and the crises they bring serve to force the issues that need attention, especially if they have been ignored or neglected. Saturn is also known as the Great Teacher, and often guides will appear under a Saturn transit. The lessons of Saturn are difficult—but they are necessary and worthwhile.

As Saturn holds back energy, its transits can indicate blocks of various kinds. Often Saturn transits are harbingers of a crisis *period* with which we must deal or suffer the consequences.

Trumps Fifteen—The Devil

Description

Most decks picture a traditional medieval Christian-type devil, complete with horns, hooves, a hairy tail, and a pitchfork. Usually at the feet of the devil there are two smaller, humanlike figures, one male and one female, with chains around their necks that are attached to the block upon which the devil sits. However, and this is important to note, the chains are loose and could easily be slipped off over the head, suggesting self-imposed limitations.

Whatever form the Devil takes in various decks, he is usually pretty scary looking, with a fierce expression. Occasionally, he is more bat-like or stylized depending on the theme of the deck and its designer's inclinations toward the figure. In some decks, he has an inverted pentagram over his head or on his brow. In one deck, there is no devil at all, only two nude figures chained to a symbolically decorated block, straining toward an open doorway at the end of a long tunnel. The variety of illustrations for the Devil card imply widely differing opinions of the card's meaning. For some, "devil" is a symbol for consummate evil; for others it is a mythical creature with no substance that is a result of human malfeasance, ignorance, and lack of personal responsibility. Thus, the illustration appearing on the card represents a point of view as well as the traditional meanings associated with the card.

Interpretation

Superficially, the Devil appears to be one of the more alarming cards of the Major Arcana, and readees sometimes gasp at his appearance as if he were going to "get" them! However, in my

view, as indicated in the previous section on the transits of Saturn, the Devil appears when one is trapped in an oppressive situation of his or her own doing. He does not represent Satanic forces with evil intent, and it is important to remember this when doing readings. He is the Horned God of pagan times, connected to the fertility rites banned by the all-controlling established Church, which feared the power of pagan rituals, especially those including sexual activity.

When the Devil shows up in a reading, depending upon his position in the spread, he is telling the readee that he or she needs to re-evaluate his or her relationship to material things, which serve to keep us "chained" firmly in one position. It's a time to review whatever is limiting you and holding you back from personal growth, especially abusive or harmful relationships. You are being called upon to confront your fears about financial security and social and material success—the things of this world. The Devil is calling you to a reality check.

You need to recognize and acknowledge whatever about yourself you have tried to deny exists—things you don't like about your personality, your body, your temperament. It's time to let go of old fears, hang-ups, inhibitions, tendencies to manipulate others to satisfy your needs instead of learning to take responsibility for satisfying your own needs in a positive manner. Often there is a sexual component involved that is having a deleterious effect on your whole life and which you know you ought to get out of but are resisting making the necessary change. Or, there could be a nonsexual relationship to which you are bound from which separation is necessary before you can grow further.

Whatever the situation, you are the only one who can change it. The two chained figures on the card represent bondage to the material realm of money and status. That their chains are loose indicates your potential for attaining your freedom by relinquishing obsessive ambition and excessive attachment to the things of this world.

Mythologically, the Devil is related to the old pagan god "Great Pan," a god of nature and the natural processes of nature, including lust and sex. The Greek form of Pan was Dionysos, known for cavorting with satyrs, in whose honor the female followers of the goddess religion held wild and uninhibited rituals annually that included a sexual free-for-all.

Also known as "Le Diable," the Devil corresponds to the number Fifteen and to the Hebrew letter Samekh.

Trumps Sixteen—The Tower

Description

The Tower depicts a stone tower of fortress-like construction such as one sees in what is left of medieval Europe today. The Tower is being struck by lightning, or is in flames or falling down.

In the Waite deck, and some others, the Tower has a crown that is being blown off by the fiery impact. Human figures are being thrown out of the windows by the blast. The implication is that the forces of heaven are angry and attacking the structure from which flaming debris is flying out in all directions.

Interpretation

Like the Death card and the Devil, the Tower tends to strike alarm and fear into anyone in whose reading it appears, and indeed many writers place a totally negative meaning on this card, which is wrong. These writers are usually coming from an old-fashioned religious point of view that believes the "wrath of God" will descend on sinners. The actual meaning is *psychological*–and spiritual. The Tower does not represent ruin and devastation, although its appearance usually does herald swift and dramatic change–sometimes shocking and extremely upsetting. As mentioned in the Uranus sidebar, those people most devoted to hanging on to the status quo will be the most affected.

However, the person has usually brought the situation on him- or herself by ignoring or denying that something is rotten in their lives and needs restructuring or deconstructioning. When we refuse to acknowledge that we need to make changes, we invite attention from the gods in the form of drastic measures. Ordinarily, the readee is already well aware of a pressing need to make changes–but is stead-

fastly refusing to take the necessary action. Then—BAM!—along comes some circumstance such as losing a job or getting a divorce, having an accident or a financial setback, that forces the person to get into reality-check mode instead of stubbornly looking everywhere but where the problem lies.

There's no question this card signifies the crumbling of an old and outworn structure, and demands that you begin to deal seriously with your life collapsing all around you instead of, like Nero, fiddling while your house burns. Any number of possibilities exist—breaking off an unsatisfactory or destructive relationship; quitting a stifling, non-creative job; casting off false materialistic values; confrontation of some long-buried issues of guilt and shame; shucking the social conventions that limit your progress; selling your mortgage-ridden house and living more simply; ridding yourself of burdensome possessions. The list is endless, but the readee nearly always knows what the issue is and, once confronted by the Tower, can acknowledge that he or she is being imprisoned by a self-created fortress, whether for protection, safety, or from fear of facing the unknown.

The message of the Tower is that you must either destroy the old structures before they destroy you, or submit to them being shattered by seemingly outside influences (which you have actually created yourself) in order to grow and reach enlightenment. In the wake of the chaos, a new order will grow. What was unsound will come tumbling down so that you can pick and choose among the rubble to decide what is worth saving, and from that, rebuild your life in accordance with who you truly are.

Mythologically, the Tower is linked with the Old Testament story of the Tower of Babel, which was a massive structure intended to reach all the way up to God in his heaven.

The lightning is also connected to the Greek god Zeus, known for his tendency when angry to throw huge bolts of lightning

Lightning, of course, strikes suddenly, quickly, and sometimes unexpectedly and can cause serious damage—or, it can be viewed as a celestial work of art. Who has not been mightily awed when viewing an impressive display of heavenly fire, aware?

Also known as "La Maison Dieu" (The House of God) and the Falling Tower, or the Tower of Destruction, the Tower corresponds to the number Sixteen and to the Hebrew letter Ayin.

Trumps Seventeen—The Star

Description

In this lovely card, a nude female figure is seen, usually kneeling on one knee at the side of a pool of water, or in a pool of water, pouring from two jugs, one held in each hand. In the Waite deck, she pours from one pitcher into the stream, from the other into the ground. In some decks, she pours the contents of both pitchers into the stream.

The background of the Star is always full of stars, usually with one much larger central star directly above the figure of the woman and the others scattered all about the sky. Most decks show seven subsidiary stars, sometimes arranged to reflect the portal or two-pillar theme, sometimes set in a circle or a halo-like form around her. The stars are set above a pastoral setting—trees, mountains, birds, flowers. If there are trees, there is usually one at either side of her, another echo of the portal or pillar symbol. The colors are always bright, often with yellow (the color of optimism) predominating. The essence of the symbolism is that, naked, she represents unveiled Truth and purity. Her jugs contain the Waters of Life, some of which are being returned to the Source, some of which are being used to infuse the land with new life.

Interpretation

The Star is unfailingly positive and its appearance can signal the end of the travails represented by some of the earlier cards, symbolizing that a new and happier phase of life is coming into being as a result of the person's having overcome the obstacles along the Path of the Tarot and reached the Star. "Reaching for the stars," is an appropriate metaphor for this card as from earliest times humans

Astrological Reference to the Tower

When the Tower appears in a reading, it can point to a transit of the planet Uranus against the client's natal chart. Uranus is best described as "a bolt from the blue." The energy of Uranus is *unexpected*, sudden, and often disruptive. Uranus represents the desire to break free of limitations—its energy works to keep things flexible by preventing too much unbending order. It is the random element of creativity. Uranian forces strive to break one out of old, outworn patterns that have become rigid and too limiting. Order is necessary, but the "old order" must always give way to a new one eventually. The power of Uranus comes in to transform and restructure lives in ways that are more fulfilling, opening the person up to new, sometimes alien, realities. Uranian energy seems to strike particularly when a person has become stuck in the status quo, unsatisfied and discontent, but not knowing how to make the needed changes.

Like a breath of fresh air—sometimes more like a hurricane—Uranus comes along and inspires the person with an urgent need to break free of the restrictions that have been limiting development. Usually this appears to come unexpectedly, but close examination will reveal that the matter has been on the back burner for quite some time.

The individual who makes friends with Uranian energies and heeds the transits of this electrifying planet is one who will continue growing throughout life. One who resists change and is utterly dependent upon the regularity and predictability of the status quo, will have much difficulty. But change must come, or we become calcified in the old, outworn pattern. Uranus will not allow attachment to the status quo.

Recognizing this power of Uranus to force change in a drastic way allows one to be prepared to take advantage of this energy's structure-annihilating opportunities. If we dismantle our old structures willingly to make room for the change that must come, we will not suffer the more serious effects of the transit. It is only when we resist that drastic action is taken. With a Uranus disruption, we have the opportunity to search through the rubble for what is worth keeping and chuck out the garbage from our psychic storeroom.

Uranus, for all his ability to intrude harshly upon our dearly beloved status quo, is a friend. His powers can recreate aliveness and re-establish touch with the core of our being. It's a fact that people feel exhilarated when facing an emergency. For some reason, dealing with disaster brings out the best and the most creative in human beings. A Uranian transit may not be easy, but it is a good tonic for hardening of the attitudes.

Mythologically, the Star is linked to all the great goddesses of love and beauty from many cultures: the Sumerian; the Greek, in which *Stella Maris*, "Star of the Sea," was one of the titles bestowed upon Aphrodite, known as "foam-born," as she arose from the sea; and the Romans renamed her Venus. And it is Venus who appears to us as the morning and evening star. Venus rises as the morning star for a period of approximately 240 days, disappears for 14 days, and then reappears as the morning star, to begin the cycle anew.

Also known as "L'étoile," the Star corresponds to the number Seventeen, which in old numerological systems was connected with immortality, hope, intuition, and self-expression.

have been awed and fascinated by the celestial display and its regular motions, seeing in the stars a cosmic reflection of life on Earth. "As above, so Below."

The Star in a reading is like looking up at the bright starry sky on a clear night and seeing there all the magnificence of the universe—it stimulates the imagination to ponder on the great potential of each and every human being—for growth, inspiration, intuition, inner wisdom, and celestial guidance.

Although the Star does not usually point to any specific planetary transit, as do some of the other Major Arcana described, it does have a strong connection to astrology in general. When the Star appears in a reading, it is a good time to have your horoscope read, or to begin studying astrology yourself. A gate has opened for you to new directions and new successes. This card portends good fortune, creative inspiration, spiritual growth, help from unseen forces, the receiving of what you hoped, wished, and worked for—perhaps for a long time. It is a time of fulfillment. So, when the Star appears in your reading, go out and watch for the first star to appear in the night sky and wish upon it. Your wish will come true. And when it does, be sure to give something back to show your appreciation and gratitude and ensure continued protection.

Trumps Eighteen—The Moon

Description

The Moon is a magical, mysterious card emblematic of what is unconscious—and what stems from the invisible realm of dreams, imagination, and psychic impressions. Usually shown with a distinct division between upper and lower parts, the Moon card is richly symbolic. In the top half is the Moon, shown both full and crescent-shaped, the crescent enclosed in the full circle, radiating pointed rays. Drops of water fall from the moon through the center of the card. Below, there are two canines, a dog and a wolf, who are baying at the moon between two towers, another reference to the portal theme. At the bottom of the card there is a pool or pond of water from which is emerging a shelled creature—possibly a crab or crayfish. The water is emblematic both of the moon's rulership of the tides, the Earth, and our unconscious realm from which emerges our awareness of ourselves as human.

Some say the animals represent our opposite tendencies—the wolf, the untamed inner animal nature, the dog the domesticated, daily persona with which we face the world. But canines and the moon have deep mythological roots that relate the combination to the underworld. In addition, the dog indicates psychic ability as it is able to follow an invisible trail with its nose, i.e., locate what cannot be seen.

Interpretation

Physicist David Bohm speaks of a "link or bridge between realms." Astrologically, the Moon represents the *Soul*, which is the link between Spirit (Sun) and Matter (Earth). The Moon is feminine: it is what we *feel* and how we *respond*. Therefore, it is emblematic of all that is *receptive* in human nature: the subconscious, the emotions, the

Mythologically, the Moon is the great symbol for the Goddess, whose three aspects represent the three faces of the Great Triple Goddess. As the newborn crescent, the Moon is Maiden, the Virgin—not chaste, but belonging to herself alone, not bound to any man. At the full Moon, she is the mature woman, sexual and maternal, giver of life.

At the end of her cycle, the waning moon about to turn dark is representative of the wise old woman whose years have ripened into wisdom.

Also called "La Lune," the Moon corresponds to the number Eighteen and to the Hebrew letter Tzaddik.

behavioral instincts, the automatic functions of the body such as the autonomic nervous system, digestion, breathing, and the like. The *lunar self* is the channel for the flow of the universal, or divine, source—as such, the Moon has great power. It affects everything and everyone on earth—from the tides of the seas to the moods of humans and the cycles of animals.

Therefore, when the Moon appears in a reading it is a statement that you should be paying more attention to your inner self, your lunar self. Symbolically, the Moon card offers you the opportunity to illuminate your deepest nature, for the Moon symbolizes the non-conscious side of human life, and in that diffuse light we can often see more clearly than in the glare of the noonday sun. The light of the sun enables us to see the world around us—what is *outside* ourselves. But the moon allows us to shine light into our inner spiritual world, to illuminate what springs naturally from *inside* ourselves. In moonlight we perceive the reality of our inner spiritual selves more clearly, we are more aware of the shadings and nuances of feelings and inner perceptions.

This is because during the hours of night our subtle senses are more open and receptive to our inner spiritual harmony. The moon has been called the "soul of life." Without the moon we would have no poetry, literature, art, music, dance, or dreams. Artists are notorious for being "dreamy," and it is at night when the moon reigns that we dream. It is a time to attend to your dreams, feelings, intuitions, and to spend time developing these faculties.

Although traditionally the Moon card refers to deceit and self-deception, confinement and undoing, these conditions are usually a result of ignoring your own inner promptings, of not paying attention to the signals coming from within. If you get "taken"—especially emotionally—it's because you were letting your rational mind override your feelings. The Moon card's appearance also notifies you to take care of loose ends connected to the past, especially to your mother or other females, especially relatives.

If the Moon card is closely related to negative cards in the spread, it can be an indication you are neglecting your lunar self,

over-nurturing others while foregoing your own needs. Many people are disconnected from their lunar selves because of pressures to conform to the outer world around them. This can be a precursor to "lunar burnout," even illness. (For a complete discussion of lunar burnout and the art of self-nurture, see Chapter 10, "The Healing Moon," in my book *Healing Mind, Body, Spirit.*)

On the other hand, if adjacent cards point to outward activities, you may be emerging from a long period of inner concentration and be bringing your creativity out into the open and presenting your inner self to the world.

The Moon, as the luminous aspect of the night, belongs to [the Goddess]; it is her fruit, her sublimation of light, an expression of her essential spirit. [It] appears as a birth—and indeed as rebirth. Such processes are the primordial mysteries of the Feminine . . . from which all life arises and unfolds, assuming, in its highest transformation, the form of the spirit.

—Erich Neumann,
The Great Mother

The Phases of the Moon

The *waxing*, or increasing, Moon brings an energy of expansion. This is a positive influence, the best time to concentrate on issues of growth or a new beginning of any kind. Whatever is seeded now will grow into fruition.

When the Moon is *full*, the energy moves toward the completion of what was previously set in motion. The lunar energy is at its strongest and most powerful. You can focus this by using meditation and affirmations. As the light of the full Moon eliminates shadows, this is an especially good time to work on conditions with vague symptoms that are difficult to diagnose. Ask for identification of the source of the problem in order to determine an appropriate solution.

During the period of the *waning* Moon, the energy moves toward decreasing and, finally, at the dark Moon, eliminating. This phase is ideal for dealing with negative issues you want to eliminate from your life, including ill health. Now is the time to practice releasing and letting go. Use the waning phase of the Moon to help you discharge all negativity from your life. Loose it and let it go.

The energies of the Moon change slowly, segueing from one phase into the next. After the night of the dark Moon, for example, the energy of the new Moon slowly increases into the expansive growth

The true mystic is not merely involved in esoteric thoughts or beautiful images of God in heaven. He is totally absorbed in a life movement, a journey in which his essential self—his real self—comes into life with and in God. This "coming to God," as it has been called, is the journey.

—Marsha Sinetar, *Ordinary People as Monks and Mystics*

phase that will culminate in the full Moon. The energy of the full Moon begins to build two days before the total fullness is achieved, and it continues in effect for another two days afterward, only somewhat diminished in power as the waning phase takes over. The energy of the waning Moon fades slowly as its visible area decreases.

You can increase your sensitivity to the Moon and your lunar self by making direct contact. To do this, sit facing the direction of the visible Moon. If you cannot see her, acknowledge her by closing your eyes and imagining the beautiful silver crescent or disk in the dark sky. If possible, position yourself in front of a window or go outside where the rays of the Moon can shine on you. Sit quietly for several minutes until you can feel the Moon's energy contacting you. Imagine her luminosity entering your body, connecting your soul to her as the soul of our planetary system. Feel the magnetic pull of the Moon on your sensitivities and allow yourself to be touched within by her softly glowing light. Let it illuminate your "dark night of the soul," inspiring and uplifting you.

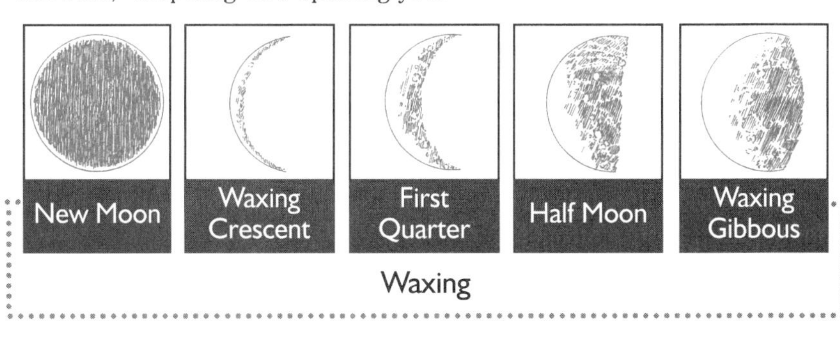

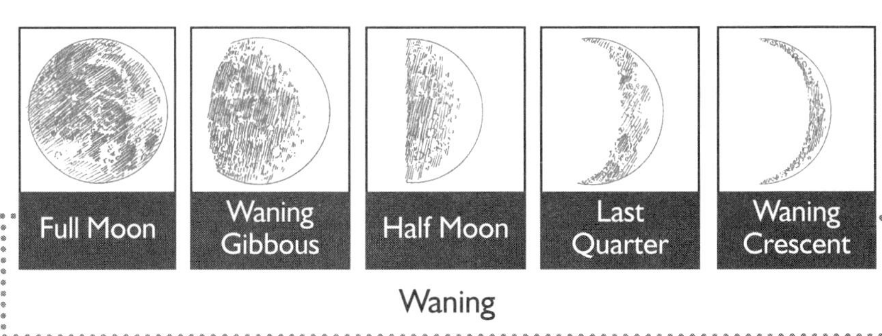

Trumps Nineteen—The Sun

Description

The Sun card features a blazing sun, sometimes with a face, beams radiating out from it. Beneath the sun a smiling nude child is riding a white horse. Behind him, a banner unfurls, held up by a winged staff. In the background are huge sunflowers growing against a stone wall.

Some decks show more than one child, usually two with their arms around each other; other decks show a young couple holding hands. The child, or children, are clearly very happy and having a wonderful time. The sun's planetary ruler is Leo, tenant of the horoscope's fifth House, which represents children, pleasure, and creativity. The Sun is also the heart, the center of the personality. It represents life itself—as indeed our real sun in the sky gives life to all on earth and without its light we would perish. The Sun card represents vitality, confidence, achievement, ego-attainment, and success in all endeavors. It is emblematic of the proverb, "May the sun shine on all you do," the implication being that sunshine brings joy.

Mythologically and historically, in the wake of the demise of the Great Mother Goddess as the sole divinity, the Sun, which represents the masculine principle, came to be worshipped as the central deity in many cultures. The ancient Egyptians, after eons of a pantheon of multiple goddesses and gods, under the leadership of the pharaoh Akhenaton, were persuaded, albeit reluctantly, to accept a single god—Ra, Amun-Ra, or Aton for the Sun—which Akhenaton believed was the god of all gods and to be worshipped as such. The Greeks called their sun god Helios, whom the Romans named Apollo.

Also called "Le Soleil," the Sun corresponds to the number Nineteen and to the Hebrew letter Quoph.

Interpretation

When the Sun card appears it is an indication that your past work is now bearing fruit, symbolized by the children who are a product of the combination of the previous card, the Moon, representing what is hidden, i.e., gestation, and the Sun, which in psychological and metaphysical terms means birth. These two cards imply the union between the unconscious realm of creativity (Moon) and the conscious realm of manifesting into life (Sun). Whether the birth is of a child or a creative project, the outcome is a happy one. It is a time of good things coming into your life–success, optimism, achievement, health, general good fortune, and happiness.

When the Sun turns up, even if there are negative cards in the spread, they are lightened up by his appearance, no matter where the Sun appears in the spread. His influence is always beneficial, representing prosperity, enthusiasm, honors, public recognition, and attainment. Pleasure is easy, and you are happy to be alive because you feel it is the dawning of a new day. Any special efforts–such as the taking of tests or examinations, will turn out favorably.

The gifts of a childlike response to everyday situations are yours with this card and you are being rewarded for your previous striving and suffering with "a day at the beach." In fact, literally the Sun card can indicate you are going to take a wonderful vacation in the sun where you can relax and let go of your worries and tensions in the wake of getting your just desserts.

Trumps Twenty—Judgment

Description

The Judgment card visually seems rather negative—a winged figure with a trumpet, whom some call the angel Gabriel, is coming out of a cloud, dominating the top of the card. Beneath him are several nude figures of men and women looking up, obviously hearing the trumpet's blast. Their arms are outstretched, and they seem to have come out of coffins or the earth itself. Their expressions are of awe tinged with fear.

Of all the allegorical symbolism of the Major Arcana, this is the most purely Christian, suggesting the feared "Day of Judgment," when God will judge all souls and apportion out rewards or punishments accordingly. However, this is not a totally Christian idea; other cultures such as the Egyptians have also expressed the notion of the soul being judged, as with the goddess Maat who weighs the soul against her "Feather of Truth."

Whether seen from a Christian point of view (which these medieval images represent) or from a universal one, the idea behind the symbols is of an awakening, what we today refer to as "a wake-up call," when events cause us to re-evaluate our way of life.

Mythologically, the Judgment card relates to classical Greek Hermes-Trismigestus in his role as *psychopomp*, or guide of souls. The activity of Hermes refers to alternatives of life, to the dissolution of fatal opposites, to clandestine violations of boundaries and laws. In other words, the overturning of the rational-mind-dictated world and the discovery of the magical powers of the inner world.

Hermes was called Mercury by the Romans, and the deeper expression of Hermes-Mercury's role as messenger of the gods is that which mediates, or delivers messages between the conscious mind and the unconscious realm.

Also called "Le Jugement," the Judgment card corresponds to the number Twenty and to the Hebrew letter Resh.

Interpretation

When the Judgment card appears, what is being awakened is the sense of a Higher Self within. Sometimes the card coincides with a person turning away from a traditional set of beliefs to one that better suits his or her personal philosophy of life. Judgment represents the end of something—an old way of life, a cycle that is finished. It is a time to seek new direction, to make adjustments that reflect who your truly are—perhaps by breaking away from your conventional way of life and belief.

It's also a time for decision-making. What's been put on the back burner is now boiling over and you can't go on ignoring this situation. Generally speaking, this is a positive card symbolizing regeneration and rebirth into wholeness after a period of confusion and a sense of confinement (the coffins). You may have been feeling "dead" in your old life. When Judgment appears, you have the unique opportunity to relive, to enliven yourself and your environment by making the appropriate changes. What is ending is doubt and indecision, depression and despair, fear and inhibition. It's a time of new freedom to be yourself.

Trumps Twenty-One—The World

Description

There is little variance in the depiction of the World card in the different decks. The central figure is a nude young woman wearing a flowing long scarf which is placed across her body like the banner beauty queens wear signifying their state or country of origin. It covers her genitals but leaves her breasts bare. In each hand, she holds a double-ended wand that points both upward and downward, suggesting, again, "As above, so below." She is surrounded by an oval-shaped wreath made of vines, leaves, flowers, or all three.

As with the Wheel of Fortune card to which the World is related, the four corners of the card have a bull, a lion, an eagle, and a man—representing the four fixed signs of the zodiac, Taurus (Earth); Leo (Fire); Scorpio (Water); and Aquarius (Air). Thus are the four elements represented and the four directions. In the Waite deck, the wreath is bound at the top and bottom by ribbons in the shape of the infinity symbol that is found over the head of the Magician and the woman on the Strength card (the figure 8 turned sideways).

Interpretation

This is the last numbered card of the Major Arcana. It represents balance and support by unseen forces, and symbolizes the end of the spiritual journey begun by the Fool. To embark upon the spiritual journey is to invite unseen forces to interact with us. These creative energies manifest in many ways, a principal one of which is as guides. Guides bring us into grace and show the way. To encounter a guide—and they come in many guises—is to enter another realm, a

Mythologically, this card can be linked to Shiva, the Hindu god who dances the world into being—and then destroys it only to once again dance it into being—in the eternal dance of life, death, and rebirth.

The World card, with its symbols of the four elements and its joyfully dancing figure, is about balance and completion.

place of great powers and, sometimes, of great secrets. This realm belongs to the invisible world, although its denizens can, like angels, comc in human or animal form. To interface with this world is to be impacted in a way that is life-changing. With guides, we enter a world of supreme power–not the power of the material world but of the invisible order that supports and nourishes our world and our lives here. It is the realm of the sacred.

When the World card appears in a reading, it is a signal that you have been guided to the successful conclusion of your spiritual journey. At this, the final stage, you will receive what is rightfully yours because you have earned it. Now, you are and feel whole and complete. You are refreshed from your long journey and ready to begin anew at a higher level. Blessings are yours for the asking.

Chapter 5

The Trumps Individually

Practical Uses

For centuries, the Tarot has been used to advise on practical matters, such as the choice of a job, or the right marriage, or economic issues. One method is to choose an individual card to represent you or another person; a group or organization; a situation or event. This card is called a "Significator." Many spreads, including the popular Celtic Cross, call for a Significator. This spread, described in Chapter 13, was recommended by Arthur Edward Waite as "the most suitable for obtaining an answer to a definite question."

To select a Significator, you must find an appropriate card that describes what you want to signify. Any of the seventy-eight cards in the deck can be used. You can use a Court card to represent a person. (See Chapter 4 for descriptions of the Court cards as representational of people.)

When using a Significator, the basic idea is to choose a card that best describes the person or matter about which you are inquiring.

When using a Significator, you can either remove the card from the pack or leave it in, according to the layout you are using. The Celtic Cross spread begins by consciously picking a Significator card and removing it from the deck. If the Significator is removed from the deck, it serves as the center, or grounding point, of the layout. If it is left in the deck and turns up, the position the Significator occupies becomes of special importance.

You can also use *only* the Major Arcana cards in a spread, in which case the Significator plays an even more important role.

Below is a listing of the Major Arcana cards with suggestions regarding how they can be used as Significators.

O The Fool

The Fool can stand for a child or young person, innocence or an innocent person, someone who is lacking experience in life. It can be used to represent an adventure of any kind, travel, or a trip. Also it can be used to signify a decision that needs to be made, especially if the decision involves risk.

I The Magician

Choose the Magician as a Significator for someone who has latent talent that he or she wants to bring to manifestation. This is a card of *potential* and can be used to represent an ideal man who has power of any kind. He can represent anyone in the field of applied sciences, such as engineering. Also, he can signify a man or woman with artistic ability who wants to put it to a practical use.

II The High Priestess

As a Significator, the High Priestess represents secrets. It could be a secretive person, or someone who is keeping a secret or who wants to reveal a secret. It is a good Significator for anyone trying to delve into knowledge, such as a scholar or researcher. It can represent someone with psychic ability or a wise woman.

III The Empress

This card signifies a woman of substance, someone who is mature and able to handle life well. She is in a position of authority, wealth, and power. She could be a female politician, or someone aspiring to public office. Or, she can signify a person who has an Earth Mother personality. Also, she can represent a pregnant woman or one with many children.

IV The Emperor

Use the Emperor to signify a man of authority, wealth, and power. He could be your boss or any public figure, or follow a profession that commands respect, like the law or medicine. He is representative of any male authority figure, such as a politician, a military officer, someone in law enforcement, a CEO of a corporation, or a government representative.

V The Hierophant

This is a teacher or mentor figure, especially a clergyman or member of an established institution, such as a university professor. He can also represent a ceremonial figure with public duties, such as the head of an awards committee or grant-giving institution.

VI The Lovers

This card can represent any two people, or a situation involving two people who have to cooperate with each other, a married or engaged couple, issues around a love relationship or a friendship, or any one-on-one situation between two people.

[There are] forces operating within that are capable of producing phenomenal results. That is, the power of your own suggestion starts the machinery into operation or causes the subconscious mind to begin its creative work [which] *leads to belief, and once this belief becomes a deep conviction, things begin to happen.*

—Claude Bristol, *The Magic of Believing*

VII The Chariot

This card can signify a messenger, or the need for a message. It can be used to indicate someone who is involved in the transportation industry or who is in the military service. Use it for any situation where conflicting elements are involved and need to be controlled, such as getting a group organized with everybody going in the same direction despite disagreement over purpose or method.

VIII Strength

Use this card to signify someone who is in control, a strong woman, or any forceful person. It can mean a man or woman with charisma and charm. It represents any situation where courage is required, such as athletics or exploration.

IX The Hermit

The Hermit is a good card to use if guidance is needed. He can be a seeker of knowledge, or an elderly person. He may be someone who prefers solitude to company, a recluse, or a wise man with knowledge to share. It can also signify anyone who is concerned about the past and looking into it.

X Wheel of Fortune

This card is not used to represent persons, but it can be used to represent situations that have already been put into motion and are playing themselves out.

XI Justice

Use this card to represent someone who is in the process of weighing a decision, or who is looking for information with which to make a decision. It can signify someone in law, such as a judge or an arbitrator, or be used for the legal and jurisprudence system. Use it for anyone involved in a lawsuit who is concerned about the outcome being fair.

XII The Hanged Man

This card is best used to signify someone who is at a turning point, or who feels he or she is at a standstill. It is representative of a person who has retreated from ordinary life, or who desires to do so. It can also refer to someone who is ill in a hospital, or for whom an illness has provided the chance to embark on a new course. It can be anyone who is at a crossroads.

XIII Death

Many people shy away from this card, and it is not usually used as a Significator, but it is a good card to use for any situation involving a major transformation, whether it involves a person or a situation, such as the ending of a relationship, the loss of a job, or any crisis that leads to a transformation.

XIV Temperance

Use this card as a Significator for a healer or protective figure such as a nurse, doctor, psychotherapist, or practitioner of an alternative healing practice, such as chiropractic or acupuncture. Temperance can be used to signify resourcefulness and conservation.

XV The Devil

This card can be used to signify someone who is depressed or in a destructive state of mind. It can signify a person who feels trapped and can't see the way out. It refers to any restrictive situation that is limiting progress.

XVI The Tower

The Tower can be used as a Significator for an explosive situation or for the presence of forces beyond one's control. It is not used to signify a person.

XVII The Star

The Star can signify someone who is of a humanitarian bent, offering help to others without expectation of recompense or reward. It can be someone who entertains others, such as an actor, or someone who is an inspired artist, or a beautiful person of either sex.

XVIII The Moon

The Moon can be used to represent someone who is "moony," or "loony." There are so many associations with the moon in life—as the Maiden or Virgin, the Mother, the Wise Woman. The Moon is associated with Artemis, the "Lady of the Beasts," and all in nature that is wild and free. Use the Moon card for anyone who strongly relates to the inner feminine nature.

Meditating on Tarot with Prayer

Everything that I believe to be true about the Spirit, I understand is also true about myself. Its Goodness is my goodness. Its Power is my power. Its Presence in me is my true self. There is only one True Self.

Meditating on Tarot with Prayer

Every day I believe I am receiving Divine Guidance and inspiration. I realize there is nothing in the universe opposed to me other than my own doubt or any negative force in my own mind. There is nothing that can hinder, impede, or impair my progress.

XIX The Sun

The Sun card is the usual Significator for children, or issues surrounding children. It can also be used when you want to "throw light" onto a situation, or to bring something "into the light of day."

XX Judgment

This is the card to use when someone either is in the process of becoming more aware of what needs to be done in his or her life at the present, or needs to develop this awareness. It represents someone seeking the truth about a particular situation.

XXI The World

This card represents a self-actualized and fulfilled person. It can signify a situation that is going especially well. Use it as a Significator for anyone involved in the natural sciences or environmental work.

Intuitive Meditations

In any kind of divinatory work, intuition is an important factor, ranging from such "low data/high subjectivity" methods as tea-leaf reading or crystal gazing, where there is little hard data to go on, to "high data/low subjectivity" systems, like astrology and Tarot, where the use of a physical tool (the chart or the cards) provides a high level of reliable information on which to base the reading. However, even in the case of these data-rich systems, it must be stressed that the development of personal intuition is a vital component of an accurate reading. This is because the symbolic nature of these systems provides the possibility of interpretation on many different levels. Therefore, it is most important that you spend time and effort learning to access your intuitive self, to the point where your intuition is eventually automatically activated when you lay out your cards for a reading.

If a particularly important consideration comes up on which you want your intuition to work, you can concentrate on that issue, setting aside some extra time to do so. In the beginning, try not to ask too much of yourself. Be patient and keep working. Be gentle with yourself, knowing that you cannot fail because this is a natural talent we all possess.

Practice Meditation

Choose a card that seems to you to represent a condition or an inner state on which you desire information or assistance. Place the card in front of you and carefully examine *all* of the symbols, even the smallest details. Be aware of your *feeling* responses to the symbols, play with them in your imagination—what if you *were* the High Priestess? Who would you be? How would you think? What would be your personality?

Keep pen and paper at hand, preferably your Tarot study journal, and make notes of your feelings and responses to the symbols on the card, being sure to title your page with the name of the card, the date, and the time of day. Spend an hour or so simply *being with the card*. See if you agree with the meanings that have been given here, or if other meanings suggest themselves to you. Make notes of this as well. Note also how you *respond* to the card—does it make you happy, cheerful, eager, lively, sad, uncomfortable, angry, or upset? Note these feelings and attempt to locate their causes within yourself.

For example, some cards—such as the Devil and the Tower—strike some people as negative. If you have negative feelings about any of the cards, or any of the specific symbols, ask yourself *why* you feel this way. This is an excellent method for plumbing your own depths where fears are hidden away. If you have positive reactions to a particular card, or a particular symbol, note *why* these feelings occur. Perhaps the Fool makes you feel free and carefree. Maybe you are yearning for that kind of happy-go-lucky element in your life.

Notice if the card strikes a chord with you—if you immediately identify with the figure, or if the figure is one you wish to become like. Or, pick a card that shows an attribute, such as Strength, that you want to develop and meditate on that. Always focus on just one card at a time.

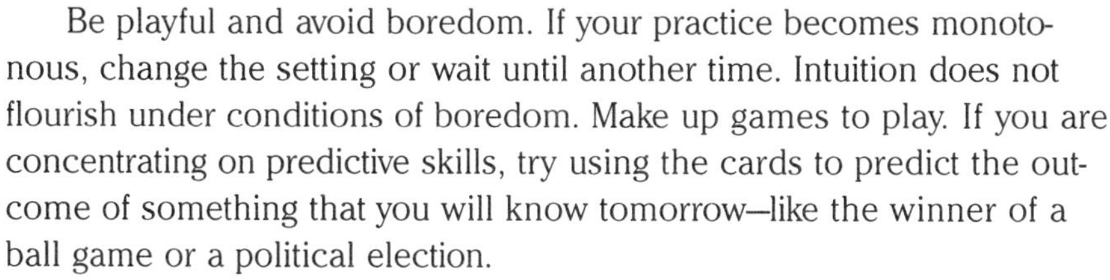

Be playful and avoid boredom. If your practice becomes monotonous, change the setting or wait until another time. Intuition does not flourish under conditions of boredom. Make up games to play. If you are concentrating on predictive skills, try using the cards to predict the outcome of something that you will know tomorrow–like the winner of a ball game or a political election.

Developing intuitive skills should be fun, not a chore. Your "hits" based on your intuition will vary from time to time. Sometimes you will get a "flow" where the information just seems to be coming into your mind, like being tuned to a radio station; at other times, there's static. When using the cards for meditation in order to access your intuition, you must be aware that there are always variables. Your mood, your health, your state of mind, the time of day, and the environmental setting can all be factors affecting how your intuition will perform. For this reason, it is important to first thoroughly acquaint yourself with the cards generally, to be sure of their meanings—even though with practice you will have the latitude to intuit the meaning that is appropriate to the situation for which you are consulting the cards.

As the use of intuition and the level that is available to any person is an extremely individual matter, it is not possible to give rigid definitions or to define precise methodologies. Psychic intuition doesn't work like an accounting system–it's part and parcel of *you* and who you are. Therefore, your moods, your intelligence, your education, your interests–the "furniture of the mind" as Willa Cather called it–your energies, your past experiences, your future aims, and your ability to be open to the experiences you will encounter are all factors in the development of psychic intuition.

As you work with the cards intuitively, choosing a meaning for a particular instance, bear in mind that this is a *process* with which you are involved, not a course of study with a definite curriculum, like math or engineering. If you are not used to doing your internal processing in an aware manner, it may take a bit of time for you to get used to doing so. The important thing is to make a commitment to yourself and follow through on it. Don't expect immediate success (but don't rule it out either). In the end, as you learn to trust your psychic responses and let them operate on their own, success becomes automatic.

How long will it take? That's up to you. Each person is an individual and results will vary. One medium I know spent five years in steady meditation before a channel opened for him. Others achieve quicker results. Much depends on your personal goals, the quality and length of time you invest, individual aptitude, and factors as yet unknown. I urge you to be patient with yourself until you reach your goal. Sometimes people work diligently for a long time and nothing seems to be happening and then, *bingo*!—what is called a "gateway" intuition occurs. It's like walking along a dull, dreary street and suddenly going through a gate into a beautiful, flower-filled courtyard hidden behind the facade of a building. This feeling is exemplified for me in *The Wizard of Oz* when Dorothy steps out of her house into the land of the Munchkins—and the black-and-white film turns into glorious Technicolor. When you have had a gateway intuition, you'll know for sure you aren't in Kansas anymore. This is also known as the "ah-ha!" experience, a moment of clear understanding of what before was murky.

Using intuition uses all of you. It is precisely the holistic nature of intuition that gives it its power. In your unconscious, you have a huge data bank of experiences upon which to draw, most of which you are not aware of. You know much more than you think you know, and your psychic intuition has the ability to come up with new and creative combinations of knowledge to produce integration of the elements of a Tarot card spread, to see it as a whole. It is an innovator with great creative ability. The results may amaze you!

There are many ways to discover your own inner dimensions. One of the best of these is the contemplation and mediation upon *symbols*, and the Tarot deck is richly full of symbols. During the study of the Tarot and its symbology, one opens the door to intuition. The personal growth that results from this study will be apparent to the student. What happens is that meditation upon the symbols on the cards awakens the corresponding archetypal forms in the unconscious, and that in turn allows us to get at the right interpretation, to see the truth in the heart of the matter. And, since every card has multiple meanings, the correct application of the intuitive process is vital to getting an accurate reading.

If you are sincere and earnest in your search for Truth, whether about practical concerns, to predict circumstances, or as a means of serious meditation, the time and energy you expend on meditation on the symbols of the cards will bring marvelous results to the aspiring student because the Tarot has a unique value as a tool for meditation. By reflecting on the deep meanings of the symbols on a regular basis, you set in motion an inward process that will reveal to you truths about yourself and enable you to look outward to grasp Universal Truth.

Meditating on Tarot with Prayer

In Spirit, all is perfect. In Spirit I am perfect. Spirit is at the root of my being. I have an intimate Source from which I may draw strength and inspiration. This universal "I Am" finds expression through me as the individual "I." It is the very essence of my being and in it I realize my true nature.

Prayer is also a form of meditation. It puts us into an altered state of consciousness not unlike the ones used for self-hypnosis and visualization. When we pray, we are actually visualizing the result desired even if we are not doing that consciously. It is a good idea to begin each Tarot session, whether for study or reading, with a short prayer affirming your faith in guidance and your innate connection to Spirit.

Spiritual Progress

Meditation on the cards activates our unconscious repository of images; these can be used for spiritual progress. Working with the Tarot opens a passageway between the material and the spiritual realms. The Tarot cards are able to be read at many levels for they symbolize our unconscious understanding of our life experience—past, present, and future. From the esoteric point of view, the cards represent all possible experiences available to human life. When using the Tarot for spiritual purposes, it is best to keep a separate deck that no others touch.

Greater awareness of your own spiritual dimension and a deeper knowledge of your spiritual self are great rewards for concentrating on Tarot as a means of spiritual development. As one writer has commented, "Tarot cards are a step forward in our evolution to perfection." Though absolute perfection may not be for this world, in Spirit all is perfect.

One of the most marvelous properties of the Tarot is that it can be used as a path to spiritual enlightenment, as well as for the more mundane purposes of answering questions in the here-and-now. If you decide to use the Tarot for your personal spiritual development, you will find that your understanding of the visual images on the cards will take on deeper meaning. You will begin to see beyond, or *into*, the symbols where the Truth resides. And, if you do a serious study of the Tarot for spiritual purposes, you will find that it will provide answers to questions that ultimately will affect the direction of your life, which may change markedly as you progress spiritually.

At the spiritual level, each of the Major Arcana represents a *state of being*, or an inner truth about yourself. It will reflect your spiritual condition at the time of use. Alternatively, you can choose, either deliberately or at random, specific cards on which to concentrate for spiritual purposes. As one of the paths to spiritual self-enlightenment, the Tarot teaches you as you go along, sometimes in very subtle ways. You might not "get it" at first, but it's happening just the same, rather like a bowlful of sourdough starter that just sits there for days seeming to be doing nothing—and then there's a *ping!* as a little bubble rises to the surface, an indication that the process is underway and working.

Another thing the Tarot will do when you are using it for spiritual purposes is to warn you of mistakes and danger, or alert you to possible wrong turns or wrong associations. For example, sometimes it will tell you in unambiguous terms that someone in your life is bad for you and needs to be either watched carefully or jettisoned altogether. Heed these warnings—ignore them at your own peril! I have said before that the Tarot is not for frivolous use, not a toy for entertainment, but an amazing tool with great power. Therefore, understand that you are taking on a responsibility, especially if you read for others. Proper preparation is essential, not only in knowing the surface meanings of the cards but in having a firm spiritual grounding for the work.

The problem with human-based divinatory methods, of course, is the *human* source with its potential for distortion, or the insertion of the reader's own bias. Just as the clarity of a radio or TV broadcast is determined by the quality of the equipment used to receive it, so sincere practitioners of the occult arts have always understood that the validity of their readings reflect the person channeling the message. Because of this, all traditions have placed enormous emphasis on spiritual and moral purity as a prerequisite for acting as an oracle. In fact, the ancient Jews considered the accuracy of prophecy to be a direct result of spiritual attainment! If the prediction came true, it showed that the prophet had penetrated to the highest levels and was in communication with the Divine Mind. Conversely, a failed one was proof that the prophet was relying on his own subjective imaginings.

The simplest way to understand the Tarot Major Arcana in spiritual terms is to think of it as an ascending staircase with twenty-two steps. Each step is a little different than the one before it—each has a different lesson to impart. Some are wider or narrower than others; some are smoother or rougher. Some have few obstacles while others have major obstacles. The time you spend with each step is an individual matter and strictly up to you. You'll *know* when you're ready to move up to the next step because you will have understood the meaning of the previous one.

The climb up the steps will vary in terms of ease or difficulty, depending upon your own inner progress. You may at times move quickly and easily, and at other times seem to be stuck on one step for an inordinately long time. This is okay, for you can only go at your

Affirmations for Spiritual Tarot Work

I am healthy, strong, peaceful, happy, and at rest.

Spirit, which is active in me, flows throughout.

I am well, buoyant, happy, free, and full of joy.

My days are filled with energy, radiance, and health.

The purifying energy of Spirit moves through me.

I give praise and thanksgiving for all blessings.

I bless myself and all others.

I invite the power of Spirit into my life.

own pace. Each step, or card, represents a barrier or a boundary which you must cross to move up to the next step. And you have to figure out how to do this yourself—there is no set system. It's *your* spiritual nature and no on else's, and no two people are the same nor are any two at the same point on any spiritual path.

Along the way you will come to "landings," places where you can stop and rest, look back at how far you've come, and then decide whether to continue or stop. There's no hard-and-fast rule that you have to make it to the top. Again, this is an individual choice. There is an analogy for this in therapy: sometimes a client goes to a therapist because he or she is in psychological pain. After working on it for a while, the person often reaches what I call a "comfort zone." The pain may not be entirely gone, but it's bearable enough to forget about some of the time. So the client terminates therapy before getting to the root of the matter, which would cause *more* pain, even if going through the old pain would finally heal it permanently. But that is the client's choice.

When you hit a landing, you may have found a comfort zone and feel that you've gone far enough, struggled enough, learned enough. That's a severe temptation. I've never climbed a mountain, but I'm sure that's how climbing Everest must feel when the weather is stormy and the body is tired. By all means, stop and rest—but do try to go on to the top. The view is sensational!

As a seeker, you begin at the bottom, asking the questions we all ask—those basic human riddles—"Who am I?" "Why am I here?" "Where am I going?" "What am I supposed to do with my life?" "Why have I suffered?" "Why is there so much suffering in the world?" "What is life all about anyway?" "Is it worth the trouble?"

As you progress, you can be advised by others who have made the climb before and you can get a general idea of what's required and how tough it gets or how easy it can be, but it's like someone telling you all about a trip they made to London, showing you their slides, and talking about the restaurants where they dined. You will know something about London—but it won't have been *your* experience of London. And when you do go, you will have different experiences than those your friends had, different reactions, meet different people, eat in different restaurants. You'll have some general guidelines, but your trip will be your own. No one can tell you precisely what to expect at each step of the way—or how to handle the experience. The whole point of following a spiritual path is that it is *your* path and your life. Guides are useful, but the inner guide *knows the way.*

With Tarot, the only thing absolutely certain is that there are twenty-two steps. You may stop at any point short of the total, and you may think you have found the answers you seek, but unless you have the courage and fortitude to continue the climb to the top, you won't have the whole Truth. It is said that all roads at the bottom of a mountain lead to the summit, and there are many spiritual paths other than the Tarot. Each of them has its dangers, each presents the possibility of failure. There will be times when you feel uplifted, and times when you feel defeated and are tempted to quit. This is when you have to grit your teeth and persevere. If you do, you will find that—amazingly—you have the inner resources you need to continue on.

We all possess marvelous potential *right now,* lying hidden within ourselves, as the latent beautiful butterfly is concealed within the chrysalis. We are at the point of being able to realize talents we as yet don't even have terms to describe properly. According to neuroscientist Dr. Manfred Clynes, humans have reached the stage where it is possible to evolve states of mind and emotions entirely new to our experience. And these potentials are not restricted to any one field of endeavor. It has been proved that expanding consciousness in one direction has the unexpected result of producing positive results in other, seemingly unrelated, areas.

Innately, we are *already* whole persons, but if we are to grow into our innate potential and become able to use more of our capacities, we must allow ourselves to grow into our spiritual selves at the deepest level. The good news is that *you already have the capacity to do this.* The Tarot cannot confer it on you—its teachings are only there for you to discover the wonders within yourself.

However we choose to define *spiritual* for ourselves, we must do so from a perspective of the whole human being acting in and interacting with a holistic universe where anything is possible. We have only to open our minds and release our fears to summon marvelous genii capable of astounding feats from the depths of our own psyches.

Meditating on Tarot with Prayer

I shall remember at all times that it is Life that gives. I am its beneficiary. Quietness, confidence, peace are mine. My every tomorrow is better than today. I now accept that I have an Infinite Power at my disposal.

Chapter 6

Astrological Correspondences of the Major Arcana to the Signs of the Zodiac

One of the most amazing things about Tarot to me is how it dovetails with astrology. Of course, there are numerological correspondences, but these are obvious since all of the cards are numbered. But the uncanny ability of the Tarot (at least in my experience) to point directly to some astrological factor at work in the life of the person I am reading for still astonishes me.

As I began to read Tarot professionally *before* I became a professional astrologer, this connection was not at first evident to me. I read the cards as the cards—eventually, they began to act as a "field" through which my intuition could function at a high level of performance. So, when I added astrology to my psychic repertoire, even though I knew there were *standard* astrological references to the cards, I realized that all metaphysical systems are intimately connected. Often, if one practices only one of these intuitive arts, it is difficult to readily see the correspondences.

Therefore, in this chapter, I am going to give you the astrological correspondences, both as they are ordinarily interpreted and with my own particular gloss on the subject, gained from years of experience. Also, to help the reader who is unfamiliar with astrology, this information will expand on the meanings of the signs. Of course, you can use the Tarot with absolutely no knowledge of astrology, but even a cursory understanding of the planets and the signs of the zodiac as they relate to the Major Arcana will enrich your understanding of the Tarot.

O The Fool

The Fool is related to the planet *Uranus*, which is the destroyer of old ideologies, concepts, and structures. Uranus represents not only the advanced thinker, modern scientist, and esoteric occultist, but also the bohemian, the beatnik, the hippie—nonconformists of all stripes including revolutionaries, anarchists, and those radical humanitarians who believe and preach that all of humanity is but one family.

Uranus was discovered in 1781, just twenty-nine years after Benjamin Franklin made his famous kite experiment. Thus, its discovery coincided with that of electricity and the subsequent development of electronics and telecommunications. Uranus produces sudden change of all sorts, and, like a thunderstorm, often serves to clear the psychic air.

Uranus Key Characteristics

Intuitive	Undisciplined
Innovator	Iconoclast
Unexpected	Explosive
Awakener	Destroyer
Liberator	Rash
Humanitarian	Anarchist
Revolutionary	Rebel

Uranus symbolizes Man's liberation from the bondage of the personality and signifies the power which may be achieved through the collected energies of truly individualized souls working toward a conscious connection with the Source of Life.

—Alan Oken, *Complete Astrology*

It is the opinion of esoteric astrologers that Uranus has to do with the unique task of each person in this particular incarnation, that he is a clue to the soul's reason for making this earth-life journey. In a sense, where Uranus is active, the soul is most free of restrictions, for old karma has already been dissolved and you are able to be most truly yourself—unique and individual. With Uranus, we tend to behave in a free-spirited way—be unconventional, knock over tradition, be an iconoclast, do the unusual thing, or produce the far-out idea.

Uranus is *exalted* in Scorpio, an indication of unusual courage and daring, of willingness to stake life itself on adventures into the unknown—as the Fool is about to do.

Uranus rules the sign of Aquarius, an air sign symbolizing mental activity. Aquarius symbolizes the idea of the individual as a cooperative member of the larger whole, which fosters the understanding that all humanity is one coherent family, a concept which can be grasped only intuitively. *Detachment* is a primary quality of Aquarius, conferring the ability to deal with large issues that would be painful to others who lack emotional objectivity.

Aquarius tends to be radical and forward-looking, even futuristic, and will go out of its way for new experiences, even if danger is involved. Traditional ways of thinking and being bore Aquarius, which wants to shape the future in line with its personal vision of how things should be. Strongly individualistic, Aquarius can be a rebel and a free spirit, willing to experiment freely with life.

Magic is constructed on the mental plane. [Learn to] create such structures on the mental plane in order to work magic power. Magic is SYSTEM. Not hocus-pocus. ORDER. Not mental (intellectual) order as in logic or an orderly thought process but on the mental plane. Not *in the mind* but OF MIND. Understand difference between MIND and mental or thinking.

—Channeled communication from the Woodstock Shaman to the author

I The Magician

The Magician is related to the planet Mercury, and it is interesting to note that Uranus, known as the "cosmic magician," who rules magic and invention, is called the higher octave of Mercury, and as such represents the mind's pattern-maker who tries out everything mentally and sets goals based on mental preoccupation. Mercury is the planet of the mind, representing how the mind works, how we learn, and how we communicate.

It is also of note that Mercury is *exalted* in the sign of Aquarius, which is ruled by Uranus, thus relating it to the cosmic consciousness inspired intuitively by the Higher Self, which often expresses in flashes of insight.

Mercury Key Characteristics

Idea producer	Overintellectual
Logical	Pedantic
Communicator	Gossip
Messenger	Gadabout
Teacher	Clever
Analyzer	Superficial
Adaptable	Nervous

Mythologically, Mercury is the messenger of the gods, personified as being fleet of foot and quick of mind. On the metaphysical level, Mercury mediates, or delivers messages, between the conscious mind, altered states of consciousness, and the unconscious mind. Dual in nature, Mercury represents the archetypes of both the Eternal Youth and the Wise Old Man. Far more complex than astrologers generally credit, on a spiritual level, Mercury is Thoth-Hermes, guide of souls.

Mercury is multifaceted, a god of many attributes. He governs all aspects of communication—writing, speaking, learning, commerce, and messages of all sorts. The planet is quintessentially of the *mind*. In psychological terms, Mercury determines our level of ability to communicate both what we think and what we feel. It illustrates the process by which we link our internal realm of both feeling and thought to the external world.

Mercury Attunement

I am Mercury,
Messenger of the Gods,
the Divine Witness
of stars and starlight,
The God of Curiosity and Childhood.
As the Divine Herald,
the fastest, shrewdest, and
most cunning of the gods,
I have been blessed with laser perception
and a golden tongue.
I am the Great Mediator
reconciling all opposites,
since I see and understand
all points of view
and can explain them
always in continuous motion,
watching and collecting,
remembering and forgetting
as the Universal Transmitter.
I connect the spiritual and material
worlds, exchanging messages
and information from both,
reflecting the face of desire
or Light of the Spirit
with the speed of thought.
I am the Divine Weaver
of the Enchanted Loom of Stars.
I weave the fabric of the universe
connecting separate realities
spread out in a sea of space
into coherent, exquisitely intricate designs
of meaningful networks
and vibrant connections.
Child of the Wind God
I zoom back and forth
at a dazzling speed
from one forgotten edge of the universe
to another, threading
moment to moment.
I am the Cosmic Connector.
I am the connection to the heavens.
Lord of Divine Books,
I am the Scribe of the Universe.
I record all events seen and unseen,
all trade, travel, progress,
all knowledge, skill, communication.
I am Master of Disguises;
a joker, a chameleon,
a Thief of secrets;
nothing remains hidden from me.
Guide of Poets and Souls in Transition, I am
your Cosmic Connection,
your lifeline to the universe;
Use me.
I activate potentials
in every nerve, cell, and atom.
Without me there would only be
incomprehensible abstract:
a void, which I alone
make vibrant with life force.
Use me.

Mercury rules both Gemini and Virgo. Gemini is an air sign, and the Magician is said to rule the element of air; Virgo is an earth sign, which represents the Magician's ability to move easily between the two realms of spiritual and earthly.

II The High Priestess

The High Priestess is related to the *Moon*, which is the emotional body. The Moon is a metaphor for all that is instinctive. Cyclical and constantly changing, the Moon is called "the Soul of Life," mediator between the planes of the spiritual (Sun) and material (Earth), reflecting back to us the light of the Sun it has received into itself. Thus, the Moon is also a metaphor for receptivity, the *yin* principle in oriental philosophy, and is emblematic of the *container* of life, that matrix which nourishes the process of manifestation. It is the protective surrounding that shields the growing, developing entity–be it a seed in the soil, the embryo in an egg, the fetus in the womb, or the creative act of making art.

Moon Key Characteristics

Unconscious	Unaware
Feeling-oriented	Oversensitive
Instinctive	Automatic response
Mothering	Dependency
Nurturing	Needy
Changeable	Moody
Fundamental	Reactive

The Moon's house, the fourth, symbolizes our experience of our mother. The Moon rules the sign of Cancer, a water sign symbolizing contact with the instinctive nature, the realm of the World Mother who brings forth abundant life even in the face of death. There is mystery here–the one of the relationship between life and death. Cancer also symbolizes emotional relatedness, or the "invisible" side of life epitomized by feelings. As such it relates to the home and memory. Your *lunar self* is the channel for the flow of the divine Goddess energy, which is subtle and not always obvious–remember, the Moon has a hidden side that we never see.

Major Arcana Cards and the Zodiac

Many of the Major Arcana cards are related to the zodiac, either by sign or by planet, or both. As an astrologer, I often note that the appearance of certain cards directs me to consult the client's astrological chart. Often, I find that a planetary transit is in progress that correlates to the particular card, especially if the person is in the midst of a life crisis. Both physical and psychological crises can be indicated by the *transits* of the planets in relation to the natal chart. These constitute a *transforming crisis*, which is to say that one is presented with the opportunity—often the *necessity*—to make life-changing decisions with profound effects. Swiss astrologer Alexander Ruperti, in *Cycles of Becoming*, describes the crisis as symbolized by astrological concepts as follows:

> Cycles are measurements of change. In order for any purpose to be realized, change must take place, and change necessarily involves crises. Many have difficulty with the word *crisis*, confusing it with "catastrophe." [However] . . . it derives from the Greek word *krino*, "to decide," and means simply *a time for decision*. A crisis is a turning point—that which precedes CHANGE.

Symbolically, the Moon serves to illuminate the non-conscious side of human life, and in that diffuse light we can often see more clearly than in the glare of the noonday Sun. The Moon allows us to shine light into our inner spiritual world, to illuminate what springs naturally from inside ourselves. In moonlight we perceive the reality of our inner spiritual selves more clearly, we are more aware of the shadings and nuances of feelings and inner perceptions, and we tune in more accurately to the spiritual vibrations of others.

The Moon is *exalted* in the sign of Taurus, the Bull, and the High Priestess wears the "horns of the Moon"—the same as the horns of the bull—in her headdress. As a lunar figure, she speaks to our deepest inner needs, our memories, feelings, moods, and internal rhythms.

III The Empress

The Empress is related to the planet *Venus*, which represents the affections and symbolizes what we value in terms of our social natures. The process of Venus is through relating—to others, to one's own desire nature, to things, to the outside world. Venus is the planet of love, beauty, desire, and pleasure. Venus also represents the deeply feminine part of each of us, male as well as female, telling of our capacity to reach out to others in a loving and affectionate way, not just sexually or erotically.

Venus Key Characteristics

Values	Self-indulgence
Attraction	Sentiment
Desires	Cravings
Affections	Dependency
Sexual Love	Promiscuity
Artistic	Superficial
Love of beauty	Vanity

Venus rules both Taurus, an earth sign, and Libra, an air sign, both of which exhibit affection and love of beauty. In Taurus, she expresses herself in a more earthy, sensuous way, while in Libra she exposes her more refined and artistic side. Taurus symbolizes connection to the material plane with its reliance on the physical senses and, by extension, accumulation of possessions. The second sign of the zodiac, Taurus provides the matrix (a word related to mother) for the primary energies of life to come into being on the physical plane—such as bearing children and growing plants.

Earthiest of the earth signs, Taurus is symbolic of the soil of Mother Earth herself, and, a fixed sign, Taurus is concerned with conservation of energies. The receptive nature of Taurus is like the nature of Earth, which receives the seed, contains it, and causes it to grow.

Libra symbolizes the striving for balance in all things, and by extension, relationships, from the personal to the abstract. The seventh sign of the Zodiac, Libra has a strong love for whatever is harmonious, from love to the arts, but especially domestic harmony, and presides over both marriage and aesthetics.

Venus is *exalted* in Pisces and works with the transcendental vibrations of Neptune to make love the most transcendent of spiritual experiences. Here, romantic love is rendered more altruistic, singing in tune with the harmony of the spheres.

IV The Emperor

The Emperor is related to the sign of Aries. As the first sign of the Zodiac, Aries symbolizes leadership, initiative, action, energy, and new ideas. It relates to beginnings of all kinds, the primary energy that gets things going. A fire sign, and a cardinal, or initiator sign, Aries is a self-starter, a leader—not a follower. Willful and with a strong desire to be first, Aries is always looking for the next adventure, challenge, project, or experience.

Aries Key Characteristics

Outgoing	Aggressive
Active	Pushy
Adventurous	Foolhardy
Pioneering	Egotistical
Energetic	Impulsive
Independent	Self-centered
Enthusiastic	Headstrong

What is interesting about the recent development of Mars energy in women is not that the male-dominated military establishment *permits* women to serve, even to fly in combat, but that *women want to do it*, which proves that, given a chance, women can express Mars' sheer physical energy and daring as forcefully as men do.

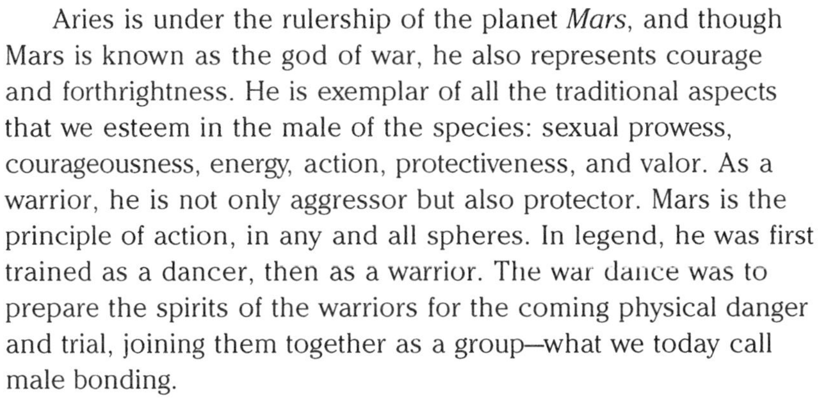

Aries is under the rulership of the planet *Mars*, and though Mars is known as the god of war, he also represents courage and forthrightness. He is exemplar of all the traditional aspects that we esteem in the male of the species: sexual prowess, courageousness, energy, action, protectiveness, and valor. As a warrior, he is not only aggressor but also protector. Mars is the principle of action, in any and all spheres. In legend, he was first trained as a dancer, then as a warrior. The war dance was to prepare the spirits of the warriors for the coming physical danger and trial, joining them together as a group—what we today call male bonding.

Though Mars is the primal male energy, we all have Mars in us, both males and females. Women as well as men have aggressive feelings, get angry, feel passion. And they can be warriors, leaders, and athletes, too.

V The Hierophant

The Hierophant is related to the sign of *Taurus*, which symbolizes connection to the material plane with its reliance on the physical senses and, by extension, accumulation of possessions. Gifted with patience, Taurus lets things happen in their own time. Like a good gardener, Taurus is content to wait until the right time comes along, knowing there's no point in pulling up the radishes to see if they are ready to eat.

The most fixed of the fixed signs, Taurus's patience may seem like slowness, but it is the slowness of certainty and self-confidence. Taurus rests secure in the knowledge that tomorrow is another day and that excess motion will not make the sun rise any earlier.

Rooted in the physical world, Taurus is quintessentially *of the earth*, which, by extension, means all worldly concerns such as institutions that endure over time, including religion, academia, jurisprudence, and so forth. Related to the second house of money and valuables, materialistic Taurus's natural instinct is not only to accumulate but to *preserve* both things and institutions. Thus is the Hierophant a representative of what is already established in the social order.

Taurus Key Characteristics

Practical	Materialistic
Determined	Stubborn
Affectionate	Possessive
Sensuous	Self-indulgent
Loyal	Rigid
Patient	Unyielding
Preserving	Unimaginative

Taurus is ruled by the planet *Venus*, who, when related to her rulership of Taurus, refers to material pleasures, enjoyment, and the five physical senses. Though associated with love and pleasure, Venus, as Aphrodite, was a Goddess of great power, just as the institutions of state are powerful and act both as helpers to the population and controllers of the people. The Hierophant represents this aspect of Taurus, which is about *relatedness*, or bringing together, in a social sense. It is our grounding in a society or community that allows us to venture forth as individuals and develop our talents. This is a card of the authority represented by social institutions and the security they provide.

VI The Lovers

The Lovers are related to the sign of *Gemini*, which symbolizes the dualistic character of humanity (male and female, left brain/right brain). As the third sign of the zodiac, and an air sign, Gemini is related to *others* in a nonparental sense: siblings, neighbors, and the immediate environment.

The most mutable of the mutable signs, Gemini's nature is to change. Represented by the Twins, its duality is clearly evident. The speed at which Gemini can change is sometimes daunting—as anyone who has ever been involved in a romantic situation with a Gemini can identify with. But the Lovers card is not to be taken at surface value—it is about the reconciliation of opposites, or duality, whether with another person or within yourself.

Gemini Key Characteristics

Communicative	Superficial
Quick-witted	Scattered
Curious	Trite
Variety-seeking	Distracted
Mobile	Fickle
Spontaneous	Nervous
Mental	Insubstantial

Gemini is ruled by the planet *Mercury* and, as Lois Rodden comments in her excellent book *The Mercury Method of Chart Comparison*, it is Mercury who "opens the gates between two people," showing a "clear picture of both the attitude and the circumstances" between them. She states, "Mercury is the planet that carries the awareness, or level of communication, from *one person to another*."

VII The Chariot

The Chariot is related to the sign of *Cancer*, which symbolizes the sheer tenacity of the life force. Its image, the Crab, is known for the ability to hold on, just as the Charioteer is holding firmly to his steeds. Cancer is the first water sign, and it represents *relatedness*, whether with others or with the opposing forces within one's self.

Cancer Key Characteristics

Sensitive	Oversensitive
Nurturing	Dependent
Intuitive	Illogical
Traditional	Living in the past
Comfort-loving	Acquisitive
Food-oriented	Self-indulgent
Tenacious	Clinging

In the Chariot, we see a man trying to hold and control two animals, who seem to be going in opposite directions. Cancer represents the process of the growth of the soul through the sustaining efforts of the life forces, which are by nature dual. Thus, Cancer's primary characteristic is *tenacity*. Its symbolic animal, the Crab, is known to never let go—if it has something in its grasp with one claw, the only way to get it loose is to cut off the claw.

As representative of motherhood and family, Cancer is an extremely powerful sign, for the pulsating life force within it is extremely strong. In the Cancer stage of development, we are required to play a larger role in our own development, to learn to master our own opposite natures, and through that mastery to win victory over whatever obstacles stand in our way.

Cancer is ruled by the *Moon* (which we have discussed at length in the section on the High Priestess), and this connection to the Great Mother strengthens the inner life force this sign represents.

As we all know, science began with the stars, and mankind discovered in them the dominants of the unconscious, the "gods," as well as the curious psychological qualities of the Zodiac: a complete projected theory of human character.

—Carl G. Jung

VIII Strength

The card Strength is related to the sign *Leo*, which, like the heart that represents it, symbolizes the center where the life force emanates, from which all energy flows and returns. It is the creative individual energizing potential into reality.

As the natural occupant of the fifth house, which concerns creativity as well as children and pleasures, Leo is the sign of the personal ego, with strong needs for self-expression and admiration. As a fire sign, Leo refers to energy, action, and creative talent. As the fixed fire sign, Leo represents the eternal flame.

Leo Key Characteristics

Dramatic	Attention-seeking
Generous	Dominating
Honorable	Keeping up appearances
Courageous	Self-glorifying
Fun-loving	Self-centered
Self-expressive	Insensitive
Warm	Overbearing

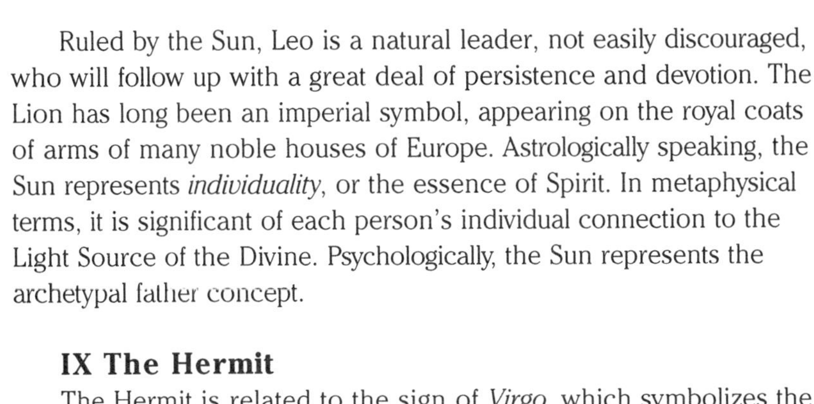

Ruled by the Sun, Leo is a natural leader, not easily discouraged, who will follow up with a great deal of persistence and devotion. The Lion has long been an imperial symbol, appearing on the royal coats of arms of many noble houses of Europe. Astrologically speaking, the Sun represents *individuality*, or the essence of Spirit. In metaphysical terms, it is significant of each person's individual connection to the Light Source of the Divine. Psychologically, the Sun represents the archetypal father concept.

IX The Hermit

The Hermit is related to the sign of *Virgo*, which symbolizes the quest for perfection, the Ideal that resides in the divine essence and the knowledge that is harvested from the fields of experience.

The most mental of the earth signs, work is its hallmark, duty its cannon. Excellent critical faculties make Virgo a perfectionist. Interested in learning all there is to know about the world, with an emphasis on practical skills and how to use tools, Virgo's aim is to be useful to others. Though Virgo has high aesthetic standards, art for art's sake doesn't interest this practical sign, which always looks toward that which serves a purpose. Totally serious, Virgo aims at what will be effective, not what will be fun. Virgo is called the sign of service.

Virgo Key Characteristics

Intelligent	Worrying
Discriminating	Fussy
Analytical	Nitpicking
Logical	Boring
Orderly	Routinized
Critical	Self-effacing
Differentiating	Lacking perspective

Virgo is ruled by the planet *Mercury*, which also rules Gemini, and has been discussed above in the section on the Lovers. Relative to the two signs, in Gemini, Mercury gathers information, and in Virgo the information is sorted and analyzed.

X Wheel of Fortune

The card Wheel of Fortune is related to the planet *Jupiter,* which is the point in the progression of the planets where we move from the realm of the strictly personal (Sun, Moon, Mercury, Venus, Mars) toward the external world and society at large. Known as the "second sun," Jupiter has generally been thought to symbolize positive energies such as prosperity, success, good luck, honor, and accomplishment. This giant among the planets is credited with being the representative of the principles of *expansion and growth.*

Jupiter Key Characteristics

Expansiveness	Overexpansion
Optimism	Foolhardiness
Abundance	Exaggeration
Ethical	Judgmental
Enthusiasm	Unrealistic
Principles	Dogmatic
Society	Hypocritical

Ruled by the idealistic sign of *Sagittarius*, this "greater benefic" serves as the interface between the individual and the institutions upon which the social order rests–schools and universities, churches, the legal system, banking, charitable organizations, government, and the like. Through association with learning and religion, Jupiter is representative of the Higher Mind, and, consequently, of the development of higher mental and spiritual attributes. He goes beyond the purely rational level of Mercury to seek an understanding of universal principles on which thought is based. This desire of the mind for the grand overview is exemplary of Jupiter's *integrative* function.

Jupiter is the ideological basis for systems of thought, be they philosophical or religious, orthodox or unorthodox. Thus, we look to Jupiter for *spiritual* as well as social development. Jupiter's *exaltation* is in Cancer, which rules the home, where the principle of learning is first established. As Jupiter also rules social conduct, and as the family is the basic unit of society, Jupiter represents how we grow

beyond the personal sphere and how we integrate the personal with the nonpersonal, or outer world.

XI Justice

The card Justice is related to the sign of *Libra*, which has as its symbol a blindfolded woman holding a set of scales, the quintessential symbol of impartial justice. Libra symbolizes the striving for balance in all things and, by extension, relationships, whether personal or abstract. Libra, the seventh sign of the zodiac, has a strong love for whatever is harmonious, from love to the arts, and presides over both marriage and aesthetics. As an air sign, Libra is mental in nature and represents one-on-one partnerships and contracts such as marriage and legally binding agreements.

Libra Key Characteristics

Relating	Approval-seeking
Peaceful	Procrastinating
Diplomatic	Indecisive
Refined	Insipid
Impartial	Inconsistent
Artistic	Conventional

Libra rules the signs of Venus and Taurus, which have been discussed above in the sections on the Empress and the Hierophant, respectively.

XII The Hanged Man

The Hanged Man is related to the planet *Neptune*, a planet difficult to define for it symbolizes all that is unreal, ethereal, mystical, otherworldly, invisible, and inspirational—in short, imaginative and creative. It is also identified with escapism, use of drugs and alcohol, avoidance of life's responsibilities, excuse-making, destructive self-indulgence, deception, fraud, delusions of all sorts, not the least of which is the self-delusion that one is the embodiment of God, or personally hears the word of God (e.g., Charles Manson, Jim Jones, David Koresh). Neptune can foster glamorization of all kinds—from fascination with celebrities' lives to involvement in religious cults.

The Presence of Neptune

Located on September 23, 1846, during the reign of Queen Victoria, Neptune's unknown presence had been suspected by two astronomers as the only logical explanation for the then unexplained erratic orbit of Uranus, which would arrive either before or after it was supposed to be due. As each planet in the solar system affects the others due to gravitational forces, Uranus's peculiarities could not be accounted for by what was already known. And, Neptune itself is so far from Earth that it can only be seen with the aid of a very powerful telescope—even then, it is only a pale greenish globe with little visible detail. It is interesting to contemplate that Uranus, the planet of eccentricity, was directly responsible for the discovery of Neptune because of its curious orbital behavior! And that Neptune was the mysterious force behind the odd orbit of its neighbor.

Only two years after Neptune's first sighting, Mme. Blavatsky, the founder of Theosophy (a new religious movement based on ancient wisdom), journeyed to Tibet and India in search of spiritual enlightenment. Afterwards, the nineteenth century set off a wave of spiritualistic, psychic, mediumistic, and table-tapping experiences all over Britain and the United States. Is it only coincidence, one wonders, that Neptune is identified with the dreamer, the artist, the musician, the filmmaker, psychic powers, mysticism, and spiritualism?

The last Neptune in Cancer generation (1938–1958) was the one that brought forth the concept of the human rights movement and freedom for all peoples of the Earth. They were also responsible for the establishment of the United Nations.

At its highest, Neptune, which is primarily involved with the emotions, being the higher octave of Venus, becomes the "celestial musician," in us who thrills to the rhythm of the Universe, unheard by physical ears but known to the dreamer and poet. This "cosmic dancer" is the progenitor of the seven Muses, those spinners of artistic inspiration. Not only patron of the creative arts, Neptune is the inspirer of prophecy and visions, which bring understanding of Universal Truth impenetrable by the power of reason alone. Through the energies of Neptune, we can contact the Universal Guides, or "master souls," who govern our planet's evolution.

Neptune Key Characteristics

Transcendental	Escapist
Spiritual	Deluded
Mystical	Unrealistic
Creative	Undisciplined
Compassionate	Self-pitying
Dreamer	Self-delusional
Inspired	Addictive

Ruler of the sign of *Pisces*, which symbolizes that which is most ephemeral in human nature, the desire to unite with the cosmic consciousness, Neptune is like a marvelous singer of songs and teller of stories who simply *flows out*. He doesn't particularly care whether his vision is made manifest in the "real" world or not. Not surprisingly, Venus is *exalted* in the sign of Pisces—but while she deals with human love, he is concerned with the transpersonal in the expression of universal love, which often means self-sacrifice.

Neptune is *exalted* in Cancer, a sign that deals with emotions (discussed in the section on the Chariot), which find their highest expression in the form of universal love, and as such represents the flow into life and illusions.

XIII Death

The Death card is related to the sign of *Scorpio*, which symbolizes the transforming powers of life and death. In dealing with the process of transformation, Scorpio relates to life's ultimate mysteries—sex and death,

Births and Deaths

As we examine the dynamics of relationships closely, we notice a subtle grammar encoded in the way events unfold for others in relation to changes in our own life. This is especially evident in the great transitions of birth and death. In the news of children being born, ours or those of people around us, we may recognize powerful signposts of new beginnings taking place in our own lives. News of deaths often carries metaphors of significant closings or transformations in related areas of our experience.

For instance . . . Astrologer Laurence Hillman has described the uncanny way the births of his two children coincided with business projects he had started. We often see the same phenomenon in the lives of prominent individuals, as when an actor's first child is born just when he has made a major new career move, or when an author announces the birth of a child just as she is offered a book contract from an important publisher. Amidst the flurry of biographical trivia to emerge during the trial of O.J. Simpson was the fact that his first child was born on the day he won the prestigious Heisman Trophy.

Deaths are similarly significant. Actor Richard Burton's death, to which his alcoholism and life of general excess contributed, occurred precisely as his long-time lover and ex-wife Elizabeth Taylor was emerging from life-transforming treatment for her alcoholism. In a symbolic sense, Burton had indeed "died" for her. The deaths of parents often seem to coincide closely with major changes or developments in their children's careers, as when George Bush's mother died near the time of his defeat by Bill Clinton; or when Russian leader Boris Yeltsin's mother died just as his authority was seriously challenged by a revolt by political opponents.

—Ray Grasse,
The Waking Dream

rebirth and regeneration. The eighth sign of the zodiac, Scorpio, the fixed water sign, is concerned with the processes of destruction and renewal. It is the most powerful sign, and its efforts will be on a high or low level depending on the motivation involved.

Before the discovery of Pluto, Mars was ruler of Scorpio, the sign of transformation through destruction of the old. Scorpio tends to increase both emotionality and inflexibility, bending energies to its prime goal of transformation. Its purpose is to probe the mysteries of the Universe by going to the limit, falling apart, and rebuilding. Its energy is catalytic. Mars in the sign of Scorpio is especially prone to risk-taking and can be destructively powerful. Today, Mars is still considered by some to be the co-ruler of Scorpio, which gives Mars a special relationship to that sign, a combustibility.

Scorpio Key Characteristics

Passionate	Possessive
Secretive	Paranoid
Intense	Brooding
Mysterious	Impenetrable
Sexual	Compulsive
Fierce	Vindictive
Regenerating	Power-abusing

Scorpio is ruled by *Pluto*, the most recent discovery of the inhabitants of our solar system. Found in 1930, it symbolizes the transformative processes of both the inner psyche and outer form. Another word for transformation is *regeneration*, which essentially breaks down the previous form and turns it into something else. Vegetation rots and becomes mulch, from which arises new vegetation. The individual sperm and ovum both "die" to be transformed into the embryo.

Astrologers associate this most compelling of the planets with the transformative process that goes on in the dark underworld of the psyche, sending up its aromas via dreams and, sometimes, compulsive behaviors. Here, we are in the realm of the ancient god Hades, as Pluto was called by the Greeks, who had great respect for the powers of the Underworld.

XIV Temperance

Temperance is related to the sign *Sagittarius*, which symbolizes the seeker after truth. It is concerned with all manifestations of the higher mind and universal values. The ninth sign of the zodiac, ruled by magnificent, magnanimous Jupiter, Sagittarius signifies the religious and intellectual institutions that bind society together and advance learning and morals. The Archer loves personal liberty and intellectual freedom and looks for the absolute truth underlying all causes, for the unifying principle at the center that binds all things into a single whole.

Sagittarius Key Characteristics

Outgoing	Opinionated
Expansive	Careless of details
Optimistic	Deluded
Ethical	Judgmental
Freedom-loving	Commitment phobe
Exploratory	Exaggerating
Straightforward	Blunt

A fire sign, this third mutable sign is far-reaching conceptually and intellectually, eclectic in the quest for knowledge, wisdom, and experience with the aim of achieving balanced actions, adjustments, self-control, and guidance by the Higher Self. Sagittarius seeks the inner teacher and guide, and is related to the angel Michael, who is the spirit of fire. Sagittarius is the sign of philosophy, religion, and law as well as of long-distance travel, usually for learning rather than recreation purposes, and symbolizes aspirations of all that is on a high plane. Like its image, the Archer, Sagittarius shoots his arrows as high as they will go, out of sight, in search of the ends of being and ideal grace.

XV The Devil

The Devil is related to the planet *Saturn*, known as "The Lord of Karma," and as the great Teacher. Saturn is the planet of discipline and structure, time and ambition, and represents where we are tested by the Universe, bringing tasks and trials to the person in the form of obstacles, which are lessons to be learned. He also brings stability, permanence, responsibility, and a capacity for self-sacrifice as well as dependability and endurance. A hard worker—and sometime a harsh taskmaster—Saturn rules *Capricorn*, the natural executive of the Zodiac. Once his lessons are learned, he grants wisdom and an understanding of practical reality. During the approximately twenty-eight years he takes to transit all the signs of the zodiac, he points to the necessary ways a person must develop in order to achieve maturity.

Sagittarius represents the stage of human development in which Man has evolved the strength to activate his vital energy to maximum mobility. His thoughts shoot out in all directions and impregnate society with their latitude of vision and wide scope of understanding.

On the intellectual plane, the higher qualities of the Sagittarian nature allow Man to create civil, legal, and theological codes of behavior for the masses to follow and observe. Sagittarius is then the moral foundation upon which civilization in its truest sense can be based.

On the spiritual level, Sagittarius is the arrow of aspiration which is released by the soul into infinity; its target is the Godhead.

—Alan Oken,
As Above, So Below

Saturn Key Characteristics

Disciplined	Restricted
Practical	Limited
Structured	Rigid
Time-conscious	Fearful
Conservative	Confined
Mature	Cautious
Wise	Restrained

Saturn's *exaltation* in the sign of Libra, which rules marriage and one-on-one relationships, deals with the interaction of the Self with the other, demanding that we learn the lesson of cooperation with others in the real sphere of time and space. In the long run, Saturn teaches us about *reality*. The world is not an easy place for anyone, but the person who has a firm sense of inner structure and discipline is better equipped to deal with life's unpredictable vagaries than the one who must always look outside for authoritative guidance. In the final analysis, Saturn teaches us how to live in harmony with ourselves, balancing emotional needs with worldly realities, using inner discipline to take responsibility for our actions, acting not only for our own benefit but for that of those we love and, by extension, for all of society.

Of all the planets, Saturn's is the most serious face, showing what we take most seriously as well as where we must face obstacles. However, by overcoming the tests he sets for us, we learn, sometimes with many trials and tribulations, what we need to know to develop spiritually, for in the end this is the purpose of any of life's trials, no matter how hard it may be to accept that idea when we are in the throes of coping with them.

It is through this process of growth—or trial by fire—that we eventually find order and security and understand that Saturn is the king of the manifest world, which is to say that he stabilizes and brings forth into Time what is otherwise ephemeral and only mental. The person using Saturn energies correctly can build castles in the air and then construct them on the ground so people can live in them.

As the ruler of Capricorn, the cardinal earth sign, and of the tenth house of social status, Saturn is much concerned with status and recognition. He represents the law of necessary limitation and that of conservation of energy and resources. Many people find the structured energy of Saturn difficult to cope with, but if they will only accept the necessity of learning the lessons concerned with the situation at hand, then they will find themselves free to become their own authorities, rather than relying on external ones.

Often, Saturn's influence seems to correspond with painful circumstances seemingly unconnected with any weakness or flaw on the part of the person but which merely "happen"–hence the title, "Lord of Karma." This idea prevails despite the ancient tradition which tells us that he is the Dweller at the Threshold, the keeper of the keys to the gate, and that through him alone we can achieve eventual freedom through self-understanding. The sad fact, however, is that human beings do not earn free will except through self-discovery, and they do not attempt self-discovery until things become so painful that they have no other choice. But, when he is encountered in the right spirit–when trials and difficult experiences are seen as opportunities for self-development–Saturn fosters the exhilaration of psychological freedom. When we have freed ourselves and are no longer prisoners of our own lower instincts, we meet Saturn anew as a guide to lead us to our own higher beings. By passing the tests Saturn sets for us, we become our own true and authentic selves.

XVI The Tower

The Tower is related to the planet *Mars*, the fire of energy. Mars is known as the god of war because it is his function to create *separateness*, in contrast to the function of Venus which is to create unity. Mars is *energy*, most particularly physical energy. It is everything we traditionally think of as masculine–assertiveness, aggressiveness, action, drive, ambition, initiative, combativeness, and courage. Mars is where our primary energy to get things done resides. When we are feeling angry, that is Mars energy. When we want to kill or destroy, for whatever reason, Mars has been engaged.

The psychic process which Saturn symbolizes seems to have something to do with the realization of this inner experience of psychic completeness within the individual. Saturn is connected with the educational value of pain and with the difference between external values—those which we acquire from others—and internal values—those which we have worked to discover within ourselves. [Like Beauty and the Beast] Saturn's role as the Beast is a necessary aspect of his meaning, for as the fairy-tale tells us, it is only when the Beast is loved for his own sake that he can be freed from the spell and become the Prince.

—Liz Green,
A New Look at an Old Devil

Mars Key Characteristics

Motivation	Self-projection
Drive	Aggression
Physicality	Impetuous
Action	Violence
Sexuality	Hostility
Boldness	Anger
Upfront	Argumentative

Mars is also identified with masculine sexuality, the forward thrust that is man engaged in sex—or war. This is an energy of unrefined power, like crude oil. In order to be useful for more than procreation and killing, it needs to be regulated, just as a furnace does. Mars energy is powerful and can be used constructively or destructively, just as sports simulates the masculine urge toward warlike action without the deadly results.

Mars is in *dignity* in Aries, which rules the first Cardinal fire sign. Interestingly, Aries was the Greek word for Roman Mars. In many ways, the planet and the sign are similar. Mars is *exalted* in Capricorn, and here the aggressive energy of Mars is put to useful, practical ends. The fiery energy of Mars is at its best when combined with a constructive goal.

XVII The Star

The Star is related to the sign of *Aquarius*, which symbolizes the idea of the individual as a cooperative member of the larger whole, fostering the understanding that all humanity is one coherent family, a concept which can be grasped only intuitively. Brotherhood—or sisterhood—is the prime concept, for Aquarius sees everyone in the humanitarian spirit of friendship.

Moon Attunement

I am the Moon,
Ruler of Blue shadows and moist
silence in
The Bowl of Heaven.
I give form to creative force.
I am Fertile Matter which sustains and
nourishes
Seeds of solar life.
I absorb the solar currents
By being passive, feminine, and
receptive.
I am the sentient substance
Of instincts, memories, and desires
Waiting to be impregnated
By the light, heat, and power of the
Sun's rays.
I am the Great Mother.
the ancient ones called me
One thousand names of mystery.
I am the Celestial Midwife
Cherishing the Child of Divine Seed.
Sister of the Sun, the caress of the
Mother,
I am the breast of Life,
Lover of Lovers,
The Wisdom of the waters,
Of instinct and ancestral experience,
Of nature and spirit, Fate and the
motion of Time.
I harbor the secret knowledge and
power of Love,
Of the subconscious, of immortality,
Of inspiration and instinctive desire.
Mother of Enchantresses and
Magicians,
I rule the function and form of matter,
Rhythms of the body and fate of the
soul,
Where one has been and what one
has yet to face.
I am the Captor and Reflector.

How is it, one may ask, that Aquarius, the Water Bearer, is an air sign? Alan Leo, in *As Above, So Below*, says:

"In order to answer this question, we have to probe into the more esoteric significance of this symbol. In the first place, the water which the Man distributes from his Urn is the water of *consciousness*. It is the understanding that all men are brothers, a concept which can be understood intellectually but only "seen" intuitively. It is the power of the intuitive aspect of mind [mind is always related to air] which is embodied by Aquarius."

Aquarius Key Characteristics

Humanitarian	Emotionally cool
Innovative	Rebellious
Independent	Disruptive
Friendly	Uninvolved
Visionary	Impractical
Tolerant	Perverse
Unusual	Individualistic

Aquarius is the eleventh sign of the zodiac, the fixed air sign. It is related to stability and stamina, and before Uranus, its ruler, was discovered, its rulership was assigned to Saturn, which also has fixed qualities. Aquarius takes as its purpose the experimentation with all established structures. It freely crosses all man-made boundaries in order to experience the new and unusual. It is related to reform within the structure of the larger group, bringing innovative ideas.

Recent scientific discoveries have shown that the human brain receives and sends messages via electrical charges. Thus, all telepathic communication and ESP phenomena are attributed to Aquarius and its ruler, Uranus. All communication is associated with air signs. Being associated with satellite communication, radio, telegraph, telephone, television, and all of the allied technical professions of the above, for Aquarius—the sky's the limit!

XVIII The Moon

The Moon is related to the sign of *Pisces*, which symbolizes that which is most ephemeral in human nature, the desire to unite with the cosmic consciousness. The twelfth sign of the zodiac and the mutable water sign, Pisces is emotional, female, and intuitive. Ruled by Neptune, it is the sign of creativity, psychic ability, empathy, illusions, poetic sensibilities. It represents the urge toward self-sacrifice to a Higher Cause and the soul's struggle with the imperfections of the material plane. Its image of two fish swimming in opposite directions suggests the dichotomy inherent in the fusion of the material and spiritual realms. Pisces is the most receptive of the receptive signs, the most watery of the water signs, the most mutable of the mutable signs, which can give a desire to know the deep spiritual truths that come from the denizens of the invisible realm of the psyche.

Pisces Key Characteristics

Sensitive	Vulnerable
Imaginative	Escapist
Compassionate	Sentimental
Subtle	Vague
Visionary	Impractical
Artistic	Illusory
Psychic	Self-deceiving

Pisces' dual image represents the finite consciousness on the one side, and the infinite consciousness of the universe, or cosmic consciousness, on the other side. The connecting point is our Earth, where the spiritual and material aspects of being meet. Thus, Pisces represents the urge to unite itself with the invisible forces of the soul's struggle to enter and control the material sphere of humans. One of the fish is the physical body, with all its limitations and mortality; the second fish is the soul and its invisible world where boundaries are almost infinite.

Astrologically the Moon represents the Soul, which is the link between Spirit (Sun) and Matter (Earth). Your *lunar self* is the channel for the flow of the universal, or divine, energy.

Symbolically, the moon serves to illuminate the non-conscious side of human life, and in that diffuse light we can often see more clearly than in the glare of the noonday sun. The light of the sun enables us to see the world around us—what is *outside ourselves.* But the moon allows us to shine light into our inner spiritual world, to illuminate what springs naturally from *inside ourselves.* In moonlight we perceive the reality of our inner spiritual selves more clearly, we are more aware of the shadings and nuances of feelings and inner perceptions, we tune in more accurately to the spiritual vibrations of others, and we are more in tune with the information universe.

This is because during the hours of night our subtle senses are more open and receptive to our inner spiritual harmony. The moon

Sun Attunement

I am the Sun of our Solar System.
I am the "Director of the Planets."
All others within my realms
revolve around me.
I am the Head of the Planetary Council.
I am the Center of the Circle.
I am the Hub of the Cosmic Wheel of Life.
All paths lead to me.
I am the Circle
whose center is everywhere and
whose circumference is nowhere.
I am the God of Gods in our realm.
When I shine, heavens are rolled aside;
new horizons are opened.
I wake Life itself from dark deep slumber.
I am the torch of the gods.
I am the lighthouse in a sea of stars.
I am the God of Light
in whom no darkness exists.
I am the God of Truth.
I am the very heart-center of being,
the Void from which all creation comes forth.
The Spirit manifests itself through me.
I am the totality of all matter;
I am the One Supreme Atom.
Out of me, the One, come the Many
for I am the Generator of Life.
I am the Heart of the Matter,
The Spine of the Spirit,
the sense of *Self*, the *I*, the *Me*,
The Will of the True Self,
The Source of Power and Authority.
My dawn is Life itself.
I am the Healer,
The Master Musician of the Golden Lyre.
I am throbbing with Life.
I am the surging Love that unifies
every part within the whole.
Every reality I have created
is conquered by my Love.
I am the spirit of conscious purpose;
of vitality and growth.
I bestow the desire to become
more than we are, to shine in the world.
I define the purpose of the individual
within the Cosmic Plan, the identity.
I am the place where
one meets with infinity.

has been called the "soul of life." Without it, we would have only the mechanical, an endless solar efficiency, which, in the end, is soul-less. Without the moon we would have no poetry, literature, art, music, dance, or dreams. Artists are notorious for being "dreamy, and it is at night when the moon reigns that we dream.

XIX The Sun

The Sun is related to the zodiacal sign of *Leo*, which it rules. (The sign Leo has been discussed under the section on Strength.) Astrologically speaking, the Sun represents *individuality*, or the essence of Spirit—it is called the Light of the Soul. In metaphysical terms, it is significant of each person's individual connection to the Light Source of the Divine. Psychologically, the Sun represents the archetypal Father concept, which may or may not have a direct relationship to the actual parent. In physical terms, it is *vitality*. The Sun is life, energy, ego, and the desire to attain.

Sun Key Characteristics

Individuality	Egotistical
Father Spirit	Authoritarian
Consciousness	Lacking instincts
Vitality	Grandiose
Will	Prideful
Drive	Dictatorial
Creative	Self-conscious

The Sun is at the center of the solar system, and it is at the heart of the astrological chart, telling us what we are *potentially*, not necessarily what we will become. The Sun determines the *conscious* sense of Self, which is concerned with the life-purpose derived from the life-giving energy of the Divine Source. The process of coming to consciousness is one that lasts a lifetime. The Sun is at the heart of *why* you think you are here on Earth, *where* you are going in your life, *what* makes you feel important. It speaks to your *purpose in life*—the sense of "I am."

The Sun's glyph, an open circle with a dot at the center, signifies the emanation of life-giving energy from the unlimited resources

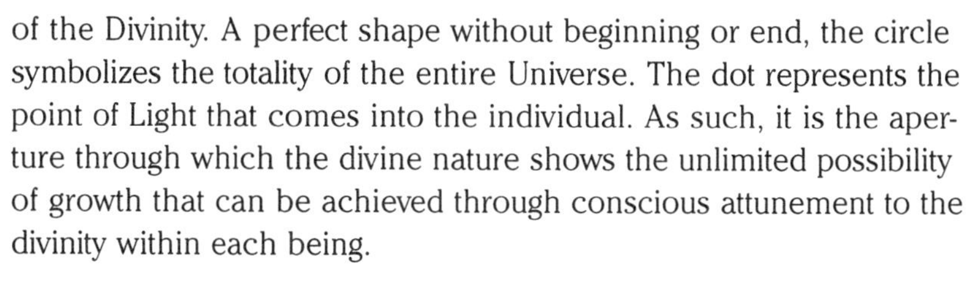

of the Divinity. A perfect shape without beginning or end, the circle symbolizes the totality of the entire Universe. The dot represents the point of Light that comes into the individual. As such, it is the aperture through which the divine nature shows the unlimited possibility of growth that can be achieved through conscious attunement to the divinity within each being.

XX Judgment

The Judgment card is related to the planet *Pluto*, which symbolizes the transformative processes of both the inner psyche and outer form. Pluto is not totally understood. Astronomers are even unsure of its true size. Some speculate that it is small and dense; others that the central sphere that can be seen is merely the light-reflecting center of a much larger orb. Though not much is known absolutely, there seems to be no question that *power* resides there, power of a most potent sort. Indeed, transits of Pluto to the natal chart are a definite wake-up call from the Universe!

Pluto Key Characteristics

Transformer	Compulsive
Powerful	Dictatorial
Regenerator	Obsessive
Revitalizer	Annihilator
Renewer	Fanatic
Metamorphosis	Ruthless
Redeemer	Eliminator

Perturbations in the orbits of both Uranus and Neptune are a result of Pluto's as yet undetermined physical characteristics. It is interesting to note that just five years after Pluto's discovery the daughter of Marie Curie, Irene, with her husband, won the Nobel Prize for synthesis of the new radioactive elements. It would not be too much to say that the resulting Plutonium, the trigger of the atom bomb, transformed the entire world forever after.

As Pluto takes some 244 years to circle the zodiac, none of us will ever experience more than a small slice of his influence, but that fragment can be powerful indeed. Ruler of *Scorpio*, the Great Transformer causes whatever he touches to become something else. King Midas evoked Plutonian energies—to his everlasting sorrow—when he wished for everything he touched to turn to gold—and then embraced his lovely young daughter. Great wealth—and the transformation of dross into gold—also belongs to Pluto realm. He is the bottom-line fundamental in our lives, symbolizing death and rebirth on the spiritual plane, as well as power struggles of all sorts—those we have with others, and those with ourselves.

Because of his long, erratic orbit (at one point coming closer to the sun than Neptune, his nearest neighbor), he symbolizes the Great Collective, the point where we connect, for good or for ill, with the rest of our society—not just our local community but the totality of humanity, which somewhere shares a single psyche, what Carl G. Jung has called the "collective unconscious." Everywhere the forms of the psyche are the same, though they manifest differently in different cultures and at different times. Pluto is known as "Mr. Moneybags," because power begets money, and the great riches of our century have come from deep within the Earth's dark interior—oil, gold, gems, and minerals. As ruler of the Underworld, he is a subterranean force to be reckoned with. He favors individual regeneration, but in the end individual karma is always linked to the karma of the society into which we are born.

Pluto is *exalted* in Leo, which is a sign of *self-awareness*. The generation born with Pluto in Leo (1938-1958) has the power to bring about regenerative changes through increasing self-awareness, which leads to awareness of all. They—we—have the task of spiritually regenerating themselves—ourselves—in order to save the planet from destruction due to overpopulation and the resulting pollution of the environment. From their ranks will come the leaders who will take the world into the twenty-first century.

XXI The World

The world is related to the sign of *Capricorn*—the world leader—which symbolizes father, authority, the social order, pragmatism, and the slow but sure ascent to the top of the heap. The tenth sign of the zodiac, Capricorn builds what is practical and useful to society, looking to authority figures to determine the right way of doing things, wanting to know exactly what the rules are.

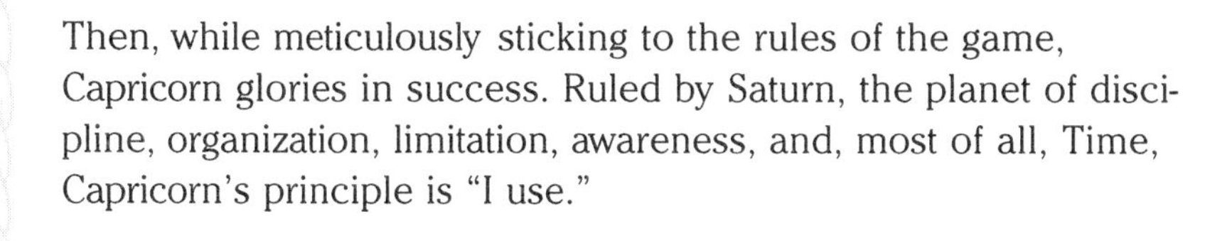

Then, while meticulously sticking to the rules of the game, Capricorn glories in success. Ruled by Saturn, the planet of discipline, organization, limitation, awareness, and, most of all, Time, Capricorn's principle is "I use."

Capricorn Key Characteristics

Organized	Overstructuring
Serious	Worrying
Practical	Restricting
Ambitious	Materialistic
Disciplined	Rigid
Achieving	Overworking
Methodical	Stiff

Capricorn is more concerned with social values than freedom and innovation. Efficiency is its watchword. What works is accepted and applauded, what does not work is discarded without a backward glance because everything must serve the same end: usefulness. Capricorn asks, "Will this work?" and if the answer is, "No," it turns away without a backward glance.

Capricorn has always been regarded as a sacred sign, for within its boundaries the winter solstice takes place, bringing an increase of daylight to the Northern Hemisphere. It is for this reason that the Christ–the world savior–is born in Capricorn. Christmas is celebrated as a symbol that the newborn Babe promises arrested death and continued life, and the old pagan religions held ceremonies celebrating the winter solstice, marking the return of the Sun, which was considered a divine being.

Capricorn marks the winter ingress of the Sun (0 degrees of Capricorn), giving it a very special place in the branch of astrology concerned with worldly affairs. At that time, a horoscope is cast for the various longitudes and latitudes of the nations of Earth in order to help astrologers interpret the coming planetary influences that will affect the entire world in the coming year. Capricorn is indeed the most *worldly* of the signs of the zodiac.

Chapter 7

The Trumps in a Reading

When doing a reading, it is important to realize that each of the Major Arcana has many layered meanings. Not all of them will apply to a given situation. In Chapter 5, we discussed the three levels of Tarot reading: 1) practical, or mundane; 2) intuitive, or meditative; and 3) spiritual progress.

However, many people will want to use the Tarot for divinatory, or predictive, uses. This is called "fortunetelling," but because that term has unfortunate negative connotations, I prefer not to use it. Moreover, as a psychotherapist, my own approach to a reading has more to do with the inner state of the person for whom the reading is being given. And perhaps it is because of this that the cards work for me in a way that points to the psychological issues, sometimes very deep ones, that underlie practical problems with which the person is concerned. As I have only my own experience to go on, I cannot say how any other individual will read the cards. But I do believe that we inevitably bring to our use of the cards—whether in doing readings for ourselves or others or using them for meditation and/or spiritual reasons—our own particular point of view, philosophy, interests, and emotional coloration.

Though we can study standardized "meanings," and there is general agreement upon these for the individual Trumps, only the individual reader can use the *art of interpretation* as it applies to the immediate situation. The development of intuition is as important in the use of the Tarot as is study of specific meanings. (For a thorough discussion of how to develop your intuition, plus many helpful exercises, see my book *Your Psychic Potential.*)

As you use your deck, or decks, of cards, shuffling and mixing them eventually some cards will become reversed. Some readers deliberately reverse cards by turning half of the deck opposite the other half when shuffling. My preference is for the cards to be reversed only at the time of the reading; therefore, I always begin with the entire deck of cards in the upright position. Other readers leave the deck as it was, partly reversed, from the previous use, and in the shuffling process some cards that previously were reversed will then become upright. How you feel about this upright/reversed process is up to you. The choice is yours.

0 The Fool

Upright

At this time, you are out of sync with the rest of the world, but in a positive way. You may want to go out on your own, "Full speed ahead and damn the torpedoes." Or, you may feel somehow isolated from the general group, a loner. Your experience of the current situation is different from those around you, which may make you feel as if you are marching to a different drummer, and you probably are. You need to honor that "different drummer," for that is the true beat of your authentic self trying to get your attention.

Reversed

The time for independent action may not be right. You must discriminate between your personal fantasies—of going off into some asocial situation or chucking it all for a new track—with reality as it actually is. As the advice given to people who want to become writers or artists stereotypically is given, "Don't quit your day job." This is not to say that what you want to do is invalid, only that you must consider all of the pros and cons carefully in the light of present reality.

At every moment we are dying and renewing ourselves. Each moment we see that a new consciousness, a new thought, a new hope, a new light is dawning in us. When something new dawns, at that time, we see that the old has been transformed into something higher, deeper, and more profound.

—Sri Chinmoy,
Death and Reincarnation: Eternity's Voyage

1 The Magician

Upright

This is a situation of new beginnings and new choices. It indicates someone who is willing and able to manipulate the situation in order to achieve the desired ends. It indicates leadership potential, ambition, desire for action, and new relationships coming into being. The tools for whatever action is desired are already at hand, as is the knowledge for using them correctly. This is a key point: any use of the Magician's power for improper end will backfire. It is a time to evaluate the tools you have at your disposal and relate them properly to your aims.

Reversed

The time for change is not now. It may be that you are not ready internally, or that you are not fully prepared in an external way. However, new directions are in the making, but patience is required for the proper working out. You may be experiencing self-doubt about any new venture, or your spirits and vitality may be too low for the action required. There is a sense of creativity

being in the latent stage, like a caterpillar in its cocoon, and there is no sense in rushing things prematurely. The key here is waiting until the time is ripe.

II The High Priestess

Upright

You are experiencing a high degree of awareness of what I call "the invisible world," where inner change takes place before it manifests in the outer, material world. Your attunement to these inner, invisible sources is acute now, and you are in a position to take advantage of this fact. You may want to remove yourself, literally, from your day-to-day life in order to go deeper into your inner core and tune into your inner voice and spiritual awareness.

Reversed

Something within you is seeking a greater recognition of your inner needs, which you may have been neglecting, although at a deep level you are aware that something is stirring. You may be tuning in to yourself in a very private way, not wanting others to know about this activity. Those around you may notice that you seem "vague," or "not quite yourself," and you may be fending off comments about your not being "here." Ignore them. You are in the process of finding your own personal way into your inner world and the riches it contains.

III The Empress

Upright

Your are in a position of nurturing someone else, or several others. This could be taking an obvious form, as in caring for children, or the sick, or being supportive of a spouse or friend in need. It could also refer to a pregnancy, or the desire for a pregnancy. It is appropriate for you to be giving nurturance now, for you have the inner strength and the ability to do so without harming or depleting yourself.

Reversed

This is a time for you to be nurturing *yourself*. You may have been spending too much time nurturing others (or you may have recently had a child whose demands have worn you out). This is an indication that you need to take time out for yourself. You may be on the verge of what I call "lunar burnout"—a condition that happens when we are depleted from nurturing others and have been neglecting our own personal needs. This is a call for self-love and the awareness that we deserve the same care and attention we give to our loved ones in order to maintain a balance between the needs of others and our own, equally valid, needs.

IV The Emperor

Upright

This is an indication that you are involved with the established order, or involved with someone else who is a representative of the "establishment." You may have a need to identify with a powerful group, whether religious, ideological, intellectual, or political. You may be attending meetings related to a particular culture, social group, institution, economic group, company, or community that enable you to identify with this power. You may be feeling a need to *belong*—to be "one of them." Or you may be associating with someone else who has this need.

Reversed

This is a situation where you may be in conflict with the established order of things—perhaps at your job, or with your traditional religion or ethnic base. You may be feeling pressured to accept responsibilities you don't want, or don't feel up to handling. You may have recently experienced a loss of power, such as "downsizing," or you may be feeling a lack of energy to reach your goals. You may need more experience or drive, or a physical check-up may be indicated.

V The Hierophant

Upright

There is a traditional factor active in your life, whether it is a religion, a philosophy, a social organization, or any other authoritative group. You feel a great deal of loyalty to this tradition or group and find it supportive. You choose to live in accordance with the beliefs you have in common with the group or organization. You may aspire to become a leader, or you may have a close relationship with the leader. This group or tradition serves

It is clear that civilization cannot evolve further until the occult is taken for granted on the same level as atomic energy.

—Colin Wilson,
The Occult

you in many ways, inspirationally, as a teacher, as emotional support. There may also be a judgmental quality involved where you are expected to follow a certain set of beliefs and, if you fail, you are called to account.

Reversed

You may wish to overthrow an old tradition—religious, ideological, intellectual, or whatever—that you feel either is suffocating you or simply no longer serves your needs. You want to choose to live by whatever philosophy or belief structure that resonates with your true nature, not be told *ipso facto* what is permitted in terms of belief and a way of life. You want to direct your actions your own way, even if this puts you into conflict with some established tradition. You may find that your faith is being challenged in some way and that you have to re-evaluate tenets heretofore taken for granted. You want to be accountable to yourself alone.

VI The Lovers

Upright

This is a card of cooperation, of working together in coalition with others to accomplish joint purposes. It stands for attraction of any kind, not only of the romantic variety, and for any venture requiring harmony, union, and cooperation. There can be an indication of a choice being required between two factors of equal worth—but the choice you make will be the right one. Or, two or more forces or people may have come together in your life in pursuit of a common goal. This may be a temporary conjoinment for some specific purpose.

Reversed

This is a situation where your own disparate parts are in cooperation with each other, where warring factors of your own personality are coming together—such as your realizing you can be beautiful and brainy at the same time, or assertive and gentle simultaneously. Whatever the case, you are finding a way to bring together what was not working well together and melding these differences into a system of mutual support for yourself. There could be an indication of a delay of some project that needs mutual cooperation, or of trying to force cooperation among basically incompatible elements.

VII The Chariot

Upright

Victory is assured! Things are moving fast, and transition is occurring rapidly. You are holding things together successfully, uniting opposite energies to stay on track. This is a situation where you are completely, totally involved, and happily so. You are feeling together with yourself and whatever task is at hand to be accomplished. Though the pace is faster than usual, you are attuned to the rhythm of it and keeping up with the changes that are happening—at your job, in your relationship, with your career, or in some community or worldly involvement. You are sensitive to the minor adjustments you must constantly make to keep things going right.

Reversed

With the Chariot reversed, the changes and transitions are happening *internally*, but at a rapid rate. You may feel things are moving so fast that you are out of control and feel that you are struggling to keep your head above water. You may feel pulled in two directions at once and be stressed out by the pressure. It's a time to choose direction carefully, to accept the process of inner transition as a positive one, but to do so with an effort of mental clarity about your direction in life. The more you can tune in to your own transition process, the more control over it you will feel able to exert.

VIII Strength

Upright

You have come through severe trials and triumphed. You have found your deep inner strength, and it will from now on see you through whatever comes your way. You are firmly connected to the instinctual world (represented by the lion) and you are able to make friends with it and control it for your own benefit and that of others. Emotionally, at a gut-level, you are connected positively to your animal self, and this will protect and care for you. Your inner drives are in harmony with your outer needs and your instinctive nature is supporting all that you do or hope to do. At this time, your logical mind—if it is in conflict with your intuitive knowingness—is not as important in making decisions as is what you *feel* to be right for you. Whatever decisions you make, or actions you take, will be successful.

Symbol is myth's vehicle, the chariot by which legend and story, and myth's higher form, religion, is drawn through the heart and mind, and through time, the pages of history. Symbols express underlying patterns of thought and feeling stemming from the mythological roots that still affect us in a very real way.

Reversed

You are struggling to gain your own in a situation that is difficult and which may be inimical to your ultimate good. As a result, you are experiencing an upsurge from your inner, instinctive nature that is calling upon you to pay careful attention to your own needs and not put your ambitions on the back burner in order to attend to the demands of others. It is a time of travail, but you will eventually overcome the difficulties and come out on top. Others may find you are behaving in a way that seems to them illogical or contrary to what is "normal" or generally accepted. But, you are being put on notice by your basic instincts of survival that this is a time for change and expression of your individuality.

IX The Hermit

Upright

The Hermit is a guide figure. Depending on where he appears in the layout, he is either nearby waiting for you to call on his wisdom, or he is waiting patiently for you to turn to him for advice. Usually, you are aware of his influence, but you may be ignoring it. At this time, you may be involved actively in seeking guidance from the "invisible world." This may take a physical form: you may be isolating yourself in some way, going out of town for a few days to be alone with yourself, or, if staying home, turning off the phone and seeking solitude. You want to gain some perspective on your life, and you are open to the inner guidance that is available to you upon request.

Reversed

You have been putting off giving yourself the solitude you need to sort out your life and the issues you are currently confronting. You may have engaged in staying extra busy, a form of denial, but the inner Guide is still tapping at your interior door, for he knows you need him even if you are avoiding looking within for fear of what you will find there. It is a time—or long past time—for you to engage in some self-evaluation about your life, your aims and goals, your associations, your relationships, your career, your life path. You may find yourself wanting to withdraw into yourself to think things through, but you are avoiding it even though you know this needs to be done.

X The Wheel of Fortune

Upright

Things have been put into motion that are now unstoppable and will run their course no matter what you do. You have done something—quit a job, made travel reservations, ended a relationship, opted out of a friendship or other situation. Destiny has been set in motion and all will turn out as it is intended. There's very little more you have to do except to go with the flow. There may be unexpected turns of events—such as meeting people while you are on a journey or being made an offer of some sort, a new opportunity—but they too are part of the grand plan for your life. This is the precursor of good fortune.

Reversed

You are holding back your own destiny by your refusal to make the necessary changes or take the required actions. You are refusing to set things in motion, which is leading to stagnation and frustration. You are rationalizing the fact that you are standing still, but you are uncomfortable with the situation. You think you are waiting for the propitious time, but fear of the unknown is standing in your way. You are bringing problems upon yourself by your foot-dragging. You may be fantasizing about what you want to do, but you have to take the action before anything can happen. This is the time to send out a call to the Universe to show you the way and to fearlessly follow the direction you are given. You may experience delays in your projects because of lack of commitment. It's time to quit being wishy-washy and get on with what you already know you need to be doing.

XI Justice

Upright

You are concerned with external circumstances, waiting for the time for action to be right. You may be seeking justice in personal or business affairs, or be involved with a lawsuit. In any case, it is important that you work to resolve the situation in a way that is fair to all participants. You must crate a balance, not only of power but of emotional reactions to the situation at hand, which could involve jockeying for power at work or the division of material possessions between yourself and others. This is a time for moderation in all

things, for creating harmony to facilitate relationships. You may be called upon to arbitrate for others, or be subject to arbitration. Your judgment is good at this time and you are not swayed by personal considerations or bias.

Reversed

Justice in reverse indicates delays in legal matters or unfairness in some other situation. The danger is becoming angry and hostile. There is a lack of balance here and the possibility of abuse of power. If you are the person in power, you may be unduly severe in meting out punishment. If you are in the powerless position, you may be festering with resentment over being treated unfairly. The antidote is to create a balance within your own life and become less dependent upon outside influences. Your state of equilibrium is out of whack and you may be swinging from one extreme to another. It is a time to work at achieving psychological balance.

XII The Hanged Man

Upright

You are in suspension between the past and the future and a new direction for your life is in the making. It is a time for a new perspective, making significant changes. Look at things from a different angle in order to make necessary readjustments. Cosmic consciousness is calling to you and enlightenment should be your goal now. You need to make a clean break with the past and concentrate on becoming spiritually attuned. Readjustment is needed but there's no hurry. Take your time and make the right decisions about where you truly want to take your life at this time and for the long term. Pay attention to your inner development and be prepared to dance to a different drummer in the future.

Reversed

You are at a crossroads and are in a standstill because you have become stuck on the material plane and are neglecting your spiritual development. You may be in denial about your real needs which could be affecting you with depression and a sense of dissatisfaction which in turn is producing apathy, the feeling that any effort will be futile. This is because you are not being true to your inner Self. You may be sacrificing some part of your life unneccessarily because of a martyr complex and/or a refusal to make decisions. It's a time to end such behavior and commit yourself to a worthwhile goal that will lead to your higher good. This may require turning your world upside down in order to march to your own drummer and not someone else's tune.

As you examine your cards and do practice layouts, be sure to record in your notes, or preferably a Tarot study journal you keep for the purpose, what Major Arcana cards appear, whether they are upright or reversed, what position they occupy, and how you interpret them in relationship to each other. This is especially important for the beginner who may become confused by cards that seem to be saying different things in the same spread.

XIII Death

Upright

Contrary to the grim illustration, the Death card is actually positive, for it indicates a transformation for the better. It does *not* portend actual physical death. Usually, the person is experiencing a metamorphosis of some sort, a destruction of the old, outworn circumstances that have been holding back new development. Something is being regenerated at a deep level and superficial changes won't cut it. It's time for a total change and no doubt about it. Patterns you have found workable are no longer working. They have to be destroyed to make room for the new that is coming into being.

Reversed

You are putting off making the necessary changes, usually out of fear. You feel that others are standing in your way, but it's really yourself blocking you. You're stuck in old habit patterns that you know need to be changed, but you don't want to put forth the effort even though you are unhappy with the current situation. Whether you know it or recognize it or not, you *are* going through some internal changes that will eventually lead to external reforms. But at the moment you would rather not actively participate. You may be depressed or in a state of apathy, the result of refusing the necessary process of psychological death, which leads to rebirth. The way out is to face up to your stagnation, frustration, and unhappiness. Jettison any relationships that aren't working. Begin to make the decisions that will throw out the old and ring in the new.

XIV Temperance

Upright

You are being asked to blend things in a harmonious way, and you have the ability to use your creative talents to achieve this goal. Like the alchemists of old, you are mixing the streams

of the spiritual and material in a positive way, creating new forms. You are using your energies positively and have a good deal of self-control which comes from trusting the inner self's guidance. You are learning to temper your ego needs with the legitimate needs of the spirit within. This is a time of inner growth and outer harmony. You have patience and can accommodate disparate elements—whether they are raw materials, resources, personnel, or ideas—into a harmonious whole.

Reversed

Things seem stalled. Previous combinations aren't working well. There's not much you can do at the present except to let things work themselves out, which they will in time. Patience is the key, for trying to force together inharmonious elements will only result in bad feelings and poor results, like mixing oil and water. This is a time to concentrate on blending the different parts of yourself together into a new form—of combining your own personal psychological, emotional, and spiritual elements into a new *you*, of tempering whatever inner conditions you have that make you feel out of balance.

XV The Devil

Upright

The Devil is a mythical creature with no real substance, but symbolically it represents the bondage that we create and maintain for ourselves. There may be obstacles in the environment that you find frustrating, or you may feel your options are narrowing. Someone else may be involved, but you have the ability to free yourself from the situation by using your will power. Everyone faces limits and boundaries, but it is our own self-bondage to the material world of possessions and status that is usually at the root of the problem. Even in the most restrictive of situations, we still have *spiritual* choices. And, everyone needs structure to create a solid foundation for growth and development.

Reversed

You feel trapped in a situation over which you feel you have no control, but close examination will show that it is your own attitudes and belief systems that are causing the problem. You have established

certain conditions, based upon these belief systems, that are now limiting you. The solution is to carefully examine your belief systems to learn how they are serving as restrictions. Be careful of any "quick fix" to your problems, which are structural not superficial. If you are willing to do the hard work, both on the inner and outer planes, you can solve the issues and achieve success on your own. Remember that Saturn rules the Devil card, and Saturn's influences are long-term. Also, the appearance of this card can often be related to a transit of Saturn to a planet in the natal chart.

Remember that it is human nature to be multifaceted—and that therefore different strands of the person's life will show up in the cards. This is good because it opens up issues for discussion and resolution. If, for example, the Hermit appears upright and the Devil appears also, it is an indication that the person needs to seek inner guidance (the Hermit) in order to resolve the problems or restrictions of the Devil.

XVI The Tower

Upright

Many people interpret the Tower as representing catastrophe, but whatever disruption or adversity is to be faced is for the best. The Tower represents the overthrow of false ideas and old habit patterns that need to be gotten rid of. In this sense, it is *not* a negative card but a positive one. However, since most people are afraid of anything that upsets their regular routine, it may represent distinctively uncomfortable feelings. Sometimes, there is indeed some kind of loss–personal or financial, or the breakup of a marriage. But, careful examination of all of the factors will generally show that the catastrophic event could have been foreseen if one had only been aware and willing to face facts. Though the Tower is related to the planet Mars, I often find that its appearance coincides with a transit of Uranus, the planet of unexpected, lightning-fast events, to the natal chart. The combination of Mars/Uranus is extremely powerful and can be destructive. But what is destroyed is what has served its purpose and needs to go. Uranian energy seems to strike particularly when a person has become stuck in the status quo, unsatisfied and discontent, but not knowing how to make the needed changes, firing an urgent need to break free of the restrictions that have been limiting further development.

Reversed

You are refusing to change the old habit patterns and you will suffer continued disruption in the form of unforeseen difficulties until you finally get the message that it's time to make some far-reaching changes in your life. You may suffer from confusion about just who and what you are. At a deep level, you are being

prepared for the changes that *must* eventually take place, but you are resisting what your own deepest self knows already. You may have the feeling that some particular identity—such as a family or career position—was basically and fundamentally true. Yet, it is possible for you to alter that fixed belief and accept that you are larger than any such limited identity. Once you do, there will be far-reaching ramifications in your life.

XVII The Star

Upright

At this time you are experiencing a new flow of energy and self-confidence, and are feeling good about yourself and your place in the Universe. You are at a significant point of departure, for which you actually have been preparing yourself for a number of years. You are receiving assistance both from the invisible world and from the material world. Good things are in the offing because you are freely flowing with the pure energy of the Universe. Full of faith and trust in life and its many processes, you are setting new goals for the future and opening the door to new opportunities in career or relationships. Because you are in tune with the natural abundance of the Universe, the likelihood is that you will be getting benefits coming from the material world in the form of money, possessions, recognition, or assistance.

Reversed

When the Star is reversed, it represents an inward condition where you are seeking your own path in a private way, without regard to the outside world and its benefits. You may be feeling particularly withdrawn, even resentful of outer obligations at this time, because your inner need is great. You may recently have experienced some disappointment, an expectation on which you counted that went unfulfilled, and this may have brought on a mood of pessimism that has caused you to turn inward for comfort and sustenance. There's nothing wrong with this, for it is a necessary step you must make in order to get your life in order to achieve the goals you have set for yourself. You need "repair time," including silence and solitude to retune yourself with your inner needs. When you do, you will begin to re-energize yourself more in concert with who you truly are.

XVIII The Moon

Upright

The Moon is a mysterious card and many readers find negative vibrations in it. Perhaps because I am an astrologer, I generally feel that the Moon is positive. It is saying that you are aware of the need to tune in to your lunar energies. Symbolically, the Moon serves to illuminate the non-conscious side of human life, allowing light to shine into our inner spiritual world, to illuminate what springs naturally from *inside ourselves*. You are now perceiving the reality of your inner nature more clearly, becoming more aware of the shadings and nuances of feelings and inner perceptions. It is a time you can tune in more accurately to the spiritual vibrations of others because you are more connected to the information universe of the invisible world the Moon lights. It can also indicate heightened psychic development.

Reversed

Your soul is calling for help, and your attention. You may have been ignoring your lunar needs—for self-nurturance, for artistic creation, for lingering with your dreams. The demands of the day are overwhelming you and you need time out to address your inner lunar self, which is the channel for the flow of the divine Goddess energy as well as the soul-satisfying feminine side of life—a softer, gentler way than the sometimes harsh requirements of the daily grind. You are out of balance inside because you are neglecting your inner needs, because of pressures to conform to the outside world. You feel disconnected from your true self and need to restore the inner balance.

XIX The Sun

Upright

Generally considered a positive card, the Sun relates to energy, vitality, confidence, success, and good times. It's a time of new beginnings, of things going well, of accomplishment, success, contentment. Material well-being is indicated and an optimistic and happy frame of mind. You feel cheerful and self-confident, full of life and vitality, ready to undertake new projects and make changes for the better. Whatever you are planning, you feel a great deal of enthusiasm for it and aren't worried about the outcome. You may

As you work with the cards and notice the juxtapositions that occur, you will begin to understand how they all relate to one another, enriching the information flow and giving substance to the reading.

be starting more than one project, or upgrading something in your life, such as moving to a better-paying, more satisfying job, remodeling your home, or moving to a sunnier climate.

Reversed

All of the above apply to the reversed Sun, because it is never a negative card. However, the reversed position indicates that there will be delays, that you will have to make some adjustments you hadn't planned on. Basically, you feel fine just the way you are, but circumstances are presenting you with the need to make some minor changes. Maybe you need to spruce up your appearance for that new job—get a new haircut or a new wardrobe to show yourself at your very best. You are finding new and more effective ways to express who you are to the outside world.

XX Judgment

Upright

You've had a wake-up call from the Universe and are now ready to step into a new phase of your maturing process. Your life is fairly settled now, and you are letting things grow and mature at a steady pace, not trying to hurry up the process. You are realizing that you are being guided by a Higher Power and feel faith in that realization. A new phase in your life is coming into being as the natural result of your maturity—like a tree that has gone through the flowering stage produces fruit, the product of its maturity. You may get important news that will prove beneficial, or acquire new knowledge that will bring you joy and a sense of fulfillment. Health improves, and problems are easily solved.

Reversed

There are interior biological and psychological factors at work over which you have little or no control—your hair may be getting gray. You may be thinking about making some changes, which are being signaled by these inner timing mechanisms. This process may be throwing you into a state of confusion as you aren't sure just how to handle the process of getting older. Nonetheless, you are facing a new phase in your life and must make your peace with it. Emotionally, you may be being called upon to grow up. Judgment in reverse may also indicate frustrating delays or postponements, a materialistic view of life, refusal to take charge, possible loss or separation, and the need to cope with these life changes in spite of not wanting to face reality.

XXI The World

Upright

A wonderful card! Success in all endeavors is assured. You are—or soon will be—"on top of the world." Everything is available to you—completion of projects, attainment of your goals and aims, happiness, harmony. Whatever you do now will succeed—a career change, a move to another place, a new relationship, recognition, rewards, acclaim. This is the end of an old cycle and the beginning of a new one. You have mastered the complexities of your own inner nature and feel supported by your inner resources. It is a time of supreme self-confidence and of victory. You have put your trust where it belongs—in the Higher Power—and you will reap the rewards. At this time, many possibilities and opportunities are available to you and you are completely free to choose what pleases you and make it work well.

Reversed

You are being presented with a multiplicity of choices and aren't sure which one to make. You may be experiencing new facets of your own self or investigating different levels of reality. Or, you may be rejecting new ideas being offered out of fear or a purely materialistic view of life. Now is the time to face the fact that the Universe is a more complex place than you have been willing to admit, that there is more in heaven and on earth than meets the eye, or that has been provided for in your philosophy.

Relationship of the Major Arcana to Each Other

Often, more than one of the cards of the Major Arcana will come up in a reading layout. They can come up in any order, and must be considered in terms of their position in the spread you are using. Therefore, it's important for you to know how they interact.

There are no hard and fast rules here, and whether the cards come upright or reversed is also a factor in their relationship. Often, a person being read for will have conflicting emotions or situations in his or her life, and the Major Arcana cards are likely to reflect this fact.

Part III

The Minor Arcana: Symbolic Interpretation

Chapter 8

The Minor Arcana

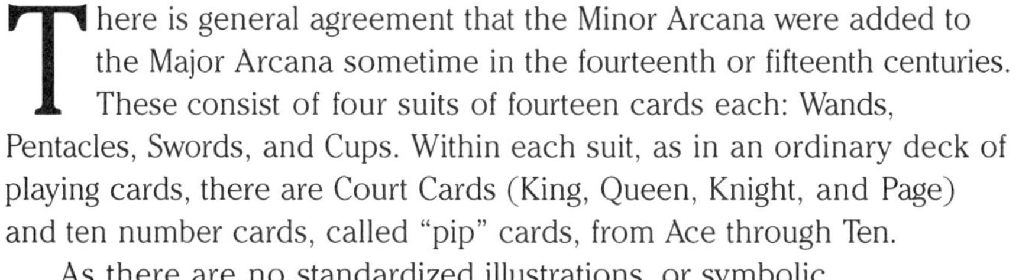

There is general agreement that the Minor Arcana were added to the Major Arcana sometime in the fourteenth or fifteenth centuries. These consist of four suits of fourteen cards each: Wands, Pentacles, Swords, and Cups. Within each suit, as in an ordinary deck of playing cards, there are Court Cards (King, Queen, Knight, and Page) and ten number cards, called "pip" cards, from Ace through Ten.

As there are no standardized illustrations, or symbolic renderings, of the Minor Arcana, as there are with the Major Arcana, interpretations vary. Some writers about Tarot pay little attention to the Minor Arcana; others approach them from a point of view of numerology since, aside from the Court Cards, they are number cards.

As number cards, they are illustrated many different ways, often without any distinct activity connected to the specific number. In many decks, the pip cards do not display *any* symbols for interpretation but merely show a stylized corresponding number of their suit symbol. For example, the Three of Cups may be merely three cups, arranged in an arbitrary manner.

The exception to this is the Waite deck, where each of the pip cards shows a definite activity being performed, with people in relationship to the number of objects representing the suit. When specific illustrations are found, as with the Waite deck, there is the problem that they may cause confusion in terms of interpretation as the illustration can seem contradictory both to the meaning of the suit involved and to the number being represented.

Some say the pip cards were illustrated as a memory tool rather than as representative of the meanings of the cards. And indeed a vivid illustration—such as three Swords stuck through a large red heart—does help the Three of Swords stick in the mind as meaning heartache and separation.

The Court cards are usually quite similar in design to those on ordinary playing cards—straightforward illustrations of a King, a Queen, a Knight, and a Page. Though there may be some variation in costume, depending upon the philosophical orientation of the designer of the deck, sometimes the only way to differentiate the suits is to note the symbol of the suit, which is usually shown on the card, or the bottom has a label with the applicable word.

Again, the Waite deck is an exception. Each of the Court Cards is quite definitely recognizable as to which suit it belongs. And, to my mind, the Court cards in the Waite deck are designed so that they pictorially represent the *meaning* of the suit they represent. For example, the

King of Cups is a benign figure holding a large cup in one hand and a scepter in the other, and the colors are bright and cheerful, while the King of Swords is a stern figure holding a sword upright as if willing to strike, and the colors are dull and forbidding.

Whether or not the number cards in a deck are illuminated, or merely an attractive or ornate rendering of the numbers, there are not many traditional elements in the Minor Arcana to use in interpretation. Although five hundred years' worth of Tarot students and masters have produced some agreement on the meanings of the Minor Arcana cards, there is also a good deal of disagreement. To resolve this, I prefer to base interpretations of the pip cards on the *number* rather than on any particular illustration, unless, of course, my intuition hooks into the picture and it reveals something.

Despite this seeming confusion, the Minor Arcana cards can be extremely accurate in answering questions about the here-and-now—they were originally used for fortunetelling exclusively—as they refer to specific areas of life and human experience. There is in them no specific reference to spiritual growth, but each of the areas to which they refer can certainly be incorporated into a pattern of spiritual development, such as one's livelihood or one's love relationships, referred to by the Wands and the Cups, respectively.

Understanding the Minor Arcana

In order to understand the Minor Arcana, it's important to realize that they serve as an *adjunct* to the Major Arcana—a sort of commentary within the context of the reading. It is not that they have no real significance on their own, for as numerological references they can be extremely useful, but that they are an integral part of the context of the entire reading.

As such, there is no need to search for some mystical meaning to attach to them. They are what they are, and their own intrinsic meanings are full of significance in terms of the specific question, life situation, or problem for which the Tarot reading is being consulted.

Their function is to relate the readee (person being read for) to the elements of the everyday world, which, after all, exist for all of us no matter how "spiritual" we are or how seriously we pursue a spiritual path. In this context, everything can have a spiritual meaning—every action of every day can serve as a spiritual celebration, as I have written extensively about in my book *Awaken to Your Spiritual Self.*

The divine is everywhere. We have only to look and listen. Most magnificently, the sacred is inside each of us, nestled in the most interior part of our beings. Alas, our perception of the sacred within ourselves and all around us is too often buried beneath an encrustation of the demands and expectations of others—family, teachers, society and its institutions, which serve to obscure our ability to realize and recognize the divine spirit glowing within ourselves. But, no matter how faint the ember, we have only to go deeply within to find its eternal spark and fan it into new and vibrant life.

To know one's self deeply and intimately is to know the divine spirit.

The Royal Court of the Tarot is composed of a King, a Queen, a Knight (or Cavalier—usually on horseback), and a Page (or Valet). These personages should be understood as literal representatives of the type of authority each carries.

King

A king is a powerful ruler who exercises absolute authority over the territory he rules. He is, so to speak, at the top of the heap. Thus, the King of any suit represents a completion point: there's no higher position to attain. A cycle has been completed that began with the Ace and it's now time to either consolidate your position or begin a new cycle. The level of the King is where one releases and lets go, completes old things, and prepares for a new and more fulfilling way of life. An example of this is a man who is a highly placed corporate executive, who's reached the pinnacle of success in his field, who's made a lot of money, who decides that it's time to "give back" to the world. Ex-president Jimmy Carter is a good example of this.

Queen

The Queen is a mature woman who has all the strengths and weakness of the King of the same suit, but she is also a ruler in her own right, not just the King's consort. As such, she represents a woman who embodies her own feminine qualities of rulership, or leadership. She has developed skills and has the wisdom of years of experience. With the Queen, you are at a level of complete maturity and the self-confidence that comes with it. You know when to compromise, or when to take a firm stand. You are not intimidated by any situation. Yet you remain able to grow and evolve, and be flexible through understanding.

Knight

A Knight is someone who has been singled out by the ruler as a person who has performed valuable services. As a Knight, he takes on even more responsibility to the Crown he serves. At the level of the Knight, you are fully aware of your direction and your aims are clear. You want to get on with it in the most direct way possible, not waste time on irrelevancies. You are feeling a sense of dedication—to a project, an idea, a person—that is very intense. You've taken risks and "gotten yourself together" for the task at hand and you are focusing your energies totally to accomplish your goal and make the risk worthwhile. This is a time of vertical thinking, for the point of our devotion is where the divine enters.

Page

The Page is a personal attendant of the royal family, often an errand boy (or girl). It's his job to *serve* in order to advance. The page represents a level of taking risks in order to succeed at something. It involves being willing to be in a subordinate role—as younger people often are—and to learn about commitment, even when commitment involves taking risks to reach a new level. The Page is about challenging yourself, developing your inner resources, and taking something to a greater stage of development. There may be hesitancy, or a feeling of not being fully prepared for the task, but you still hope the situation will turn out as you anticipate.

Interpreting the Minor Arcana

As the Minor Arcana do not have the symbolic meanings of the Major Arcana, they have been used primarily to represent real life situations and to point to solutions to real life problems. They are very effective for this purpose, if interpreted correctly.

As you begin to study the Minor Arcana, especially if you read different books on the subject, you will find a mixture of interpretations, some of which conflict with each other. Some experienced readers have developed their own particular interpretations; others seem to follow a general trend toward sameness. There can even be overlap when one source will agree with another on the meaning of a specific card but disagree on the meaning of another card. This is not to say that a valid interpretation cannot be had.

As mentioned earlier, your *intuition* is a significant factor in interpreting the Minor Arcana, as is your experience over time in the study of Tarot and practice of doing readings.

As you proceed, you will begin to develop your own renderings of the cards, discovering by trial and error what works and what doesn't work. Bear in mind that what works for one reader may not work for another reader. This is mainly a result of two things: one is the reader's point or view; the other is the readee's state of mind during the reading. Timing is another factor. In one reading, a Minor Arcana card may represent one meaning; later, another.

Working with the Tarot cards, allow yourself to be flexible. Learn the basic definitions of the Minor Arcana, but then let yourself "go into" the reading when you lay out the cards in order to activate your intuition. Beyond the Court cards, the number cards, or pips, fall into general categories—once you learn the basic significance of the numbers and the suits, you will be able to combine these into your own interpretation, based upon the card's position in the layout.

Remember also that people are at different levels of development in different areas of life. One person may be at a high career point (Wands) but be having emotional problems (Cups). None of us moves smoothly from one stage of development to another in all areas of life simultaneously. The captain of industry who controls the fates of thousands of employees may inside be a little boy who has never grown up and still wants his mama. A woman who does not have a job or career may be possessed of extraordinary maturity in matters of interpersonal relations—and so on.

Sometimes, a person leaps from one level to another by skipping over a few in between. As you explore the suits and the numbers and begin to test interpretations in actual readings, you will become aware of an overall system operating. It's kind of like learning to play the piano: you first have to learn the notes (symbols), then practice the scales to get familiar with fingering (reading), and then you begin to understand how the composer created a piece of music. In time, you may even write your own music.

Astrological Correspondences of the Minor Arcana: Fire, Earth, Air, Water

Astrology is a complex and deep subject, one that considers the *whole person*. Inside each of us are many and varied energies, one of the most important—aside from the planets themselves—is the *elements*: **Fire, Earth, Air, Water**. These refer to the most basic energies within us, essential dynamic life forces. The elemental makeup of the chart is the energy pattern of the individual. A grasp of these life principles and how they operate is a major step toward understanding one's self or another.

Every person relates variously to the four energies symbolized by the elements. One person may be a "natural" swimmer, while another finds mountain air restorative. Thus, we each express the elements inherently in us in a way that complements our individual nature.

Each of the four suits of the Minor Arcana relates to one of the elements. Below, I'll describe how each element functions, as well as to which suits it relates, so that you can begin to get a picture of how the suits, regardless of numbers or the Court cards, operate on an elemental level.

Fire: The Wands

Fire is the basic life force. Its zodiacal signs are Aries, Leo, and Sagittarius. The energy of Fire is radiant. It is excitable and enthusiastic. Fire people are spontaneous, quick, full of flowing energy. They can appear to be self-centered, or too objective. They have high spirits, self-esteem, strength that comes in spurts, and a strong desire to express themselves, as well as a great need for freedom. They tend to impatience, especially with the Earth and Water elements, fearing that Earth will smother them with practicality or that

Water will drench their Fire energy. Fire likes Air, which fans the flames of their ardent nature and inspires them with new ideas for their active natures and minds.

When Wands appear in a reading, there is a lot of Fire energy around the person, or around other people in the environment. Wands indicate much mental activity related to the outside world, usually of work and career. The Wand Court cards refer to people with the Fire signs in their charts, often the Sun sign but sometimes other planets as well—such as Mars or Jupiter.

Earth: The Pentacles

The energy of Earth is solid, related closely to the physical plane and senses. Its zodiacal signs are Taurus, Virgo, and Capricorn. Earth signs are known for hard-headed practicality, based on experience and the observance of reality. They don't usually go for the flashy or superficial, preferring something more substantial than inspirations, theoretical considerations, or the intuitive flights of fancy. They prefer money in the bank, so to speak. They want results of a practical nature and are patient and willing to discipline themselves to get them. They have an innate understanding of the world and its many forms as well as the stamina to persist until the goal is reached. They have enormous endurance at their disposal and the strength of this gives them persistence. They rarely give up, no matter how hard the road or tiresome the journey. Sometimes slow to start, like the tortoise, they have the fortitude to go the long mile, carrying on after the competition has dropped by the roadside in exhaustion. Earth likes Water and finds Fire difficult but attractive, but Air, with its endless intellectual fancies seems foreign to them.

When Pentacles appear in a reading, there is a lot of Earth energy around the person, or around other people in the environment. Pentacles indicate concern with money and material possessions, or a lack thereof. There may be issues around security. The Pentacle Court cards refer to people with the Earth signs in their charts, often the Sun sign but sometimes other planets as well—such as Venus, Mercury, or Saturn.

Air: The Swords

Air is the realm of the mind. Its zodiacal signs are Gemini, Libra, and Aquarius. The energy of Air is ephemeral, constantly

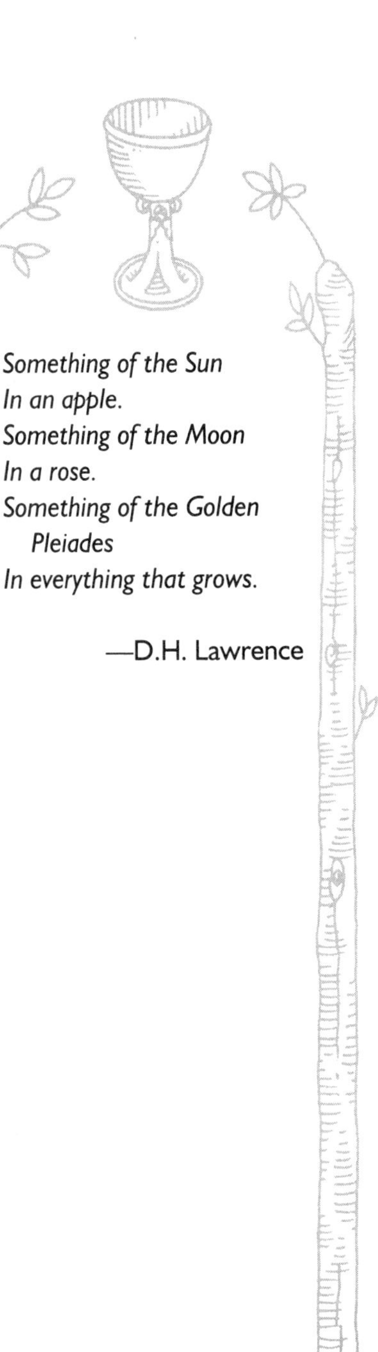

Something of the Sun
In an apple.
Something of the Moon
In a rose.
Something of the Golden
Pleiades
In everything that grows.

—D.H. Lawrence

shifting, like the blowing of the winds. The realm of Air is the realm of the mind freed of all physical restrictions (imagine if you could fly!). It is the non-material, where form does not yet exist and is only "in the mind," but it is compelling nonetheless. Ideas must precede manifestation. Every building on earth was once nothing more than air, an idea in the mind of the architect, then a set of mere drawings on paper, before it was translated into the hard reality of stone, brick, and mortar. Air emphasizes theory and concepts, which leads to finding compatible modes of expression in words, usually through abstract thoughts. Air is detached and doesn't find it necessary or profitable to become involved in other people's emotionally messy lives. Air likes to float above it all!

Air likes Fire and finds Water difficult but attractive while Earth bores Air because of its practical nature and lack of inspiration.

When Swords appear in a reading, there is a lot of Air energy around the person, or around other people in the environment. Swords indicate the Self, obstacles one is facing, and spiritual issues. The Sword Court cards refer to people with the Air signs in their charts, often the Sun sign but sometimes other planets as well—such as Mercury, Venus, or Uranus.

Water: The Cups

Water represents the intangible world. Its zodiacal signs are Cancer, Scorpio, and Pisces. The energy of Water is flowing and various intangibles play a large part in the element of Water. Water is intuitive, psychic, imaginative, and tuned in to feelings, its own and other people's. Water is an element of deep emotion, and feeling responses can go from extreme compassion to total self-pity. Water is very aware of unconscious processes, seeming to just *know*. Water trusts its inner promptings and acts on them, sometimes flying in the face of ordinary reality. Water represents the mystics and dreamers, the artists and those in touch with the deeper dimensions of life. Water tends toward insularity at times because of the need to spend time alone in the inner realm.

Water likes Earth because it grounds them. It finds Fire and Air both difficult but attractive because Fire boils Water and Air lacks sympathy.

When Cups appear in a reading, there is a lot of Water energy around the person, or around other people in the environment. Cups indicate the emotions, love and romance, the unconscious

processes, dreams and visions. The Cups Court cards refer to people with the Water signs in their charts, often the Sun sign but sometimes other planets—such as the Moon, Pluto, or Neptune.

It is important to note that if the cards appear reversed or in the obstacle position in the layout there may be an indication of a *lack* of the element represented.

The Court Cards

The Court Cards often represent actual people in the person's life, or can personify the readee. They can also be used as Significators.

By and large, the Kings represent mature male figures with the qualities of the suits to which they belong, usually someone in a position of authority, or a father figure, or the querent's actual father. A King is someone with wisdom and experience. A reversed King could represent a woman with the qualities of that particular King card.

The Queen cards almost always represent women with the qualities of the suit to which the Queen belongs, a mature woman or a mother image, sometimes the person's real mother, an authority figure who is nurturing and understanding. In certain instances, reversed or upright, a Queen card can refer to a man who has the qualities of the Queen—in other words, a man who is deeply attuned to his own feminine nature, such as an artist or a sensitive.

The Knight, who is generally considered a messenger, can refer to a woman as well as to a man. The message will be related to the suit to which the Knight belongs.

The Page cards can represent either sex, but usually refer to a young person, or to a child, who is involved in the experiences related to the suit to which the Page belongs. Pages can indicate messengers, schoolchildren, young adults, or immature adults.

In addition to representing actual people in the person's life such as family members, spouses or lovers, friends, bosses and colleagues, or others with whom the querent is having dealings, the Court cards and symbolize *influences* in the environment, or they can refer to ideas in the mind of the readee.

Because of the new diversity of our society, and the equalization of women with men, it is possible to see a woman through a

Pythagoras, a famous Greek philosopher, metaphysician, and mathematician, pursued the mystical significance of numbers as a science in the sixth century B.C. He studied numbers for their mathematical qualities; he also venerated them, believing that each number contained specific mystical significance. In Pythagoras's philosophy, numbers were an expression of the fundamental laws of the universe.

Over time, the secrets of Pythagoras's number system were passed along from teacher to student, as each student achieved mastery, he in turn initiated others in the mysteries of numbers and their spiritual significance. The tradition continues to this day in the study and practice of numerology.

male card and vice versa. Here, feedback from the readee is valuable to identify to whom a Court card is referring.

The Number Cards from Ace Through Ten

The first characteristic of the pip cards of the Minor Arcana is their relationship to *number*. Some decks, like the Waite deck and certain others, also have illustrations from which one can draw meaning; many decks, however, only indicate the number and the suit, and it is this combination that provides the essential information in a reading.

Symbolically speaking, numbers are not merely arithmetic or math used to express quantities—each number also has its own individual power, applicable both to the spiritual and the material worlds.

The roots of numerology go back thousands of years—all cultures with an esoteric tradition have honored and understood the sacred symbology of numbers, for numbers are symbols, and each possesses its own special characteristics.

With the number cards of the Minor Arcana, the *suit* will tell you the area of life to which the number refers. It will signify the nature of the influences and forces at work about which the specific number is commenting. By combining the two, you can achieve an interpretation and recognize how and where it is applicable to the particular situation for which the reading is being used.

Ace (One)

The essence of *One* is new beginnings. It implies something *coming into being*, the starting point of a whole new cycle. It represents self-development, creativity, action, progress, a new chance, a rebirth.

With the Ace, a seed has been planted, something has begun, though you may not yet know where it will lead. The Aces symbolize potential growth. With an Ace, you are at a starting point, are being offered a new opportunity. It's up to you to follow through on the new direction—it won't automatically happen. The Ace is an indication that you have the *choice* to initiate something, that the time is ripe for new development.

The energy of One is solitary. It may indicate being alone or going into isolation in order to nurture the new before going public with it.

Two

The essence of *Two* is duality. It is the number of two coming together in some kind of union. It indicates a second factor coming into play, following the Ace. Two is about *balance* of polarities such as yin and yang, male and female, private and public, separate and together. Two can indicate a need for this balance with whatever new factor is being added to the situation. Whether favorable or unfavorable, this addition will be of importance to you, either increasing the chances of a desirable outcome or presenting obstacles to it. The purpose of the Two is to further the direction presented by the Ace, to stabilize and affirm the new opportunity.

The Two vibration may expand your sensitivity to others to the point where you consider their needs over your own. "Two-ness" can also indicate a state of being self-contained, either with another person, or with an idea or a project.

Three

The essence of *Three* is the trinity of Mind, Body, and Spirit. It is the number of *self-expression* and communication, of expansion, openness, optimism, and clarity. With the Three, you begin to open up and see the big picture, understanding the details of how One and Two combine in your own process of growth and evolution. This is the point where whatever was started begins to take on form, whether it is a creative project or a relationship. Three says "Go," but if unfavorable elements are involved, caution is advised.

With the Three, there is danger of expanding too fast, of scattering energies, of spreading yourself too thin. There is a tendency to leap first and think later, or buy now and pay later. However, properly handled, the Three vibration is cheerful, optimistic, and fun so long as you pay attention to what you are doing.

Four

The essence of the number *Four* represents the *foundation*. Four is the number of the elements and the directions, so it is a fundamental number that is about working hard and planning for security. Four is a time for self-discipline through work and service, productivity, organization, unity. You should know what you are doing in this situation so that you can work effectively to make it turn out positively. If you are in a place that's where you want to be, you have to work to keep it stable; if you are in a place where you don't want to be, you have to make the appropriate plans and do the work to make changes. There is also the possibility of an unexpected new factor entering into the current situation, which you will have to evaluate carefully before making a decision as to whether it is good or bad.

At this time, life can seem like all work and no play, but sometimes that's necessary for the time being, and nothing lasts forever. If your goals and purpose are clear, you won't mind doing the work, for you see the end result as beneficial.

Five

The essence of the number *Five* is freedom and creativity. There is excitement, adventure, challenge. Five is *active*, physical, impulsive, dramatic, resourceful, curious, playful. It might indicate a roller-coaster ride! Five indicates a time to "go for it," but with due consideration of the risks involved. With the Five, you are willing to take risks, there's even a "devil take the hindmost" attitude because you love the excitement involved in the situation. The cards around the Five will indicate whether there is real danger or if things will work out to your advantage.

Sometimes, Five can be too much to handle, especially if your nature is quiet and placid. There may be so much excitement in your life that you feel you are caught in a whirlwind—or a hurricane. You might need to slow down a bit and get some perspective before you return to the fray. If an important decision is involved, "take five" before you make any commitment.

Six

The essence of the number *Six* is service and *social responsibility,* caring, compassion, community involvement. Six is the number of peace and quiet after the storm of Five. It is a time to be simple and attend to everyday needs, to rest and get into harmony with yourself and your surroundings. Any misunderstandings that occurred during the period of upheaval can now be resolved harmoniously. Six is a time to stop and catch your breath, realizing that you have created a comfortable pattern in which you can reap the rewards of

your previous planning and chance-taking. With the Six, you feel centered after the upheaval and you are comfortable with both yourself and your circumstances. However, unfavorable cards in the reading may indicate difficult circumstances yet to be faced, but Six indicators are rarely negative.

The Six vibration is geared toward service to others. You need to make sure that you also take care of your own needs. The comfort of the Six situation can also tend to reclusiveness—just vegging out at home for long periods. This is fine for a time; just don't let it go too far.

> The whole world is an omen and a sign. Why look so wistfully in a corner? The voice of divination resounds everywhere and runs to waste unheard, unregarded, as the mountains echo with the bleatings of cattle.
>
> —Ralph Waldo Emerson

Seven

The essence of the number *Seven* is the inner life. It is about *solitude* and soul-searching. The number Seven is a mystical number symbolizing wisdom—there are seven heavens and seven chakras. It is a time of going within to find out what is the meaning of what has been happening. It is a time of searching, on a psychological or spiritual level. Seven refers to birth and rebirth, religious inclinations and resources. You may at this time take vows of some kind, or begin to practice ritual as part of your inner development. As the path of solitude, analysis, contemplation, Seven marks a time when you are exploring your own individuality in your own way.

This is not a time for beginning projects related to the material or the making of money. Your energy is focused on the inner rather than the outer realm. You may want to make a retreat instead of taking a regular resort vacation.

Now is a good time to create a sanctuary for contemplation, a private place where you can analyze your experiences from the past and evaluate those in the present. You may feel an intense need to be alone and try to achieve that condition. You may study or do research into metaphysical subjects, start paying attention to dreams and ESP experiences, whatever will help you to find your own true path in life.

Unfavorable aspects in the reading may indicate that you are spending too much time alone and need to socialize.

Eight

The essence of the number *Eight* is *abundance*, material prosperity, worldly power or influence. The number of leadership and

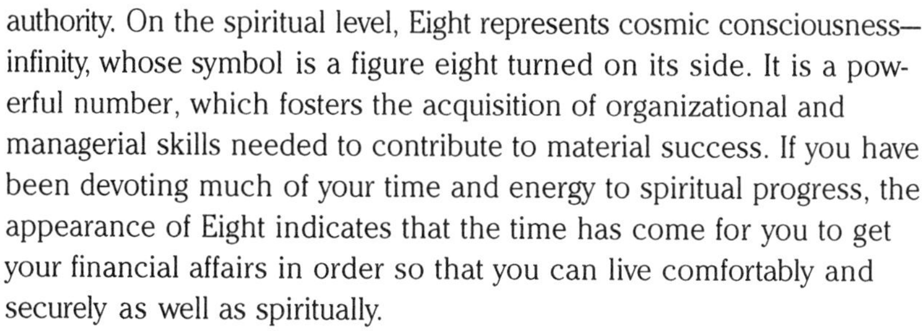

authority. On the spiritual level, Eight represents cosmic consciousness—infinity, whose symbol is a figure eight turned on its side. It is a powerful number, which fosters the acquisition of organizational and managerial skills needed to contribute to material success. If you have been devoting much of your time and energy to spiritual progress, the appearance of Eight indicates that the time has come for you to get your financial affairs in order so that you can live comfortably and securely as well as spiritually.

The Eight vibration can bring honor, respect, equality, awards, public recognition, power, and abundance in all areas of life. As the infinity symbolizes wholeness, the Eight points to the development of multiple aspects of your life—physical, mental, and spiritual.

Eight also issues a caution to consider the welfare of others as well as your own, and if there are unfavorable elements in the reading, there is an indication you have to be careful of your finances lest you lose money or possessions. Several Eights reversed indicate that you have many issues around abundance—or the lack of it—to resolve.

Nine

The essence of the number *Nine* is *humanitarianism*. It is about having reached the level where you are comfortable with dedicating your life to others' welfare, or to some worthy cause such as a nonprofit organization. Nine represents universal compassion, tolerance for the many differences among different peoples, and the attainment of wisdom through experience. Nine indicates *integration*, a time when you have established your life priorities and are clear about where and how you want to go forward now. You feel a flow of vitality between all the different parts of yourself, and how they form a whole. You are able to see the interaction between you and the world as a continuing process of living, being, moving.

The Nine vibration allows you to see beyond the boundaries of the Self into the totality of the universal. You are able to give freely of yourself because you feel complete within yourself. Nine is a wisdom level indicating that you have accomplished what this cycle now ending concerned. It's a time to tie up loose ends.

The challenge of the Nine is to not lose sight of the needs of individuals. Don't allow yourself to get so wrapped up in "the big picture" of the greatest good for the greatest number to the extent that you ignore or neglect what is closest to you. This admonition extends to your own personal needs—in your zeal to live the overarching whole, you may neglect some small but significant part of yourself.

Ten

The essence of the number *Ten* is that it is both *an ending and a beginning*. Nine is actually the number of the completion of the cycle; Ten can be reduced back to 1 (1 + 0 = 1), so it actually represents the point of transition from the completed cycle to the new cycle, which has not yet manifested. With the Ten, whatever you have been working on or involved with is over—you've got whatever you are going to get out of it and now it is time to bring in the new cycle waiting in the wings.

Whether the cycle now ending has been good or bad, you know that it's over now, which is especially important if you have been going through rough and rocky times. It's also a pointer, if you have become complacent during a good period, that now's the time to challenge yourself and develop to a higher level.

As a compound number, Ten, though it is a form of One, has more impact and therefore adds an extra dimension. The Ten is like ascending to a higher level of a spiral staircase—you can look down at precisely where you were at the beginning and chart your progress. This is a time when you have a choice to either stagnate in familiar and comfortable territory, get deeper into the established order of your life, or you can take a chance and start something new and different.

As in any period of transition, there will be discomfort about making the decision to stay put or move on. Both options are available and both require thought and consideration. You might feel like you are sitting on the fence, with one foot on either side, not sure whether to jump all the way over. Transitions are like that, and sometimes it takes quite a while to get both feet on the same side of the fence. However, you know that "he who hesitates is lost," and though you have the luxury of postponing both decision and action for a little while, look for the handwriting on the wall and heed what it tells you.

Chapter 9

The Suit of Wands

The four suits of the Minor Arcana in medieval times were representational of the four main classes of people—the nobility, the clergy, the merchant class, and the working class. Though today these "classes" presumably no longer exist, there are still correspondences in our modern society. We have an elite, or old money, class that is our "nobility"; our version of the clergy has expanded to include the professions and academia; our merchant class is a product of the corporate institutions; and our "blue collar" folks are the "working class."

The suit of Wands represents the working class—those who were originally attached to the noble houses as serfs. They had little choice but to follow the trade of their fathers, and were usually apprenticed out at an early age to learn some difficult and unpleasant task. Thus, today the Wands have come to represent whatever work you do as well as the ability to overcome tremendous odds to achieve success.

The Wands are related to mental activity, the outer world, and work or career.

How the Wands are depicted varies considerably from deck to deck. More than the other suits, Wands symbols tend to be mixed within the same deck: some Wands are sprouting or flowering branches; some are wooden staffs; others are crude clubs, heavy and thick at one end and narrow at the gripping end. Sometimes these characteristics are combined.

Wands deal with situations involving the potential for success, usually related to business and work; financial achievement may or may not be a factor. Wands generally indicate both opportunities and possibilities for success in the area indicated, despite obstacles having to be met and overcome. Generally speaking, Wands are positive cards—the colors tend to be bright (yellow stands for optimism and red for action) and cheerful in composition. Wands stand for worldly activities, enterprise, and success in terms of fulfilling your potential, whatever it may be.

King of Wands

The King of Wands is usually shown as a dignified man and is seated on a throne, robed and crowned, sometimes with armor, sometimes even shown as a prosperous merchant king. A positive-looking figure, he is clearly in command of the situation, confident and at ease. He holds a full-length staff or rod, usually upright but sometimes leaning against his shoulder.

Upright

This King represents a man of status and wealth, an influential and independent person inclined to help. He may be a boss or a mentor, a senior business partner, or an advisor. You can rely on his honesty, intelligence, fair-mindedness, and you are sure to get good advice from him. If the King does not represent an actual person in your life, he can refer to a situation, which then is exactly as it appears to be with no hint of deception. He can indicate that good fortune is coming your way, perhaps in the form of unexpected help or advice, unexpected good news, a promotion, or an inheritance.

Reversed

The King of Wands reversed indicates delays in any business project you are starting. If it involves another person whose advice and cooperation you need or solicit, the man will be available but won't go out of his way to help. He won't block your efforts and he may approve of what you are trying to accomplish on your own, lending moral support. You may not get overt help, but there's really nothing standing in your way now.

This King ordinarily faces sideways, and whether he is facing toward or away from other cards will have a bearing on his relationship to what they represent.

Queen of Wands

The Queen of Wands is a statuesque woman, tall and imposing, of regal bearing, and holds a tall staff in one hand, a symbol of her authority. Usually she sits on a throne, robed and crowned. However, some decks show her as a well-dressed matron figure.

Upright

Socially prominent, this Queen represents a woman who is in a position of authority and likes to shine in her endeavors. She is a lioness, socially and in her personality—warm, generous, and loving. She is honorable, intelligent, friendly, mature. Her advice is well worth taking, and she will be a loyal confidante or provide valuable assistance. A good money manager, her advice is valuable. If this Queen does not represent an actual person, she indicates that now is a good time for you to move forward in any business venture you are planning. If the Queen represents you, she is an indication that you have the qualities within yourself that you need to succeed.

Reversed

If the Queen of Wands is reversed, she can represent a powerful woman who demands control over your affairs in return for her advice and financial assistance. She wants to control social situations for her own advantage. If the Queen does not represent an actual person, the reversed card is a cautionary warning to be careful in any business deals with a woman, to avoid giving offense to the socially powerful, and to be aware of deception, greed, and jealousy.

Knight of Wands

The Knight of Wands is usually depicted as a young man on a rearing horse in a mode of forward action. He is brandishing the wand like a weapon, but it seems more for show than to give a blow. He is in a suit of armor that is fairly ornate. His position indicates that he is riding toward some encounter, more like jousting than fighting.

Upright

Knights are messengers, and the Knight of Wands is bringing good news concerning work or social activities. His glad tidings may relate to almost any anticipated happy event—a journey or vacation, a change of residence or job, an engagement or marriage. If this card represents a specific person, it will refer to a young man who is a relative or friend with the same qualities as the King and Queen, who are his parents in the royal family. It also indicates that the person bearing the message can be trusted and is faithful.

Reversed

None of the Wands reversed are particularly negative, but the reversed Knight can indicate a delay in a message or communication you have been expecting. It can be a case of "the check is in the mail," if you are waiting for money. The news of delay can bring on frustration either on the job or in a social situation. A trip may be canceled because of bad weather, or an engagement or wedding postponed, or even broken off. The reversed Knight betokens separation.

Page of Wands

The Page of Wands is a youth facing sideways (in most decks, including Waite) and holding a tall staff before him with both hands, perhaps leaning on it. His attitude is expectant but casual. He is wearing garb similar to the rest of the royal court, but because he is a youth he is in short pants with bare legs above his boots.

Upright

The Page of Wands indicates a message of importance to your current project or situation, usually affecting work. The information is positive and if the card represents a person in your life, it will come from a younger relative or friend, or it could indicate a younger person who is eager to experience work and social activities. This Page is an eager beaver and he is related to international travel, meetings with foreigners, and philosophic interests.

Reversed

When reversed, the Page of Wands is bringing news of a delay, which could cause trouble. Something you were expecting will not arrive on time—perhaps a part for some business machine—thus causing problems. Or, the message he brings may be unwelcome news causing some disruption in your life or requiring you to travel to put things right. If he represents a person, this is someone not to be trusted, or a bringer of false or misleading information. Be on guard.

Ace of Wands

The Ace of Wands cards shows a hand, usually emerging from a cloud, firmly grasping a heavy yet elegantly shaped stick that is vaguely phallic in that it has a knob at the top end. Out of the wand, or club, new shoots are growing with leaves also floating around it. The Wand is held directly upright, pointing upward.

Upright

This Ace indicates a new beginning of an enterprise involving business or finance. It shows that you have planted the seeds for a new birth—possibly a creative or money-making idea. The key idea is freedom from restraints that have hampered you in the past, enabling you to take on a new role or forge a new identity through your work.

Reversed

The Ace of Wands reversed indicates that the process of creating a new identity or a new endeavor is still in the interior of your mind and has not yet made its appearance on the world stage. Delays in getting started may be being experienced, or you may have to rethink your plans to make sure they are workable. You have a sense of your potential to do something new, but are hesitating because of lack of resources or confidence.

Two of Wands

The Two of Wands is an ambiguous card. It shows that a second, probably unexpected, element is entering into the situation at hand, something for which your plans have not allowed. There is an element of surprise.

Upright

You are saying "Yes" to new enterprise with the expectation that you will achieve ownership, wealth, and good fortune. You are in a sense "waiting for your ship to come in." You've started something and are awaiting results. You may, however, have to deal with some unforeseen problems or encounter unexpected obstacles and opposition, such as a bank loan not coming through, or a partner defecting, the failure of a support you were counting on. Still, you have definitely decided to pursue this new course as a means of validating your Self.

Reversed

This position emphasizes the element of surprise, perhaps a nasty one. Nonetheless, you are affirming your new self-concept whether you have told others about it or not. Whether the surprise element portends good or bad will be indicated by the surrounding cards in the reading. If it appears with a Court card, for example, it may mean the person the Court card represents will disappoint you or make an unexpected appearance which will change the picture.

Three of Wands

The Three of Wands indicates someone who is ready and willing to hang on to what he or she has achieved by remaining in calm control of the situation, knowing there is no need for impulsiveness. This is a time for acting in a mature and responsible manner based on experience and common sense, and taking things firmly in hand.

Upright

You have consolidated your situation, business, or enterprise and now can expect financial gain. By a clear definition of the role you want to play, you are presenting a positive picture to the world at large. This attitude may draw toward you helpful people or circumstances. You've established a solid foundation for your business or occupation and can expect cooperation from others to succeed. At this point, you are clear about who you are and others will respond positively to your confidence.

Reversed

You are doing most of the work on an internal level, clarifying your needs and formulating your sense of self-direction. You have resolved most of the problems connected to the situation or enterprise, negotiated the tricky bits, and can expect things to go smoothly when you go public with your ideas.

Four of Wands

This is an extremely positive card indicating that your troubles of getting something established are over and that now you can relax and enjoy life. It's a time of respite.

Upright

You are enjoying pleasure and prosperity. You are reaping the rewards you have earned. Finances are in good shape and you are in harmony with your environment and the people in it. You are showing the world who you truly are in a general situation of comfortable prosperity. It's a time for celebration and good times. Give a party!

Reversed

As this is a totally positive card, the reversed position means only that you are doing your celebrating of your good fortune in a quiet way, not flamboyantly. Your financial gains may be more modest, but you are satisfied with the sense of a job well done. You may be expanding your property holdings without any fanfare. Your new sense of self may not have a public showing, but you are feeling fine about who you are.

Five of Wands

The Five of Wands is about competition in the global economy. It signifies the mad scramble for money and power, with its concomitant excesses of greed and corruption. This card represents struggle in the marketplace.

Upright

New factors moving into the situation are demanding that you change, adapt, and grow. Life's not as simple as it was. New competition has moved into the neighborhood—or the industry—and you have to put forth a lot more effort to keep what you have gained in terms of financial gain and material goods. Depending on the rest of the reading, you will either suffer hardship and loss or go on to greater heights of success and the acquisition of wealth.

Reversed

When the Five of Wands is reversed, the indication is that you must challenge yourself in order to change and adapt to different and difficult circumstances. The new competition may be cutthroat, even dishonest or underhanded. There could be litigation to resolve disputes over contracts and suchlike. Your public self-image may suffer.

Six of Wands

The Six of Wands is a card of triumphing over adversity and being victorious. It indicates good news as a result of your having met the challenge to your identity and come through with flying colors.

Upright

Victory is at hand. You have overcome or conquered that which was opposing you. You feel secure with your identity in the world, and "in the groove." Past self-doubt has been resolved and you are in the process of winning some significant battle. Having brought your affairs to a point of success, you can expect to have your desires gratified. Gifts may be received, awards and recognition.

Reversed

The hopes and wishes you have for your success are being delayed, often by factors over which you have no control. You feel frustrated and angry, ready to do battle to get things set right. You're being challenged by circumstances to take a stance about who you are and what you intend to accomplish. You may have experienced some kind of betrayal that has caused you to re-evaluate your self-image.

Seven of Wands

The Seven of Wands is about courage and determination. It indicates someone willing to fight for what he believes in, and stand his or her ground no matter what. You might have fallen into complacency but now are more vital and active.

Upright

A card of profit and gain after some determined holding off of competition or enemies. You may be outnumbered, but your determination will win the day. You are discovering inner resources you hardly suspected you had and putting them to good use to overcome obstacles. Thus, you have the advantage and will eventually achieve success by sheer force of will and personality.

Reversed

A time of confusion. You don't know whether to hold on or back off. The Seven of Wands reversed is a statement that "He who hesitates is lost." Now is the time for firmness and decision. Even if you're not sure which way to go, it's one of those situations where any decision is better than none at all, even if it is a wrong one. Stay flexible, but don't stagnate. Get moving in one direction or another.

Eight of Wands

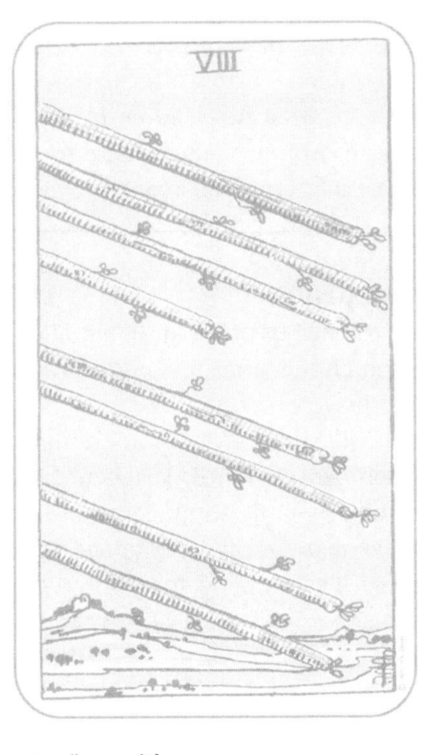

This is a card of movement toward your goals, which are assured. It's a time to follow through on what has already been put in motion and to make plans for your next moves.

Upright

You have shot your arrows into the air and they are heading right to the spot where you aimed. Now is a time for action, for initiating the next phase of your enterprise. This may involve considerable air travel, landings and taking off again. It's a busy and hopeful situation with things moving very fast. Move with them but stay who you are. Establish the roles you want to play and let go of those you no longer feel comfortable with.

Reversed

Movement may be unwanted or unpleasant, as in being transferred across the country by your company when you'd rather stay put. It's a time to "go with the flow," wherever it leads. Today's unpleasantness may be tomorrow's celebration. Allow yourself to be open to new experiences, but be prepared and try to know exactly what you're getting into. Relationships may suffer–marriage, partnership, family. You may be required to reprioritize your schedule to accommodate other people's needs.

Nine of Wands

The Nine of Wands is a card representing the defending of one's legitimate territory. It's a job that's been done well by dint of effort and determination. Success is at hand. This person has shown courage under fire.

Upright

As nines represent completion, the Nine of Wands in a reading indicates that the job is done. You have had the discipline and the ability to plan well and wisely. Your relationships are developing positively and you are moving forward with a sense of purpose and direction. If there is still opposition, your skills, strength, and courage will prevail over all opponents.

Reversed

You may be fighting a losing battle. If so, it's time to cut your losses and get out. Whatever it is, it is *over*, and if it hasn't worked out for you then go on to something else. Learn the lessons of failure—for failure is but success's opposite and the wheel always turns—and get on with your life. Recognize that you are part and parcel of the problem—your strength can be obstinacy; your determination, sheer stubbornness. Learn to use these qualities wisely and don't get locked into a static self-image that will do you no good.

Ten of Wands

The Ten of Wands indicates taking up new responsibilities appropriate to the new cycle coming in. These may seem burdensome, but you have the strength and character to carry them, for you feel you can do anything at this point, even if it is an extremely difficult task.

Upright

Your labor may have gone for naught, or you may be carrying burdens that really don't belong to you. You feel weary, as if the whole world is on your shoulders, but it's up to you whether the heavy responsibilities you have undertaken are legitimately required or if others are shirking their part. Sometimes, one member of a family or organization gets all the dirty work for the simple reason that they are willing to do it. Make sure others are doing their fair share. Ask for help if you need it; don't let pride stand in your way.

Reversed

The burden is lifted—sometimes unexpectedly, and there is a feeling of freedom from undue responsibilities. Either you have taken the appropriate action or are about to do so. In any case, the load on you has been shifted, re-proportioned, or removed entirely. You are learning to delegate and take on less. There is now reduced pressure and stress on you and you are able to enjoy life more. Sometimes, however, depending on negative influence in the adjacent cards, you may be suffering the consequences of overload—either with ill health or burnout. You may need a recovery period.

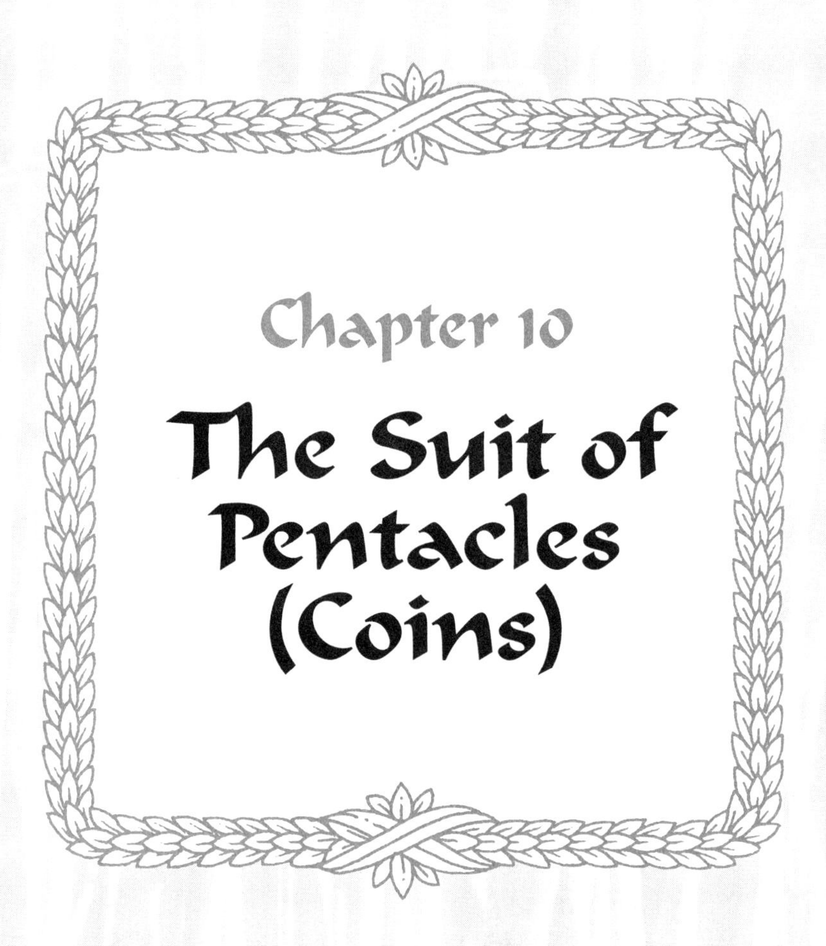

Chapter 10

The Suit of Pentacles (Coins)

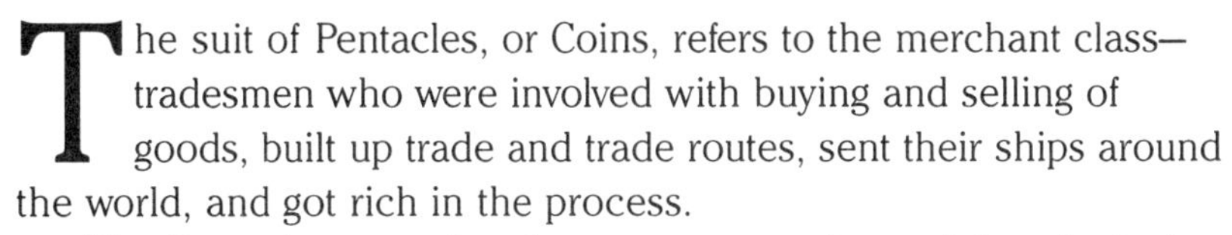

The suit of Pentacles, or Coins, refers to the merchant class—tradesmen who were involved with buying and selling of goods, built up trade and trade routes, sent their ships around the world, and got rich in the process.

The Pentacles are related to money, security, and the physical and material world in general.

How the Pentacles are depicted is fairly consistent in most decks, which show one or more discs of gold with a five-sided design in the center, usually a pentacle (five-pointed star). Interestingly, the pentacle is a powerful symbol in magick of protection against harmful influences, so that there is in this most practical of suits a suggestion of a deeper meaning here that money can serve higher purposes such as philanthropy. And, since the number five is intrinsic to the entire suit it is important to remember the symbolic meaning of the five (in the astrological chart, the fifth house is ruled by Leo and governs creativity and pleasure as well as children). Though the Pentacles represent Earth, Leo is a fire sign. Hence, the number five suggests adventure, creativity, dramatic excitement, and the enjoyment of worldly pleasures.

As coins (mostly gold) represented the buying and selling of goods, and thus the merchant class—aristocrats didn't handle money; it was considered beneath them! The suit of Pentacles (or Coins) has come to represent those who deal in our money-based economy, whether captains of industry, professionals, technocrats, entrepreneurs, shopkeepers, or those engaged in doing business in general. It includes bankers, lawyers, businessmen and women, stock traders—in other words, most of today's middle- and upper-middle classes. Money is the byword of the Pentacles, but it can also include those who desire to upgrade themselves financially, who understand money and how it works, the power it confers. Pentacles in a reading usually point to an increase in the finances of the querent—success in business, a raise, or relief from previous lack of funds.

Therefore, in general the appearance of Pentacles is a positive note on a temporal basis. As Pentacles represent the element Earth, they also indicated *groundedness* in the material and physical world. Or, they may indicate concern with financial security, career, or whatever work you do in the world that is your livelihood.

King of Pentacles

The King of Pentacles is usually shown as a royal figure seated on a throne. He may or not be crowned, but he displays someone who is comfortable with the power money grants. Generally he holds a single coin upright in one hand and a scepter in the other and is sometimes represented as a prosperous merchant. He is seated on a throne—often decorated with animal figures such as lions, a bull, an eagle, or a griffin.

Upright

This king represents a mature man who is not only wealthy but also courageous. His nature is that of a solid citizen, reputable and kind to others. He symbolizes worldly power in a positive sense; he is experienced in the handling of money matters. His stability is a major factor. It makes him one who can provide reliable counsel on matters of money and finance, and someone who is cultured, refined, and a dispenser of patronage.

If he represents an actual person, he is likely to be well-disposed toward the querent—possibly a corporate head where the person works, or a banker from whom the querent is soliciting a loan. If he is not an actual person, then his appearance indicates that the querent is engaged in some worldly enterprise that will meet with success.

Reversed

Some find this King reversed to be an extremely negative symbol—representing danger or an unwise business move—but my view of him reversed is simply of a warning to watch all your "P's and Q's" in business dealings, to be aware of all the small print in any contracts being negotiated, to make sure the "i's" are dotted and the "t's" are crossed. He can indicate unfair competition or shady business practices.

Queen of Pentacles

The Queen of Pentacles is a benevolent figure, usually seen holding the pentacle coin in her lap and gazing fondly down at it. She may also be seen standing, leaning against an ornate throne or chair. Like the King, her throne is decorated with animal figures. She has a regal and kindly bearing, someone who understands and respects money as a tool but does not worship it as a god.

Upright

This Queen represents a generous woman who is also an excellent manager of money. As an adviser, she favors the querent, or will at least be fair. She is practical and well-grounded and wants to see the money she distributes produce tangible results. If not a person, she represents harvest after much labor, security, the acquisition of wisdom through experience, and prudent use of wealth.

Reversed

In the reversed position, this Queen may represent someone who will try to block your efforts to attain her help. She may be merely indifferent, or actively hostile. If she is a relative or an older friend, mentor, or boss, she may be a superficial person who only pretends to want to help you. Or the price of her help may be too high—she wants to control everything. She may lack confidence and try to compensate for her own shortcomings by a display of her wealth, or she may be hiding a lack of money. If not a person, she represents a situation where you must take due caution about where and with whom you place your trust.

Knight of Pentacles

This Knight brings news concerning money, usually good news. He is usually depicted on horseback, facing sideways, wearing armor, and holding the Pentacle before him as if offering it to someone ahead of him. Unlike the Knight of Wands who is on a charging horse, the Knight of Pentacles' horse is at parade rest, calm, stable, often black. He is poised on the point of adventure—travel, either a departure or an arrival.

Upright

If a person, this knight represents someone with the spirit of adventure, but who is materially minded. He is good at performing any task set for him, but not likely to be a self-starter. If he is not a person, he suggests a situation involving arrivals and/or departures. You may quit a job for more money elsewhere, move to another locale for the same reason, or experience other changes in your life relative to your money.

Reversed

The Knight reversed brings an unwelcome message about money, a loss of some kind, or a disappointment or frustration due to an unforeseen delay. Existing plans may have to be aborted; delays could cause failure. If a person, he may be a young man who is unemployed or uninterested in employment. If not a person, he shows a situation where there is an element of depression, inertia, and problems with money.

Page of Pentacles

The Page of Pentacles is mostly shown as a youth standing in a meadow or countryside. He is holding the Pentacle before him, as if in admiration. This attitude suggests that he has the desire for money, or to achieve the means to gain it, whether this be schooling for a career or striving to reach the pinnacle of a profession. This card is called the card of the student or scholar; someone intent on his lessons to the point of oblivion to what is going on around him.

Upright

The Page of Wands indicates a message regarding the acquisition of money or material goods. The news is good—he is the bearer of good tidings. His appearance suggests someone who is intelligent, refined, sensitive to the arts, and appreciative of the good life. Ambitious and determined, he is goal-oriented. If he does not represent a person, this card indicates your own worldly ambitions and/or a message concerning them.

Reversed

This page in the reversed position reflects the opposite of the upright. Someone who is lazy, lackadaisical, uninterested in furthering himself through education or goal orientation. If not a person, the message may be bad news about money matters or some sort of disappointment such as the querent's failure to qualify on an exam or to gain admission to the college of his or her choice. More effort and focus are needed.

Ace of Pentacles

The Ace of Pentacles shows a large Pentacle as the central focus. In the Waite deck, a hand is coming out of a cloud with the Pentacle resting in its palm; underneath is a pastoral scene or garden. Other decks show the coin in a decorative manner, sometimes with the decorative elements growing out of the coin. The Ace of Pentacles is *the* card of new success, new money, new enterprise, attainment.

Upright

This Ace is extremely positive, predicting success for some new enterprise you are starting. You are involved in planting the seeds for a new venture involving the getting of money or increasing your financial security. The Ace is a strong indication of prosperity coming toward you. Its key idea is being open to receive.

Reversed

This Ace in the reversed position indicates that your new adventure is still in the idea stage. You are working on being more grounded and centered in order to achieve a greater level of security and prosperity. Your material gain is coming, but it is being delayed and you must be patient and not get discouraged.

Two of Pentacles

The Two of Pentacles suggests either money coming from two sources, or having to juggle finances to make ends meet. Still, it is a positive card indicating good fortune and enjoyment. You may be experiencing financial difficulty.

Upright

A message about money is on its way to you, probably in written form. You are still in the stage of deciding which of two different options to choose. You are concerned with issues of abundance and may be holding down more than one job, or "moonlighting" to make extra money. It's a time to make a choice and stick with it even if you aren't sure of the outcome.

Reversed

You may be having financial difficulties while pretending that all is well. You are juggling not only sources of income but options for change. This isn't the right time to make a change. It's a time to hang in there until the right moment presents itself. You need to overcome doubt and worry.

Three of Pentacles

The Three of Pentacles is an indicator of the craftsman, someone who has already developed skill in a profession or trade. It's time to turn these skills to profit, and success is assured. Threes indicate planning, and the Three of Pentacles cards usually show people who seem to be conferring about future action, such as cooperating in a business venture.

Upright

You are acquiring marketable skills, preparing yourself for action in the "real" world. You might be a recent graduate, or have gone back to school to upgrade your skills or change your career. You are enterprising and interested in some particular area of commerce, or a specific trade or business. You can anticipate a rise in prestige and earnings.

Reversed

You aren't making the effort to acquire the new skills you need in today's changing marketplace. You may be stuck in a job you really don't like but be too stuck in your ways to strike out and change things for the better. You need to get going–thought without action is invalid.

Four of Pentacles

The Four of Pentacles indicates someone who is holding tight to what money and material possessions he or she already has. You may be feeling threatened that loss is in the offing and trying to prepare yourself by closely guarding what you have.

Upright

You are hanging on to something—either your possessions or a situation—in a stubborn and inflexible manner. There may be fear of change involved, or you may simply be comfortable where you are, but change is part and parcel of life and you have to be able to accept that it will come.

Reversed

You may be trying to make something happen prematurely, or you are holding on too tightly to current circumstances. You may be quarreling with someone over money, such as in divorce proceedings or legacies. You need to loosen up and have more faith and trust in the Universe to provide.

Five of Pentacles

Of all the Pentacles, this is the only one that has a basic negative connotation. It suggests financial losses, business problems, material lack. It can also indicate that spiritual bankruptcy is at the root of this unfavorable condition.

Upright

This Five is a warning that money may soon be very tight, that losses may ensue from ill-advised investments, or that support you had counted on won't be forthcoming, such as a grant or stipend.

Reversed

You are being advised to get your house in order financially. Cut your losses any way you can to avoid further deterioration of your finances; if you are in debt, which you probably are, focus on getting it cleared out. Be extremely careful of any future investments. Don't risk.

Six of Pentacles

With this Six, past financial problems are solved. You now have, or will have, plenty to "share and spare." You can afford a charitable act because your income is steady and your security stable. You are in a balanced position concerning income and outgo. You are using your prosperity to help others.

Upright

This is a time of good coming to you and good going out from you in material terms. You are in a position to take some action in a good cause, perhaps contributing financially to those struggling upward, such as providing a college scholarship for the disadvantaged. You are experiencing abundance, prosperity, and personal gratification.

Reversed

You need to recoup after a period of loss and confusion. You want to help others, but don't have the means, and that makes you unhappy. It's a time when you are required to find the pattern that will create a sense of security for you so that you can find peace of mind.

Seven of Pentacles

The Seven of Pentacles is about reaping what you have sown, realizing the legitimate gain that you have earned by your own hard work. Like a farmer harvesting crops that he has nurtured through bad weather, you are getting your just desserts.

Upright

You've put in the time and effort, paid your dues. Now you will gain in your business or other enterprise. Not only that, but you feel great satisfaction from a job well done. Growth and good fortune are yours, well earned.

Reversed

You are experiencing disappointment or failure in some enterprise and having financial difficulties, usually the result of an unwise investment or a loan unpaid. It's a time to adjust your own attitudes toward how you use your money and look into how you yourself are responsible.

Eight of Pentacles

Like the Three, the Eight is a card of craftsmanship. It suggests, however, learning a new skill or taking up a new career. But your new venture augurs success because you are in the process of training yourself intensively with a clear goal in mind.

Upright

You are integrating old skills into a new form, and/or adding new skills. You've tried various means of making your living, and are now finalizing how you want to use your personal resources to realize a material sufficiency that will fulfill your needs and allow you to expand. Your sureness of purpose guarantees success. Your craftsmanship will be rewarded by commissions and new business.

Reversed

When this card is reversed, there is an indication that the querent has not finished the task of mastering the necessary skills to achieve his or her ambitions. There is desire to begin some new enterprise, but either a lack of ambition or a lack of clear identification of goals is the obstacle.

Nine of Pentacles

The Nine of Pentacles suggests independence from financial concerns and worries. There is abundance here gained from proper management of the affairs. It is a time of arrival, of having accomplished and of feeling secure.

Upright

You have integrated the factors of your life into a secure base. Now you are enjoying money, resources, and physical energy as a smooth combined flow. There is plenty all around you—material well-being, order, safety, success. You are experiencing life as a well-coordinated totality.

Reversed

Your security base is shaky and you may be dependent on someone else—like a spouse or relative—for your financial well-being. Some circumstance may have caused you to lose your independence, which you need to figure out how to regain.

Ten of Pentacles

The Ten of Pentacles is a happy card, one that signifies you have established a solid and secure life, both in business and with your family. Your work and planning have paid off and you are enjoying the fruits of your labor.

Upright

You are emphasizing home and family at this point, having succeeded in establishing a business or form of secure income to support them. You may be planning to build a new home, or buy a second vacation home. Family matters are at the forefront and you have the leisure to concentrate on personal affairs.

Reversed

You may be so established at this point that you are stagnating. Maybe you have retired comfortably and are just sitting there doing nothing but watching TV. You need to activate some growth in your life to avoid mental stagnation. Take up a hobby or start a new business.

Chapter 11

The Suit of Swords

Swords represented the knighthood, or noble houses, which ruled absolutely by the power of the sword. Yet, this class was also aware of its obligations to the people—the *noblesse oblige*, or obligation of the noble class to better those under their control.

The Swords are related to self, obstacles one is facing, and spiritual issues.

The Suit of Swords most often show unsheathed double-bladed sabers of the kind seen in medieval pictures. Although these are battle swords, there is about them a quality of power and authority wielded for some purpose other than physical fighting. Although some writers paint the Swords as totally negative, others, myself among them, see a spiritual factor in the Swords as well as obstacles, pain, and difficulties. This is because it is most often the case that we come to a spiritual path through or after intense suffering of some kind, be it physical, mental, psychological, or emotional.

The Swords represent events or obstacles, or conditions or states of mind, that are often extremely difficult to deal with. However, as a result, they also represent the growth and development of the *conscious mind*. Swords symbolize Air, and Air symbolizes mental activity. With the Swords, you may be experiencing serious problems, but these are making you *think*. There's an old Chinese proverb that says, "Life is pain. Pain makes you think. Thinking makes you wise. And wisdom makes life endurable." It is this point of view that the Swords represent.

King of Swords

The King of Swords is an august, somewhat stern, figure that can be interpreted as someone in absolute command, but fair in his judgment and decisions. He is enthroned, armored, helmeted, and crowned, a combination of symbols that suggests not only power and authority but a willingness to use it forcefully if necessary.

Upright

This King represents a man—or a power—of great strength and authority. In one deck, he holds a set of balanced scales suggesting both justice and the sign of Libra. Some decks attest that his sign is Gemini. Regardless of which zodiacal sign he refers to, it is always Air. Therefore, his appearance has to do with your mental processes. If he represents a person, it is someone who is involved with mental work, such as a professional, a researcher, a lawyer, or a military officer. As such, he is a good counselor with acute mental dexterity. He has the gift of thinking clearly and rapidly, and he is able to express his thoughts with considerable eloquence. If not a person, he represents a situation in which these qualities are called for. When he appears, you may be on the verge of a spiritual breakthrough about which you are ready to communicate.

Reversed

When reversed, this King shows the negative qualities of the Air signs—fickleness, using words as rapiers to wound, gossiping, superficiality, playing one against the other, or being of such fixed opinions that he is impossible to deal with. If not a person, he can represent a situation in which you are caught amongst people who are antagonistic to your inner philosophy or your spiritual quest. You may have to keep these matters quietly to yourself and not advertise them to those who are unsympathetic.

Queen of Swords

The Queen of Swords is the female counterpart of the King, except that she represents the emotional component of the mental processes. A mature woman, who sits on an ornate throne and wears beautiful robes, she holds her sword upright and reaches out with the other hand in a gesture suggesting permission to rise and come forward. In the Waite deck, she faces sideways; in other decks, she faces straight forward. Either way, she is a formidable figure of power and authority either in the mental world or in the spiritual realm. She represents emotional loss and bereavement.

Upright

When the Queen of Swords appears in a reading, depending on her position relative to other cards, she can indicate personal emotional loss and separation, such as a divorce or widowhood. She may also be a single woman with authority and power. If a person, she is strong-willed and has the ability to cope with her loss and go on with her life. If she does not represent a person, she can indicate the querent is going through an emotionally devastating experience, which will open new vistas if he or she uses it as a means to become more spiritual in his or her approach to life. Eventually, the painful experience will be seen as a source of positive growth. This is especially true if an Ace appears as well.

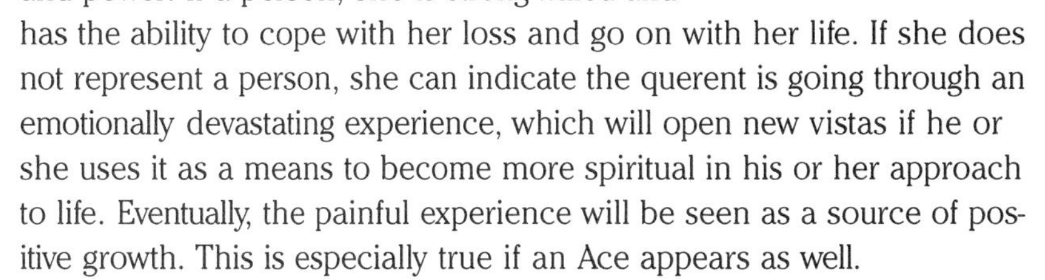

Reversed

When this Queen is reversed, the person she represents is not dealing well with whatever loss is involved. There may be sadness, withdrawal, mourning beyond reasonable limits. If not a person, she can represent a situation in which the querent is bogged down emotionally, wallowing in his or her pain, constantly bewailing an unkind Fate. Other cards in the spread will indicate the way out of the dilemma.

Knight of Swords

The Knight of Swords is leaning forward on a fully charging horse, his sword held both upright and forward as if he is about to encounter the enemy. He is definitely on the attack and by his expression he expects to win the battle. He can represent a person who is overly aggressive, who lives in attack mode. Or, he can mean that you are aggressively pursuing a lifestyle that will allow you to live out your own philosophical ideals.

Upright

As a messenger, the Knight of Swords may bring bad news, which relates to you personally or to someone close to you. Some kind of conflict is at hand, not usually physical but mental. There could be violent differences of opinion around you, with angry messages being sent and received. Or, if not a person, you may be so focused on your intellectual pursuits that you are neglecting other facets of your life. You may be being too forceful in expressing your ideas and getting negative feedback or opposition.

Reversed

When reversed, this Knight loses his aggressiveness and becomes passive about a situation that requires action. He is delaying doing what is necessary, like not sending off information about some business affair or project. There could be serious repercussions from withholding information. If not a person, this card can indicate that the querent is mentally closed off from a situation that desperately needs attention and is thereby creating bad feeling and opposition.

Page of Swords

The Page of Swords is a card about risking on a mental level. It might mean you are taking up some new line of thought. Most decks depict a young man standing, leaning slightly forward, looking over his shoulder away from the sword he holds upright with either his right hand or both hands. He wears a short garment, leather or padded cloth, instead of armor. He appears to be self-confident, as if he knows he can easily defeat any enemy who appears.

Upright

As a messenger, this Page brings news of problems and difficulties, perhaps relating to a younger person you know. An offspring may have failed college exams or be in trouble with the law. There's an element of experimentation here and either you or someone else is taking a risk or behaving in a risky manner that might cause problems. The Page is motivated by unconventional activity which can cause strife.

Reversed

When reversed, this Page is having trouble "getting it together." Although this young person is attractive and charming—eager, confident, active—he or she isn't strictly on the up and up. If a person, this Page could represent someone who is "sponging" off others, maybe parents or friends. Or, it could indicate someone who is anxious or capable of spiteful action.

Ace of Swords

Like all of the Aces, the Ace of Swords indicates a new beginning. Most decks depict the upright sword, which is crowned at the tip, held in a hand coming out of some clouds. The Sword and crown are decorated with living vegetation—vines, flowers, leaves, fruit, or berries.

This Ace indicates a triumph over difficulties by mental means. It is emblematic of a major breakthrough.

Upright

A brand new lifestyle is coming into being for you, and you have achieved this opportunity by dint of will and using your mental faculties at a high level. Prosperity, new development—especially spiritual growth—are sure to follow in the wake of your new direction in life. There may have been a birth—of an idea, an enterprise, or a child. You now are in a position of power with the possibility of manifesting your philosophy in a new way.

Reversed

As this is an extremely positive card, the reversed position only indicates delays or glitches coming along. What you planned for on the mental plane may not be coming into manifestation on the physical plane as quickly as you had hoped, and this may be causing frustration and tension.

Two of Swords

This card, shown in the Waite deck as a blindfolded woman holding two swords crossed over her breasts with a crescent Moon above and the ocean behind, represents a situation in which it appears impossible to move forward.

Upright

The person is in a period of stasis, maintaining the situation in a state of balance by ignoring the underlying tension that exists. This is an uncomfortable position to be in, but the person isn't yet ready to do anything about it. There is a need to "speak up" and communicate about the circumstances involved—perhaps a couple who really do not get along but are putting up a perfect façade to the outside world. There's a determination to pretend that things are fine—psychologically, this is called *denial*. Eventually, however, change must take place for the continued tension is unbearable. Choice is available—remove the blindfold and look squarely and honestly at the situation.

Reversed

When the Two of Swords appears reversed, it exacerbates the above situation, except that the person actually feels helpless to make the necessary changes. If a husband and wife are at odds, one party may be unwilling to admit to the truth of the situation, making discourse impossible. This may result in deceit or disloyalty, lying or duplicity.

Three of Swords

The Three of Swords signifies separation and sorrow, perhaps the breaking up of a love relationship. It is a card of severance. However, there is the sense that the separation or break-up was needed—a relationship or friendship or alliance of another sort had outworn its usefulness, and, although there is sorrow or regret, the end result is positive.

Upright

You are feeling the pain of separation right now, quite possibly in the area of love, or a "love triangle." A third party has entered into the formerly stable situation and caused the break-up, but it was ready to happen anyway. It's time to let go. Whatever has "died" needs to be allowed to disintegrate within your psychic structure. Don't try to hold on to the past.

Reversed

You are taking this separation too much to heart and not thinking clearly about the truth of the situation. You are blaming someone else instead of looking to see how you were a party to the break-up. You may be suffering depression over the event and be unable or unwilling to pull yourself together and get on with your life. This is a time to keep a clear head and not get bogged down with the what-might-have-been's.

Four of Swords

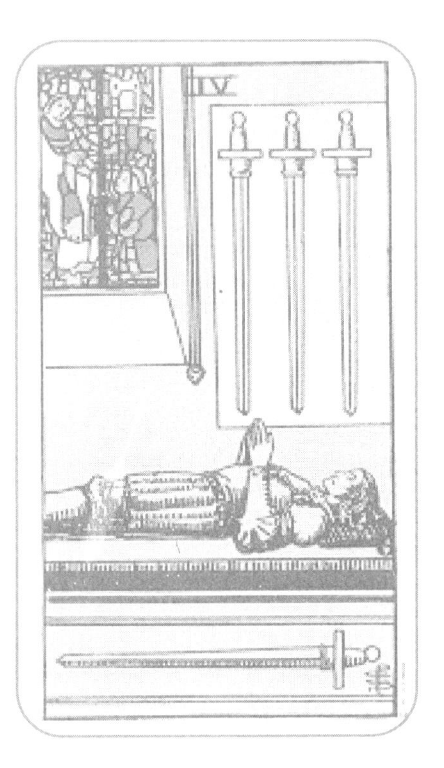

The Four of Swords is a card of respite after the sorrow or misfortune of the Three. It is a time of rest and recuperation, of working on your problems quietly and with faith. You feel the need for introspection and solitude, a necessary period of aloneness and contemplation in order to get a solid perspective on what happened and why.

Upright

You have been in pain, but now you are in the first stage of recovery, whether from emotional upheaval or physical illness. You are at rest and are taking the time out to think things through and plan your next moves more wisely. This is the calm after the storm, and you may want to go into a time of exile, away from other people. Perhaps an extended vacation to a quiet place, or a retreat. You feel monastic. During this time of R & R you need to think, plan, and re-evaluate what you had been doing before the crisis. It's a time to get your inner house in order.

Reversed

You are not allowing yourself the rest and respite you need, and if you continue this way you may well make yourself ill. Everyone needs a period of calm and quiet in the wake of any kind of disruption of regular life, and refusing to take time to recuperate, both mentally and emotionally, will only worsen the situation. So, take heed and take time out.

Five of Swords

The Five of Swords suggests the double-edge of the sword—one is of defeat, misfortune, betrayal, and loss. The other is of learning to accept the boundaries we all must face and live with, of not flying in the face of life's unavoidable limitations. Someone may have disappointed you, but you were expecting too much.

Upright

Fives are about adjusting, and this Five indicates you are in a period of adjusting to some kind of change brought on by distress or loss. It's an uncomfortable process but a necessary one. Change is part of life, and the more you resist it the more difficult you make it for yourself. Whatever is being challenged or calling for change—your lifestyle, your philosophy, your inner beliefs about yourself—now is the time to get to work and bring those changes into your daily life.

Reversed

Your losses have hit you hard, and you are in a state of great unhappiness. You feel hurt and betrayed, angry and discouraged. This is a time of agony, but only you can get yourself out of it. You may feel confused about why the crisis occurred, but deep down you are already aware of the reasons. You just don't want to face them.

Six of Swords

The Six of Swords indicates that you are moving away from past troubles, putting them behind you. It's the beginning of a new phase after a time of upheaval. You have stabilized your situation and are feeling a new peace of mind. This is the calm after the storm and you are into a period of smooth sailing with relatively few problems.

Upright

This is a time of integration—or reintegration. Harmony and lack of tension prevail. New friends and relationships come into your life, ones you can trust. After some intense suffering, you are back in harness with yourself, feeling fine and together. This card can also indicate a move or a journey over water. The destination may be unknown, or the effects of the move may be uncertain, but luck is on your side and any change you make will go smoothly.

Reversed

As this is a positive card, the reversed position simply means delays, or that the harmony you are experiencing is purely internal and not being expressed externally. You may have come to a new way of thinking about your life, or you may be affirming your old beliefs and attitudes, accepting what is as a necessary condition.

Seven of Swords

When the Seven of Swords shows up, it is a statement that caution in all dealings is called for. There is the suggestion of roundabout action, or indirect communications. Nothing is quite what it seems to be, and you have to use your wit to achieve your aims. There is a warning to void overconfidence—you may appear to be in the top spot now but lack of proper prudence could still do you in.

Upright

You have got the upper hand over a tricky situation, but you still need to exercise caution in handling your affairs. This is a time when you can begin new attempts to overcome previous failures, but you can't go at it in a bull-in-the-china-shop manner. Discretion and discrimination are required, as are diplomacy and evasive tactics. You may not like this oblique approach, but it is more likely to achieve success. You may get good advice.

Reversed

When the Seven of Swords is reversed, it emphasizes all of the above but includes the possibility of deception. Maintain caution and vigilance in all things during this period and keep mentally flexible so that you can respond to changes speedily. You may be experimenting with different plans of action, getting various points of view.

Eight of Swords

The tension of the Eight of Swords is related to that of the Two with the difference that with the Two the person was in denial, but with the Eight he or she is completely conscious of the choices available. Despite this, there is a feeling of being trapped—either of being unable or unwilling to make a choice, therefore maintaining a painful state.

Upright

Most writers view this as an extremely negative card. In the Waite deck, a bound and blindfolded woman is surrounded by the seven Swords stuck into the sand around her, like a barrier. There is a situation that causes great unhappiness, but the person is not without resources to change matters. The bad situation is temporary and, if the card falls in the "future" position, can even be avoided.

Reversed

This card reversed is a warning that what is already wrong can get worse, or that some difficult situation is approaching. It is a time to make sure all your affairs are in the best possible order without delay. If you've been putting off paying your taxes, or getting insurance, or settling some legal matter, take care of it. Material security depends on your using your head and preparing for emergencies and unexpected calamities.

Nine of Swords

The Nine of Swords is a card indicating extreme anxiety, nightmares, tension, unhappiness, regrets over past mistakes or misfortunes. When it appears, the person is in an unhappy and tense state of mind whether or not the facts bear out the fear. It is possible the fear is based on reality, but, as the saying goes, "What you fear the most is what never happens."

Upright

The Nine of Swords indicates that the person's mind is being troubled by bad dreams or horror fantasies. Where these are coming from may be an unknown factor, but some probing will reveal that there are deep-rooted causes at work trying to come to the surface to be recognized and resolved. This card can indicate the need for psychological counseling.

Upright

This is a time of extreme mental torture as you are being forced to change your attitudes and beliefs by crisis circumstances. This is not all bad, however, no matter how painful it seems. Remember that Nine is the number of completion. Thus, this card indicates that the changes you are being required to make forecast a better future.

Reversed

When the Nine of Swords is reversed, it amplifies the mental anguish while at the same time demanding that you get to work on belief systems that no longer apply to your life and that are standing in the way of your progress. You are suffering because you cannot perceive the cause of your problems. Resolute honesty is called for to achieve the insight that will resolve the situation.

Ten of Swords

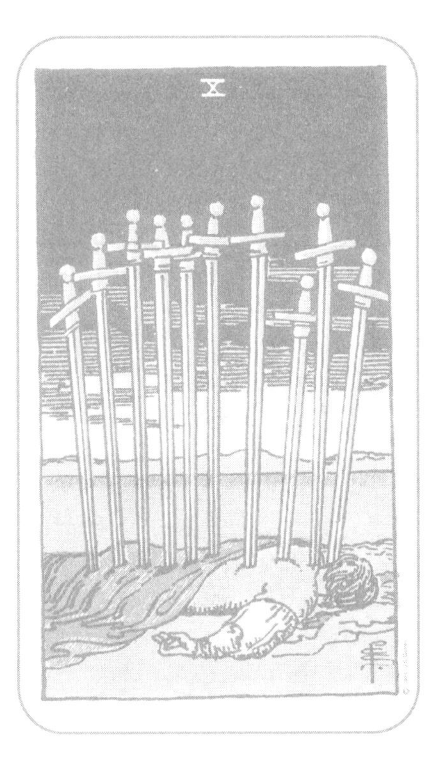

Although the Ten of Swords is another difficult card, its appearance marks the beginning of the end of a period of trials and tribulations. It also signifies the beginning of an entirely new cycle. In order for the new cycle to come in, you have to clear away the debris of the old cycle now ending, and often this process is extremely painful.

Upright

When the Ten of Swords appears upright, it is a statement that you need to make a clean break from the past and all its attendant pain and suffering. Whether this means a divorce, quitting a job, changing careers, moving across the world, or changing a traditional belief system, it's now necessary to make the break, and make it cleanly, leaving no loose ends. It's a time to see the situation clearly without previous illusions that have clouded your vision.

Reversed

When the Ten of Swords appears reversed, it is an indication that you are hanging back from taking the necessary steps to move into the new cycle. You are delaying actions or deceiving yourself about the truth of the situation. You may be making excuses for yourself or someone else in order to maintain the status quo, but you are only prolonging your agony. Make a choice, even if it's the wrong one.

Chapter 12

The Suit of Cups

The Cups in medieval times were representative of the clergy, second in influence in the society only to the nobility—in fact, it was common practice for the second or third son of a noble house to enter the Church. Although the clergy often fell short of its obligations, the local priests were often good people who used available resources to alleviate the sufferings of their flock. For this reason, the suit of Cups has come to represent love, harmony, good faith, and benign influences.

The Cups are related to emotions, love, romance, the unconscious, and creativity.

The Suit of Cups is a happy one—which may explain why in most decks they are pictured as large, beautiful, sometimes ornate vessels or chalices. They are double-ended as if they could be filled from either side. The center part is wide so as to be easily grasped by a hand, and the bottom part forms a stable base. Unlike the other suits, the Cups are usually positioned upright on all the cards, suggesting good cheer, such as is offered when a toast is made.

As the Cups represent love—in all its forms, not just romantic love but friendship and love of one's fellow humans as well—they are a strong suit, symbolically stating that the only true and enduring riches we have are built from love, kindness, and compassion. Thus, the Cups are almost always positive, and if there are negative elements in the reading a Cup card will mitigate the bad omen, or help to make a situation better, or point the way to a solution.

King of Cups

The King of Cups has a loving demeanor. He is a mature man, usually seated on a throne, often with water in the background. His crown is more like an elaborate hat than a bejeweled regal headpiece, suggesting that he stands *with* rather than above his subjects. Rarely is he shown wearing armor—usually just plain robes; so there is nothing of the militant about him. His expression is bland, his attitude relaxed and nonthreatening.

Upright

The appearance of this King indicates a man who is kindly disposed—a kind father figure, who may represent your own father or someone who takes that role for you. He can also represent an older man with whom the readee either has or wants a love relationship with. Whether as a friend, advisor, or lover, he is utterly trustworthy and dependent, and can be relied upon to come through for you when you need him. Most interpretations consider him to be a man of culture, knowledgeable about and interested in the arts, possibly himself a creative type. If the King does not represent an actual person, he indicates a situation that is favorable, especially if it is an artistic pursuit.

Reversed

Your involvement with some kind of love situation is ending, but the process should not cause much pain. You have reached a phase in your life when it's time to move on from dependency on an older person—perhaps your father or a mentor or teacher—and strike out on your own. Whether the circumstances are related to a person or to your own inner psychic process, the result is the same. It is also possible that this King reversed represents someone who is trying to get rid of *you* for some reason, romantic or otherwise. You need to let go and if necessary mourn the passing of something that was good once but is now over.

Queen of Cups

The Queen of Cups is a beautiful figure who is full of benevolence. Her Cup is an ornate chalice, and she is holding it with both hands, gazing at it as if she could see visions of the future. She wears robes that appear to be filmy and flowing and her crown is elaborate but dainty. Usually there is water flowing at her feet. An affectionate and loving woman, whether wife, mother, friend, or lover, she is wise in the ways of love and the human heart. Her attitude is one of receptiveness and approachability.

Upright

The Queen of Cups can represent any kindly woman in the querent's life, usually someone with a water sign in the chart, if not the Sun, then the Moon or Venus. If the readee is a man, she may signify his wife or the woman he loves. She is creative, perhaps an artist, with visionary tendencies. Her psychic ability is highly developed, and tends to be accurate. However, she tempers her intuitive nature with mature judgment. If she represents the querent herself, the above qualities apply to that person although they may still be in the nascent stage and need to be developed. If she does not represent a person, the situation is one concerning creative endeavor or circumstances with an emotional tone that is positive.

Reversed

This Queen reversed can indicate a love relationship gone sour, or someone who is having trouble expressing emotion. If a person, it can be a dishonest advisor. There is a warning here to be careful whom you trust, with your secrets and your emotional life. If the card represents the querent, it can mean that you are playing with possible dangerous psychic matters you don't understand.

Knight of Cups

Portrayed as a handsome young man sitting upright on a white horse—in parade or dressage position—he holds the cup straight out in front of him. His helmet may be winged, a symbol of his being a messenger, in this case, of love or good tidings. Usually depicted in an outdoor setting, with water under the horse's hooves, he is armored only lightly.

Upright

The Knight of Cups is bringing you a message about love, or he may represent your true love—the knight on the white horse! His appearances indicates you are deeply involved in an emotional situation, to the point where little else matters. You may be awaiting this message—such as a declaration of love or a proposal of marriage—with such anticipation that everything else seems insignificant. All other relationships pale by comparison with this one. If he does not represent a love, he is certainly a friend, honest, intelligent, and willing to aid you.

Reversed

The message you hope for has been delayed or may never be received. The relationship you yearn for may be based on deceit or be superficial on the other person's side. You may be obsessing about someone who really doesn't care that much about you and who will never make a commitment, even if he has led you to believe he is sincere. This is a young man (or woman) who is fickle, likes to flirt, but belongs to the "love 'em and leave 'em" school of romantic encounters.

Page of Cups

The Page of Cups shows a young man in decorated but short garb with an elaborate hat. His attitude is relaxed and open and he seems well-pleased with himself. He holds the cup out in one hand–with a fish sticking out of it–as if he produced the fish like a rabbit out of a hat. He likes what he sees and seems to expect approval.

Upright

This Page is a young person, male or female–possibly a son or daughter, or a younger sibling–who is bringing you a message about love. It might mean an engagement or a wedding–some situation wherein there is inherent emotional risk. The circumstances may be exciting yet scary at the same time, as with a sudden elopement. If the card represents the querent, there is the idea that you have already decided to take an emotional risk and aren't interested in being dissuaded. You feel it will work out.

Reversed

The Page reversed is a "fishy" situation, something you need to look at carefully. If a person, there may be deceit, flattery for gain, an unwanted pregnancy, or secrecy in matters of the heart. Someone may be trying to seduce you and you are blinded to the reality of the falseness of his or her intentions. Or, you may yourself be in the role of the seducer, playing around carelessly with someone's emotions. If so, take care–you might get hurt yourself.

Ace of Cups

The Ace of Cups shows a single large cup with water flowing fountain-like out of it. Supported by a hand usually emerging from a cloud—either resting on the palm or grasping it at the center, this Ace suggests itself as the fountain of Love. Other symbols may decorate the card, such as a dove (in the Waite deck) or flowers (symbols of love), or another water motif.

Upright

The Ace of Cups indicates a new beginning—a new love or a one-on-one relationship of any kind. There are previously unfelt emotions coming into play now, perhaps a new way of seeing a relationship. Or, a birth—of a child or an idea. This is a fertile time, for emotional or creative growth. This Ace symbolizes the consummation of something hoped for.

Reversed

When reversed, this Ace indicates delay or disappointment in love or a new beginning that won't go anywhere. Difficulties in getting any new relationship or creative effort off the ground, or things you are trying to set in motion meeting unforeseen and frustrating obstacles. It's perhaps not the right time to be starting something new.

Two of Cups

A lovely card! The two of Cups adds one to the Ace, creating a coupling of some sort—a marriage, a partnership, a union of any sort. Harmony is in the air—you may be in the "honeymoon" stage of a relationship or endeavor when all seems right and good and you think nothing can go wrong. Alternatively, an old relationship can gain new harmony.

Upright

You are moving in tandem with another person now and all is going smoothly. Whether it is love or friendship, there is plenty of accord, lots of mutuality—you are in the "Mutual Admiration Society"—full of good will toward each other. Ordinarily, this card refers to a love match between the sexes, but it can also indicate a joining of another sort.

Reversed

Fortunately, this card has such a vibration of harmony that its reversed position isn't much different from the upright, except that there may be delays or the relationship may have to be kept a secret for some reason.

Three of Cups

The appearance of the Three of Cups signifies that something has been brought to completion. There is victory and success. The act of falling in love signified by the Two of Cups may have resulted in a baby, or a creative venture has produced a salable product. It's time for a celebration!

Upright

You are experiencing success and plenty, a time of merriment and celebration is at hand. Your feelings, which may have been murky, are clearer now and you are understanding your emotional patterns in a positive and growth-producing way. You're on your way now to great things.

Reversed

The Three of Cups reversed remains a positive influence, except that the gratification you are getting may be more sensual than deeply emotional. You will still have success, but your achievements may be in small things.

Four of Cups

The Four of Cups represents a state of apathy and withdrawal. However, this may be a necessary rest from the hectic excitement represented by the Three. It's a time to get away by yourself and just drift and dream for a while before getting back into your daily grind.

Upright

You are in a state of withdrawing your emotions from a situation or a person. After intense emotional involvement, you may need some "space" in which to be yourself. There's a feeling of let-down after build-up, as in the postpartum blues or when you have to face the daily grind of ordinary life, dealing with all the nitty-gritties of making a marriage work.

Reversed

You may be experiencing displeasure, disappointment, or dissatisfaction with a relationship or the way a creative project is turning out. You want to tune out in order to get away from your negative feelings. That's okay—it is a necessary respite to regain perspective and balance.

Five of Cups

The Five of Cups signifies that you are brooding over past wrongs, losses, disappointments, or hurts. It symbolizes a state of mind that is looking backward at a painful past and refusing to look forward to a positive future.

Upright

Your unhappiness is a result of your attitude, which you can change. This is a card of choice. You can continue to brood over what went wrong, or you can turn around and contemplate what can go right in the future. You don't have to be miserable unless you enjoy misery.

Reversed

You are in a state of indecision. There's some issue about which you are refusing to make up your mind. You are refusing to face facts. Just because there have been past losses doesn't mean there can't be future gains. But if you continue in this negative state of mind, you will only make things worse.

Six of Cups

The Six of Cups signifies nostalgia and happy memories of time gone by. This card refers to a sentimental remembrance of things past. These pleasant and comforting memories can be used to better your future, to build on. Knowing that you have been happy in the past will enhance your ability to be happy in the future.

Upright

You are experiencing some feelings that are connected to your past that will shed light on your future. You are feeling calm and collected about past events, putting them into perspective, and beginning to understand how they can engender fruition in the present—a future renewal.

Reversed

A happy card, the Six of Cups reversed suggests changes in the immediate environment that will make you feel more secure. These may involve meeting new friends or making new associations. You are developing new emotional tools that will aid you in the future—an important event soon.

Seven of Cups

The Seven of Cups signifies a time of great creative potential along with the energy to make use of it. Many options are available: the difficulty is in choosing the right one. This card is about fantasy and imagination, about building castles in the air.

Upright

You are looking at a number of possibilities now—too many to make an easy choice. Like the proverbial kid in the candy store with just one penny, you are dithering over which way to go. With so many choices, you are like Walter Mitty—living out different roles in your imagination but having a hard time deciding which to manifest in reality.

Reversed

You are in a state of total confusion. There's just too much going on. Variety is the spice of life but your life has become too much like hot Mexican food. You need a calm space where you can sort through the multiple choices confronting you. Let your feelings be your guide.

Eight of Cups

The Eight of Cups indicates a situation where the only solution is to turn your back on it and go in another direction. What's there either isn't working as expected or isn't all that important any more. The eight neatly stacked Cups represent effort that was made in vain and now needs to be abandoned.

Upright

You are wishing things might have been different, but, knowing they aren't, you know that you have to let go. It's time to cut your losses and get out of the situation that has failed despite your best efforts. Unfortunately, this usually refers to a relationship that has reached such a state of deterioration that the only solution is to walk away from it.

Reversed

You are walking away without facing the facts behind the problem you want to escape from, taking the coward's way out. Things haven't worked out as you planned and wanted, and you want to cut and run without giving the situation a second chance. If you don't, you may regret it later.

Nine of Cups

This is the best "pip" card in the entire Tarot deck. Called the "Wish Card," it indicates great joy and happiness, all your dreams coming true, getting what you wish for. It's like winning the lottery and meeting Mr. or Ms. Right all on the same day.

Upright

Even the most negative interpreters have nothing bad to say about this card. It means success, triumph, everything you want and hope for. When the Nine of Cups appears ask yourself, "What is it I really want?" The answer is that you will get it!

Reversed

As above, it's hard to say anything negative about this card, even in the reverse position. The worst thing that can be said here is that if you refuse to believe in your own good fortune and take a negative attitude you can mess things up for yourself.

Ten of Cups

The Ten of Cups indicates a situation of lasting contentment, real love, domestic bliss, complete satisfaction in all your endeavors. It symbolizes people living harmoniously together, sharing their love and their lives unconditionally. This ten is so favorable that it can offset any negative cards in a reading.

Upright

This card is an indication of everything that most people wish for—love and harmony, happy family life, true love and compatible companionship. It's a time of completion, of reaping the rewards of what you have sown. It does not necessarily mean wealth, but it symbolizes an abundant life in the true sense.

Reversed

Delays and obstacles are standing in the way of your achieving the happiness you long for. Circumstances beyond your control may be the cause, and at the moment there's nothing you can do but keep a positive attitude and hold tight while waiting them to change. They will change.

Part IV

How to Do Readings

Chapter 13

Ten Spreads

To do readings successfully, you need more than just knowledge of standardized meanings of the cards and how to make spreads. As well as complete honesty and clear ethics, you must have access to your intuitive self, for the cards speak not to the rational mind but to the inner truth of one's being.

When you read Tarot cards, you are not a "reader" in the sense of reading a book. Anyone can give a mechanical reading, using the book meanings described; but only someone who has taken the time, patience, and effort to delve deeply into the Self, where intuition dwells, can truly *read* the Tarot. When you elect to do this, you bring your whole self to bear on the situation of the moment. You must have clarity of mind, spirit, and purpose—murky or unclear thinking or disturbed emotions will cloud a reading and obscure its true significance. This is why I have emphasized the importance of preparing yourself in advance.

When reading for others, conduct an interview so that the client can clarify whatever question needs answering, or the issue to be addressed by the reading.

Self-readings can help you tune in to your own inner processes and teach you *how* you tend to approach the cards. This is a highly individual matter. For example, as a psychotherapist and an astrologer I am always aware of both my own (or the client's) current psychological state of being; also I am aware of my own (or the client's) astrological chart and what transits are in progress at the time of the reading. These, for me, are valuable sources of information. One excellent reader I know is a student of numerology, so he tunes in immediately to the numbers of the cards of both the Minor Arcana and the Major Arcana. Your individualized way of interpretation will be a natural outgrowth of who you are and what you know. When doing readings for yourself, follow the same procedure as given for reading for others. Consider yourself to be the "querent," and formulate our question clearly and unambiguously.

Using intuition uses all of you. It is precisely the holistic nature of intuition that gives it its power. In your unconscious you have a huge data bank of experiences upon which to draw, most of which you are not aware of. You know much more than you think you know, and your psychic intuition has the ability to come up with new and creative combinations of knowledge. It is an innovator with great creative ability. Its products will amaze you!

If you are reading for others, the only element in the reading that does not stem from your own personal experience and world view is the querent's personality, psychological state of mind and emotions, and his or her reactions to what you say in the reading. Once you've learned the cards well and made them part of "the furniture of the mind," your intuition will do the rest if you have taken the care to put yourself in the proper frame of mind, emotions, and spirit. At first, you may want to stick close to the interpretations you read in this and other books, but as meanings are multiple and depend on positions of the cards as well as the question being asked, don't be afraid to make adjustments as they come to you. Generally, when I give a reading I feel a guide close by and I turn myself over to that power. As you become more and more familiar, not only with the varied meanings of the specific cards, but with how they affect you and your reactions to them, you'll become more at ease with letting your intuition be your guide.

Tarot is like a language, and the more you practice it the more fluent you become in understanding and "speaking" it. It's important to look at any spread first as a *whole*. Are they mostly Major Arcana cards or mostly Minor Arcana ones? Is the general color impression bright and cheery or dull and gray? Are the images powerful and dramatic, like the Tower or the Devil, or are they peaceful and benign, like Temperance or the Hermit? Is the pattern cohesive along one line or is it mixed—both calm and disturbing images? What is the general tone—one of contrasts or of harmony? Trust your immediate reaction to the overall impression you get; then proceed to analysis of the individual cards, concluding with a synthesis as you put the pieces together.

If a Significator is called for, pick it out of the deck according to the "Court Cards as Representational of People"; or consult Chapter 5, "Practical Uses" to choose one of the Major Arcana as a Significator card.

Choose a layout pattern (spread) you feel is suitable to the question or issue at hand, and lay out the cards according to the positions given, making sure you are familiar in advance with the significance of each position, as where a card falls in the layout affects the interpretation.

Next, proceed with whatever shuffling process you have decided to use (as discussed in Chapter 3). Don't worry overmuch about how the cards are shuffled or who shuffles them. Just whatever method you like and feel comfortable with, or that the querent is comfortable with. No matter how you shuffle, nor who shuffles, the cards will automatically arrange themselves as they should be—count on it! The order in which they come up is never an *accident*. However, always have the cutting done by the querent, unless of course you are reading for yourself.

In my book *Your Psychic Potential*, there are multiple methods of developing your psychic/intuitive abilities. Its dozens of exercises and meditations for opening the psychic door, integrating mind, spirit, and body, learning the practical side of being psychic, and encountering the invisible world make it an excellent adjunct for anyone studying the Tarot through which one opens the inner door to intuition.

Then, deal the spread from the top of the deck you have reassembled after the cutting. Some readers always lay the cards face down; others, face up. The choice is yours. Some writers on Tarot insist that the entire deck be kept face down at all times, a procedure that I follow. Others say that once a layout is dealt the remaining cards should be laid aside and left out of the reading. However, I hold the unused part of the deck as I read and, when it seems appropriate, for elucidation or to answer further questions regarding what has already been said, I will draw cards at random from the remaining cards of the deck. As you work with reading, you will develop your own methods. There is no *one right way*. Reading Tarot is like playing a piece of classical music—there's a score written by the original composer, but every performer plays the music slightly differently according to his or her own interpretation of the notes.

[*Note*: It doesn't matter whether the querent sits across from or beside the reader; the cards are always read as they face the reader. If you deal cards face down, be sure to turn them up from left to right so that you don't reverse uprights cards or turn reversed cards upright.]

The Traditional Celtic Cross Spread (10 cards)

The Positions and Their Meanings

In this spread, the Significator is placed on the mat and Card l placed on top of it.

*Card 1 * This covers you.*
Describes the querent's immediate concerns.

*Card 2 * This crosses you.*
Describes obstacles facing the querent.

*Card 3 * This crowns you.*
Describes what is known to the querent objectively.

*Card 4 * This is beneath you.*
Describes past influences affecting the situation.

*Card 5 * This is behind you.*
Describes past influences now fading away.

*Card 6 * This is before you.*
Describes new circumstances coming into being.

*Card 7 * This is your Self.*
Describes the querent's current state of mind.

*Card 8 * This is your House.*
Describes what surrounds the situation.

*Card 9 * This is what you hope or fear.*
Describes what the querent wants and/or fears.

*Card 10 * This is what will come.*
Describes the likely future outcome.

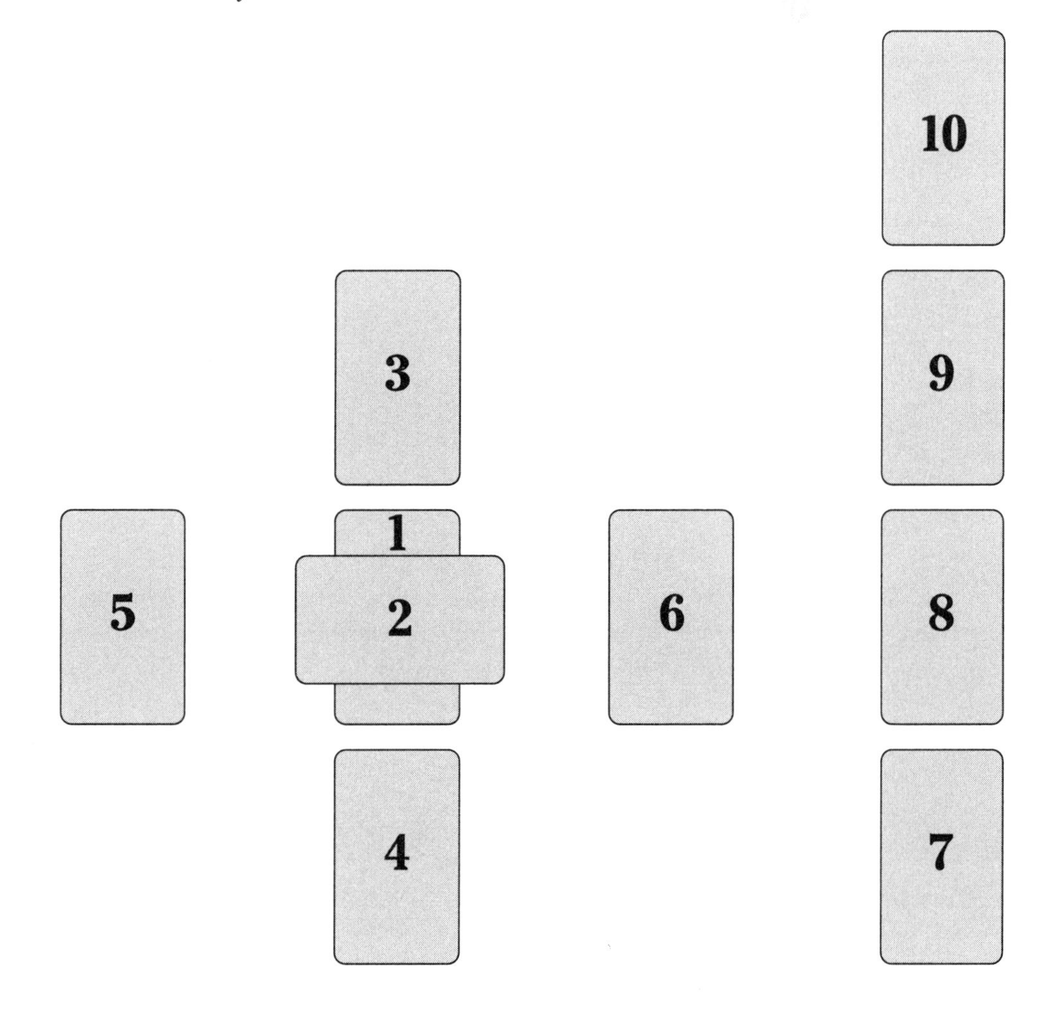

An Example of a Celtic Cross Reading

The querent was a middle-aged woman with a Pisces sun sign and an emotional nature, so I chose as her Significator the Queen of Cups.

*Card 1 * Seven of Pentacles*

She was concerned about money because she had lost her job due to ill health and was totally dependent on her husband for financial support.

*Card 2 * King of Pentacles*

Her husband was well-off and owned his own business, but he was a dominating man who held the money on a tight rein. Naturally timid, she was afraid of him because of his obvious masculine power over her and felt powerless in his presence.

*Card 3 * The Moon*

Her unconscious creative forces were at work suggesting she could, despite her ill health, work to develop her artistic creativity which she had all but squelched, and, since the Moon represents the public, perhaps eventually make money with her talent.

*Card 4 * Justice*

She was involved in a class-action lawsuit regarding her illness, which had been caused by ruptured breast implants. She was hoping for a hefty financial settlement which would free her from dependence on her husband, whom she wished to divorce.

*Card 5 * The Nine of Swords*

This card suggested that her pain and travail were coming to an end, that a solution to her emotional problems due to financial worries would be found.

*Card 6 * The Wheel of Fortune*

This card indicated that forces she had already put into motion—the lawsuit—were continuing on and that there would be a favorable result that would allow her to make significant changes in her life.

*Card 7 * Strength*

This card clearly indicated that underneath her seeming passivity and timidity she had inner strength (coming from a strong Taurus influence in her astrological chart) that would see her through this difficult time.

*Card 8 * Knight of Cups*

This card showed she was receiving loving support from her son who had recently suggested she leave her husband (his stepfather) and go to another state to live with him and his wife.

*Card 9 * The Chariot, reversed*

The Chariot reversed indicates that she was afraid of losing control over her life and that her lack of self-confidence had stopped her from making a commitment to extricate herself from her unhappy marriage.

*Card 10 * The Nine of Pentacles*

This card indicates that she will become financially independent, probably through the success of the lawsuit, and be able to live alone, her dearest wish.

The Horseshoe Spread (7 cards)

Like the Celtic Cross, The Horseshoe positions each represent a specific area of life. Note that the cards are laid out from right to left.

[Note: There is also a 10-card version of The Horseshoe; I prefer the simplicity of the 7-card layout.]

The Positions and Their Meanings

*Card 1 * The past*

Describes what past events, emotions, and actions pertain to the question being asked.

*Card 2 * The present*

Refers to the immediate past or the querent's current state of mind regarding what has just occurred.

*Card 3 * Hidden influences*

This position indicates unexpected influences or occurrences or expectations being altered.

*Card 4 * Obstacles*

Describes what is standing in the querent's way of attaining her desires, either practical difficulties or a negative attitude.

*Card 5 * The environment*
Describes other people, or another person, and their attitudes toward the querent and her issue.

*Card 6 * What should be done*
This position is an indication of action to be taken, or of an attitude to be adopted.

*Card 7 * The most likely outcome*
Assumes you will follow the advice given by Card 6.

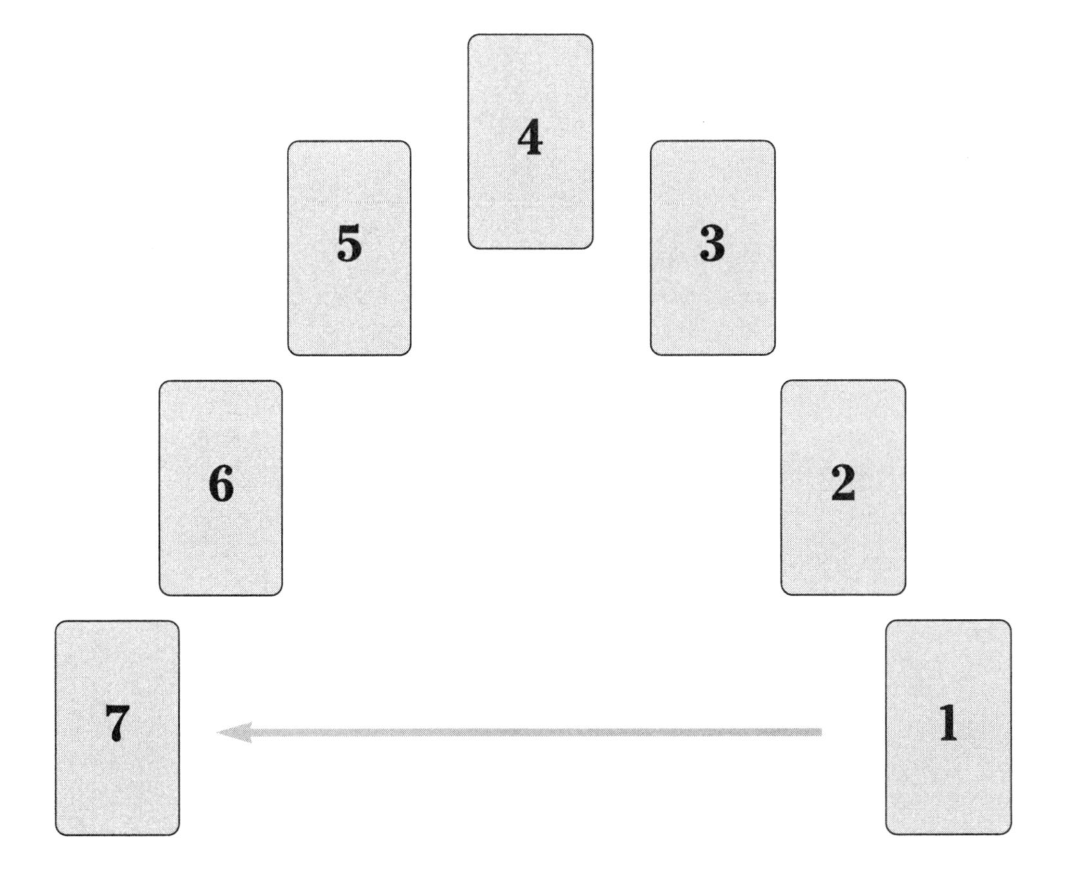

An Example of a Horseshoe Spread

The querent was a young woman involved in a romantic relationship—she wanted to know if it would develop into marriage.

*Card 1 * Three of Swords*

This card indicated that the relationship had already been plagued by separation—it had been an on-again off-again affair that had caused her much pain and anxiety.

*Card 2 * Knight of Cups*

This card revealed that she had recently had a communication from him indicating he wanted to get back together, suggesting he might be ready for commitment.

*Card 3 * The Empress, reversed*

This card warned that she was thinking of "accidentally" getting pregnant to force a marriage, a course of action that would doom her to failure.

*Card 4 * Queen of Pentacles*

This card represented her mother who strongly opposed her daughter's choice. The family was well-off and socially well-connected while the young man was from a blue-collar background and was working his way through college.

*Card 5 * Strength*

The appearance of this card indicated the young woman was ready to declare her independence, to beard the lioness in her den, so to speak, in order to marry her lover.

*Card 6 * Temperance*

This card counseled patience and self-control—not to rush into anything but to work to reconcile the opposing forces, to allow her mother to realize the young man's good qualities and to have the maturity to realize that good things often take time.

*Card 7 * Ten of Cups*

This card indicates that if she follows the advice given and does not use any trickery or deceit to get her man, there will be the result she desires of a happy marriage blessed with children and prosperity.

The Horoscope Spread (12 cards)

In the Horoscope Spread, the twelve cards are laid out in a circle that corresponds to the twelve houses of the astrological chart. A thirteenth card, a Significator, can be placed in the center if desired, either chosen or the next card that comes up.

House One begins at the left horizontal point (see diagram) and the cards are dealt around counter-clockwise until the twelfth card sits above the first card.

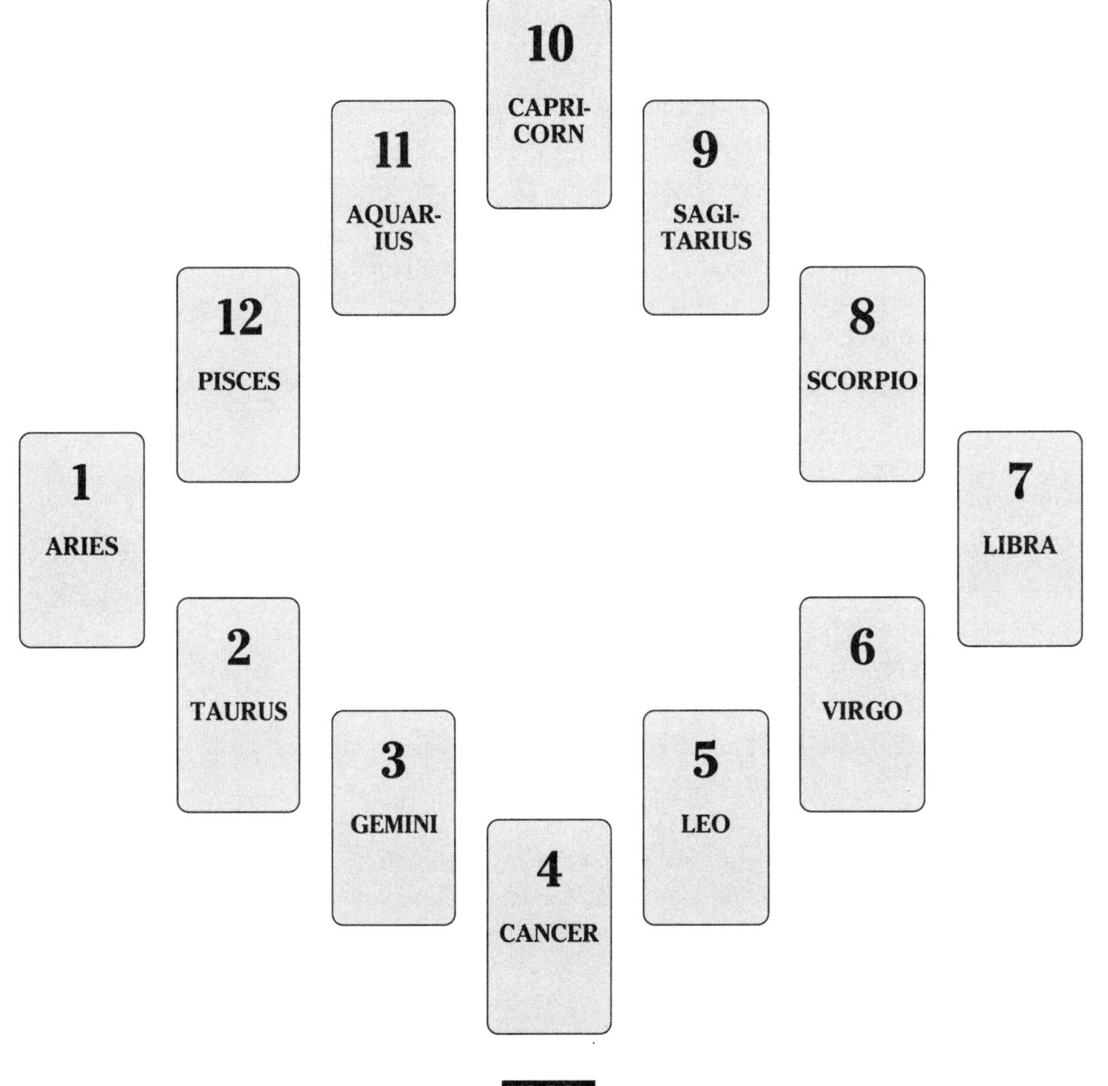

Each house refers to a specific area of life; thus, the cards are read individually in reference to each house.

This spread is not generally good for answering specific questions but is best used for an overview of where the person is in life at the time of the reading. It does not matter what the querent's Sun sign is, nor where the other planets are located in the natal chart. The houses are generic in meaning and apply across the board.

The First House: The Self

(Natural Affinity: Aries)

The first House is the quintessential "I." It is one's personality or self-projection, the physical body and appearance. The House of ego—which in this sense means that core within each of us that makes life choices—and ego development, the first House refers to *consciousness of the Self.* Basic physical vitality is also the domain of this House.

The Second House: Personal Resources

(Natural Affinity: Taurus)

The second House has to do with what is considered valuable. This includes money, personal possessions, and attitudes toward them, but it also suggests valuing as a means of identity. *I am what I value* can be extended to *I am what I own.* The process of identification with material possessions makes them a part of oneself.

The Third House: The Environment

(Natural Ruler: Gemini)

The third House covers three areas of life that at first may not seem related, but taken together represent normal daily life, what astrologers call the "near environment." The first has to do with *communications* related to the routine of everyday life—the myriad of daily telephone calls, conversations, letters, faxes, e-mail, bills, paperwork, small talk, involvement with friends, neighbors, and the community at large—as we go about our accustomed round. It is the mind operating on its customary level when performing routine tasks. This House also relates to *short-distance travel* such as commuting, business trips, weekends away, and whatever moving about we do that does not take us into unfamiliar territory but is a part of our usual routine. *Siblings and relatives* (except parents) are also the province of this House, insofar as we are concerned with routine interactions with them.

The Fourth House: Roots

(Natural Affinity: Cancer)

The fourth House is the basic foundation of one's life—home, family, parenting (especially the mother), tradition, the past, one's homeland. In short, *roots*. The cusp (beginning point) of the fourth House is at the bottom of the chart, what might be called the "Earth point." It follows that the fourth House has a deeper meaning than one's immediate family. This is the sense of support we derive from earth itself, which is the basis of our life here. It is the House of the Great Mother Goddess, as well as that of the personal mother. Cancerian images and symbolism imbue this House—nurturing, emotional support, belonging, the maternal, forebears, the ancestral land. The Moon, symbolic of the unconscious, rules Cancer, and so the fourth House also refers to humanity's collective unconscious and the symbols that link together the *human family*.

The Fifth House: Self-Expression

(Natural Affinity: Leo)

The fifth House is where we play and amuse ourselves, are creative and self-expressive, encounter romance, and have children. The fifth House is where we do what we want, not what we must. As all people know, "All work and no play makes Jack a dull boy," but the relevance of play to our growth has been overlooked. Amusements not only foster relaxation, taking us away from our ordinary chore-filled life, they release the mind and spirit to engage in creativity and self-expression.

The Sixth House: Health And Service

(Natural Affinity: Virgo)

The sixth House involves one's health and health-promoting routines, nutrition in the form of eating preferences and habits, daily work or chores, service to others, and the capacity for self-sacrifice. This House is often emphasized in the charts of nurses, social workers, and the service professions and trades generally. Propensity to illness can be found here as well as concern for health. It represents what is *necessary* as opposed to what one chooses to do for its own, or one's own, sake, our day-to-day duties and responsibilities. It is relationships based on duty rather than choice or pleasure.

The Seventh House: One-on-One Relationships

(Natural Affinity: Libra)

Traditionally the House of marriage and partnerships, the seventh House has to do with *all* of our one-on-one relationships with any type of partner, including those with enemies. In the seventh House one engages in chosen relationships, such as marriage, as opposed to those which are given, such as family. There is here a sense of mutuality, which can be extended to include those with whom we compete.

The Eighth House: The Past

(Natural Affinity: Scorpio)

The eighth House is the House of the past, transformative change, death, inheritance, and other people's money. In this case, death may mean actual physical death, but also it can mean a death of the old so that the new can be given life in rebirth.

The Ninth House: Learning

(Natural Affinity: Sagittarius)

The ninth House represents the higher mind, philosophy, religion, the law and legal matters—all of the institutions that underpin the social order—and long-distance travel, especially to foreign lands. This House, in contradistinction to the third House, is concerned with what is highly conscious in our thinking. It is the level of mind necessary for serious study and learning, for striving to relate the parts to the whole, and seeking meaning in life's experiences.

The Tenth House: Life Task

(Natural Affinity: Capricorn)

The tenth House represents social or professional status, career, life work, and parents (the father especially). This is a house of being out in the world, acting, doing. It might be likened to the process of initiation that turns a child into an adult. Whereas the fourth House is the intimate home, the tenth House is the life task that one must perform in the larger world. The parental energy here is the father-energy, or the figure of masculine authority. It is also the experience of being fathered and of difficulties with the father or authority figures. In the tenth House, we must take on a social role and achieve, becoming in our turn authority figures for others. Honor and reputation are tenth House matters.

The mysterious correspondence between the seemingly random distribution of Tarot cards in a spread and the events and/or trends in a human life has been mocked by modern science, which can't explain such phenomena. However, the principle of *synchronicity* suggests that meaningful coincidences create the impression that there is a sort of foreknowledge of a coming series of events available to the person who works with divinatory tools such as the Tarot and astrology, the *I Ching*, or runes, somehow encompassing a cross-section of the space-time continuum that is an integral part of the entire fabric of life. The Tarot spread is a picture of the moment.

The Eleventh House: Friendships

(Natural Affinity: Aquarius)

The eleventh House refers to one's friends, groups with which one is affiliated, goals, and hopes and wishes. This House is the area of life in which one must get along with large numbers of other people through becoming involved in group efforts, which in turn support the individual.

The Twelfth House: The Hidden

(Natural Affinity: Pisces)

The twelfth House has been given a bad rap by traditional astrologers who saw nothing here but mental illness, incarceration, "self-undoing," and the like. However, astrologer Bob Hand makes a very good case for the twelfth House being a place where things are just coming into being, nascent, vulnerable, still forming. This is based on the fact that planets in the twelfth House are *rising*—dawning, as it were. So, let us look at this House as that which is hidden, or not yet revealed, including our dreams and fantasies. It is true that fears, usually of the unknown, reside here, but so does spirituality. In the twelfth House we are deeply connected on an intuitive level with the powers of the Universe, themselves unseen.

An Example of A Horoscope Spread

The querent was a woman in her mid-forties, married with one child, a four-year-old girl. She worked full-time in an academic job at a university, appeared healthy and was of a cheerful disposition. Her husband's work required him to travel and be away from home much of the time.

*House 1 * The Sun, reversed*

This card showed that her natural optimism and sunny disposition were being affected by her life situation, which was yet to be revealed (to me) by the remaining cards. She was suffering from low self-esteem but trying to maintain a façade of cheerfulness and normality. However, something was clearly wrong.

*House 2 * Page of Cups*

This card referred to her daughter who had been asking questions about why daddy was never home. The mother gave the usual answers about him being away working (which was true), but the child was nonetheless delivering a message to her mother that she sensed in her heart (cups) that the family situation was amiss. Her child was the single most important person in the querent's life and her welfare was of primary importance.

*House 3 * Eight of Swords*

This card indicated that communications were being blocked and she was in a quandary as to what to do about the situation. A question from me elicited the information that she and her husband hardly ever talked about anything important, that he had withdrawn from communication with her, and she felt helpless in the face of his distancing.

*House 4 * The Tower, reversed*

The appearance of the reversed Tower indicated that the querent was trying to hold on to the crumbling structure of her home life. The situation was exacerbated by her husband's constant travel, which she thought was a means to avoid confronting their marital problems for the sake of her daughter, whom she desperately wanted to have a "normal" two-parent childhood.

*House 5 * Ten of Wands*

This card suggested that she was carrying a burden that was preventing her from enjoying life. She had shouldered total care for her daughter and resented her husband's absences and lack of concern for the little girl, which made her feel like a single parent. All responsibility for the child devolved on her, from daily care and feeding to chauffeuring her to ballet classes and other activities. She felt alone with heavy responsibilities and had little time for socializing or having fun.

*House 6 * Three of Swords*

This card indicated some kind of separation from a work situation that was unsatisfactory, and it turned out that she was in the process of changing jobs, within the university but to a new department that was much more relaxed and less pressured than her present position.

*House 7 * King of Swords, reversed*

This card represented her husband, who was a multiple Aquarius, the fixed air sign. It showed his rigid mental attitudes toward the marriage and his unwillingness to open up and talk to her due to his desire to avoid "messy" emotional scenes, a characteristic of all air signs. This card told me the marriage was over and existed in name only. At this point, she confessed that she and her husband had been using separate bedrooms for several months.

*House 8 * The Empress, reversed*

Turning up in the eighth House reversed, the Empress suggested that a past issue involving pregnancy or a maternal figure was involved in the situation. When I read the card, she told me the only reason she had married was that she had become pregnant. She and her now husband had been having a sexual affair but were not in love with each other. When she discovered herself pregnant, he "did the right thing," but subsequently was not much interested in the child he hadn't wanted or planned for.

*House 9 * The Star*

This card indicated she would have great success in her academic career (House of higher learning) and/or that she would pursue other forms of consciousness raising. She said she was very happy with the prospect of the new job, which carried much prestige; but also she was interested in pursuing a study of metaphysics, such as astrology and Tarot, and learning one of the healing arts, Reiki, in which she had been interested for a long time.

*House 10 * The Sun*

This happy card in her tenth House of career assured that the job change was a smart career move and that she would be happy and successful with it. She verified that the new job was the single really bright spot in her life at the time.

*House 11 * King of Wands*

This card represented the head of her new department who had asked her to head a task force in her specialty, which meant she would be heavily involved with group activities. That it was the King indicated her leadership style would be forthright and masculine rather than subtle and feminine. Success was assured.

*House 12 * The Moon*
The Moon appearing in the twelfth House indicated that she needed time by herself to get in touch with her deepest feelings, to access her intuitive self, to step back from the pressures of work and taking care of her daughter in order to process her feelings about her marriage situation before deciding what action to take. She needed to consult her own inner feminine wisdom rather than relying on an intellectual, rational approach to her marriage problem.

The Tree of Life Spread (10 cards)

[Note: The Tree of Life Spread is read from the bottom up; i.e., from Card 10 to Card 1.)

The Positions and Their Meanings

*Card 1 * LIGHT*
Outcome

*Card 2 * WISDOM*
Goals, Changes, Power

*Card 3 * UNDERSTANDING*
Receptivity, Creativity, Limitations

*Card 4 * MERCY*
Abundance, Generosity, Memories

*Card 5 * SEVERITY, STRENGTH*
Struggle, Activity, Destruction

*Card 6 * BEAUTY*
Love, Compassion, New Insights

*Card 7 * VICTORY*
Romance, Emotions, Desires

*Card 8 * GLORY*
Knowledge, Analysis, Discrimination

*Card 9 * FOUNDATION*
Sexual issues, Illusions, Fears, the Unconscious

*Card 10 * KINGDOM*
Physicality, Money, Practical Matters

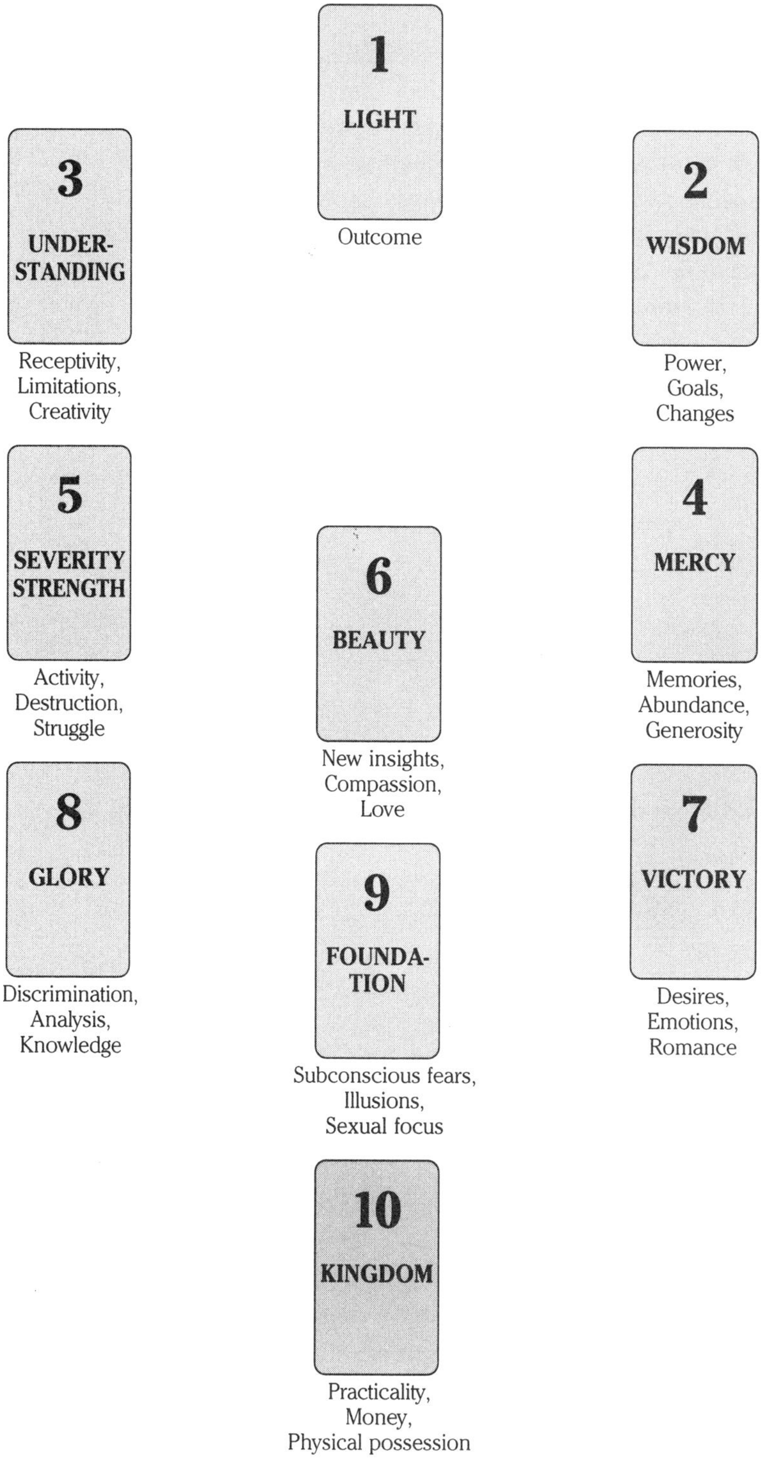

1 LIGHT
Outcome

2 WISDOM
Power, Goals, Changes

3 UNDER-STANDING
Receptivity, Limitations, Creativity

4 MERCY
Memories, Abundance, Generosity

5 SEVERITY STRENGTH
Activity, Destruction, Struggle

6 BEAUTY
New insights, Compassion, Love

7 VICTORY
Desires, Emotions, Romance

8 GLORY
Discrimination, Analysis, Knowledge

9 FOUNDA-TION
Subconscious fears, Illusions, Sexual focus

10 KINGDOM
Practicality, Money, Physical possession

An Example of a Tree of Life Spread

The querent was a man of thirty with artistic talent and ambitions. He wanted to quit his "day job" as a commercial artist to devote himself to developing his talent and wondered if this was the right choice.

*Card 10 * Eight of Pentacles*

This card in the money and practicality position signified that he would be learning new skills, becoming an apprentice at a new trade or career. It augured well for his being able to make money with his move, especially since he is full of enthusiasm and determination (Pentacles: earth) and that his nature is sufficiently practical to enable him to manage limited funds until he is making a good living at his art career.

*Card 9 * Queen of Wands, reversed*

This card represented his wife, a beautiful and ambitious woman who was against him risking their financial security. He wanted her support, but feared her disapproval and worried that if he didn't make enough money she might leave him despite their strong sexual attraction to each other.

*Card 8 * Three of Pentacles*

This is the card of the craftsman, which indicated he has the knowledge needed to practice his art and will keep developing his abilities in a discriminating way. It also suggests that he will make money with his creative talents, for he is good at what he does. His success will come through his own faith in himself.

*Card 7 * The Moon*

The Moon in the position of romance, beauty, and desire indicated that he has a strong feminine side to his nature, which makes him artistically creative in addition to having a practical side. This was corroborated astrologically by the fact that in his chart Venus was found in the sign of Taurus, an extremely practical earth sign which grounded his love of beauty (Venus) while his Moon was in the extra-sensitive sign of Pisces, ruled by Neptune, the planet of creativity, art, music, and compassion.

*Card 5 * The Chariot*

In the position of struggle and activity, the Chariot indicated that he was going to have to work hard to harness both sides of his nature, the practical and the dreamy; also that he was going to have to put effort into convincing his wife that his plans would eventually benefit her so that she would become his partner and not pull against his wishes, which would be destructive to him.

*Card 4 * Four of Pentacles*

Money has always been an issue for him with this card appearing in the position of abundance and memories. He came from a modest background where each penny had to be carefully counted and there was none to spare. Having to go to work at an early age, he worked his way through art school with great difficulty and still has painful memories of frugal living. To solve his issues of abundance, he has to have faith in himself, as was already indicated by Card 8. I advised him to perform daily affirmations to strengthen his inner belief in his value as an artist.

*Card 3 * The High Priestess*

In the position of creativity, receptivity, and limits, the High Priestess indicates that he has much talent that is yet to be developed, talent he does not himself even know the depths of. At the moment, he is suffering limitations because he has not delved deeply into himself to discover what he can do, but he is totally receptive to the idea of uncovering and utilizing his creative abilities to the greatest extent possible. As the Moon rules the High Priestess, this card is an echo of Card 7, the Moon, and an encouragement to him to express himself fully.

*Card 2 * The Wheel of Fortune*

This card appearing in the position of goals, changes, and power indicates that he has already put the wheel of change into motion by his intense desire to freelance his art instead of being chained to a boring and unfulfilling commercial job. Whether he is fully aware of the process or not, his vivid fantasies (Pisces rules imagination) of the kind of life he wants to live have already served to get his subconscious mind to work to make it happen. He is going to make this change and reach his goal—because his inner self is directing him and has already taken charge. There is no turning back now.

*Card 1 * Ace of Wands*
In the outcome position, the Ace of Wands indicates that he is starting on a new direction for his work/career and that all will turn out well. All kinds of new beginnings are in store for him related to his work, new opportunities will come his way, and new contacts will be helpful. His excitement about making this life-changing move will carry him to success.

The Quick-Answer Seven-Card Spread

The Positions and Their Meanings

[Note: the cards are laid out in a single row, face up, from left to right.]

Card 1 * Concern
Card 2 * Immediate past
Card 3 * Immediate future
Card 4 * Querent's state of mind
Card 5 * Obstacle
Card 6 * Help
Card 7 * Outcome

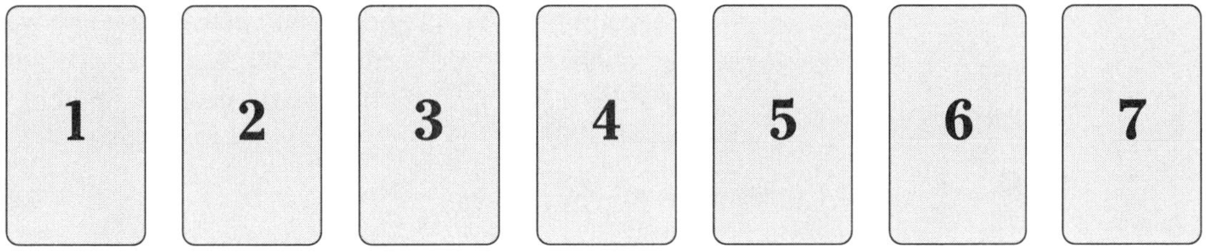

1 2 3 4 5 6 7

An Example of a Quick-Answer Seven-Card Spread

The querent was a single woman in her late twenties who had always lived at home. She wanted to live in a warm climate and was thinking of moving from New York to Florida.

*Card 1 * Four of Wands*

This card in the concern position indicated that leaving her family and the happiness and security it had always provided for her was a major issue. Being on her own for the first time, she knew she would miss her close-knit family life.

*Card 2 * Queen of Pentacles, reversed*

This card represented her mother, who had always indulged her daughter with material things but was a dominant, controlling woman. She was angry that her daughter wanted to move away and they had recently quarreled bitterly about the subject.

*Card 3 * Eight of Wands*

This card in the immediate future suggested that she would take a trip, probably by air. My advice to her was that she take her vacation in Florida and check out the job market and generally see how she felt about making her home there.

*Card 4 * Five of Pentacles*

This card representing what was uppermost in her mind was her fear that having never lived on her own, she would not being able to "make it" financially, the seed of which had been planted in her by her mother during the quarrel. It had grown into a veritable tree of self-doubt and she worried about her ability to manage money, pay rent, make car payments, and the rest.

*Card 5 * The Fool, reversed*

This card in the obstacle position indicated that she was afraid to take chances, feared risking "making a fool of herself" by not being able to manage and having to return home and admit failure.

*Card 6 * Ace of Pentacles*

This card appearing in the help position suggested that new money and opportunities for making money were coming to her and that her fears of homelessness and poverty were unfounded.

*Card 7 * The Sun*

The Sun card in the outcome position was an indication that she would be successful—in a sunny climate! The move to Florida would free her from the oppressive sense of guilt and obligation she felt to her parents for their support. The Sun card clearly said, "Go for it—I'm with you!"

General Life Conditions Spread (6 cards)

The Positions and Their Meanings

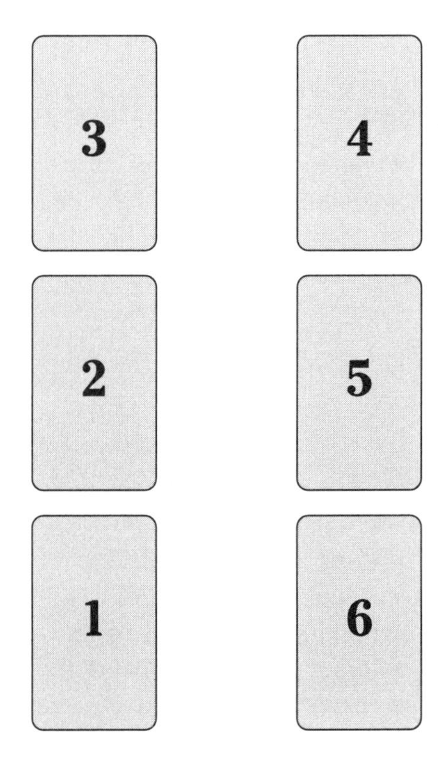

Card 1 * Who you are right now
Card 2 * What is affecting you
Card 3 * What you value
Card 4 * What's bothering you
Card 5 * The short-term
Card 6 * The long-term

An Example of a General Life Conditions Spread

The querent was a married woman with a learning disabled child and an unemployed husband.

*Card 1 * Ten of Wands*

The Ten of Wands in the "Who are you?" position said that she was carrying a full burden of responsibility on her shoulders but that she was managing the situation successfully and working hard toward bettering her life.

*Card 2 * Five of Pentacles*

Appearing in the "What's affecting you?" position, the Five of Pentacles indicated that money difficulties were a major concern. Due to her husband's current unemployment, she was the only earner and had to apply to receive food stamps.

*Card 3 * The Hierophant*

In the "What you believe in" position, the Hierophant indicated that her deeply felt religious belief was the glue holding her together during this time of trial and difficulty.

*Card 4 * Ace of Pentacles*

In the position of the short-term, the Ace of Pentacles said that new money was on its way to her and would arrive soon. She had a settlement pending as a result of an accident, and this Ace indicated it would be adjudicated quickly, that the money received would ease her situation.

*Card 6 * Ten of Cups*

In the long-term position, the Ten of Cups was a strong indication that her family would soon be moving into a new positive cycle. It indicated emotional well-being and happiness in family matters.

The Practical Advice Five-Card Spread

1 2 3 4 5

The Positions and Their Meanings

This is a simple spread made by laying the cards out from left to right in a single row.

Card 1 * Past influence
Card 2 * Present influence
Card 3 * Major influence
Card 4 * Advice
Card 5 * Outcome likely if advice is followed

An Example of a Practical Advice Five-Card Spread

The querent was a young man only a year away from graduating college. He was considering taking off a year in between graduation and starting to work and wanted advice.

*Card 1 * Ten of Wands*

This card in the position of past influence indicated that he had been carrying a heavy load for a long time, with a part-time job in addition to a full load of course work.

*Card 2 * Two of Pentacles*

This card in the position of present influence pointed to the fact that he was receiving money from more than one source as his parents helped out and he had a student loan as well as his part-time job. It further indicated that he was constantly juggling money matters, which put both external and internal pressure on him join the work force immediately after graduation.

*Card 3 * Four of Swords*

This card appearing in the major influence indicated that he was overtired and badly needed a rest. He needed time for respite and meditation, to be alone and get in touch with his inner self instead of being pushed about by outside circumstances and the expectations of others.

*Card 4 * The Fool*

The appearance of the Fool in the advice position indicated that he should have the experience of freedom and enjoy his youth, at least for a while, before buttoning himself up in the corporate venue. It was advice for him to go out and experience the world as a free spirit, to put aside his fears and worries about making the right career moves as soon as he graduated. He was being advised by the Fool to have faith, to take a leap into his unknown future, to go adventuring with a carefree attitude before settling down to the serious business of a lifetime of working.

*Card 5 * The World*

The World card in the position of the likely outcome, if he follows the Fool's advice, is that he will travel and see the world and in the end all will be well and success will be his. In other words, the world's his oyster if he goes willingly where the Fool leads.

The Immediate Situation Three-Card Spread

The Positions and Their Meanings

1 2 3

This simple, quick layout focuses on what is happening now.

Card 1 * The nature of the present situation
Card 2 * Your attitude toward what's happening
Card 3 * The key element for you to consider

An Example of an Immediate Situation Three-Card Spread

This easy layout is a good way to focus on a particular situation, clarify what's happening, and receive insight or a new perspective. This is a reading I gave for a married woman with two young children who called because she suspected her husband wanted a divorce, even though he had not actually said so.

*Card 1 * The Chariot*

In the position of the nature of the present situation, the Chariot indicated that she needed to stay centered and not get totally emotional about her suspicions, which were unproved. She had to steer a middle course between her conflicting thoughts and emotions and get at the real truth in order to get them both going forward in tandem and harmony, instead of pulling in opposite directions.

*Card 2 * Three of Swords*

The Three of Swords in the attitude position indicated that she had already made up her mind that they were going to separate. She was depressed and angry and in pain but felt no hope for mending the situation.

*Card 3 * The Empress*

The Empress card in the key position indicated that she needed to be mindful of herself as a mother as well as a wife, that she needed to address issues of communication with her husband, which were at the root of the problem. The Empress advised her to be more loving and nurturing and less critical of what she considered his shortcomings. She had Venus in Virgo, a placement with a tendency to criticize the lover. The Empress is related to Venus, which rules Libra, the sign of marriage, a sign that the marriage would survive if she would share her feelings and learn to give and receive love uncritically.

The Random-Draw Decision Spread (3 cards)

[Note: there is no formal layout for these cards; you simply shuffle, cut, fan out the deck, and draw out three cards.]

If all the cards are Major Arcana, the decision is a good one and you can make it in confidence.

If some of the cards are Major Arcana and some are Minor Arcana (Court cards count as Minor Arcana but should be considered as people if appropriate) you need to do some more thinking about the issue before coming to a firm decision.

If all the cards are Minor Arcana, the decision is a bad one and you should not make it.

Reading the meanings of the three cards will give you further information.

An Example of the Random-Draw Decision Spread

This was a reading I gave myself regarding dental surgery that had been recommended.

Card 1 * The Devil
Card 2 * The King of Swords, reversed
Card 3 * The Seven of Swords

One Major Arcana card, the Devil, and two Minor Arcana cards, the King of Swords and the Seven of Swords, indicated I needed to proceed cautiously before making a decision for root canal work. The Devil pointed me to Saturn and I discovered I had overlooked the fact that I was having a transit of Saturn, which rules bones and teeth, to my sixth House of health, which is occupied by Aries (the head). The King of Swords reversed indicated that the dentist was "knife happy" as he had proposed the surgery after only a cursory examination and one X-ray; I doubted his competence. The Seven of Swords indicated the situation was temporary, so I waited and, after the Saturn transit had passed the problem cleared up completely without any treatment. Later, a new dentist X-rayed the area and saw no problem.

The Yes/No Method

To use the Yes/No method, you need only decide which cards will represent "yes" and which "no," and then draw a single card from the deck, either from the top or at random, after the usual shuffling and cutting. There are no firm rules here, but here are some guidelines:

Major Arcana: Always YES if you are willing to work with the concept of the card.

Always NO if you are unwilling to do the work.

Minor Arcana: Even Numbers = YES
Odd Numbers = NO
Court Cards: King = NO
Queen = YES
Knight = NO
Page = YES

Upright: If YES, a definite YES.
If NO, a definite NO.

Reversed: If YES, there will be a delay.
If NO, there will be obstacles to prevent you.

Further information will be gained by reading the significance of the card that comes up.

An Example of the Yes/No Method

A client was thinking of buying a house in the country and unexpectedly found exactly what he was looking for but the price was higher than he wanted to pay. However, someone else had put a bid in and he had to make an immediate decision. He called me long distance for a "quickie" Yes/No reading. The card that came up was the Ten of Pentacles, upright. A definite YES. Since the Ten of Pentacles signifies acquisition of a home and success in money matters, I was able to advise him to buy the house in confidence that he would have the financial wherewithal. The card also indicated it was the right choice and that he would be happy there.

Creating Your Own Spreads

Now that you know what the cards mean and have seen, and hopefully practiced, a number of different layouts, you can feel free to design your own. I have created many spreads, some for general use with clients, some for a specific situation for a particular client, some for my own private use. You can do the same.

The basic idea of a spread is that it is a map of the reading you are going to do. Through the card pattern you use–like a blueprint for a house–you will build the reading. You can use as many or as

few cards as you like. You can expand on standard layouts—for example, the three-card spread can be expanded into a nine-card spread by signifying each layer of three as Past, Present, Future.

Or you can design a layout pattern yourself either by adapting an existing pattern or formulating one that is original to you. Many possibilities exist. You are limited only by your imagination and ability to risk.

To design an original layout, identify exactly what it is you want to know and examine those issues carefully. Then organize those issues into an ordered plan, marking each card's position in terms of what it will signify. By doing this, you are making the statement to your unconscious that you want specific answers to your questions, and telling it the method you are going to use to gain the information you are requesting.

Let's say a person has had an accident and thinks there is some deeper reason than bad driving and wants to explore that issue in depth. By dialoging with the readee, you go through a process of clarification by asking questions, such as "What role is this accident playing in my life now?"; "How did I participate in having this accident?"; "What purpose is the fact of the accident and its results serving in my life?" "Why did I have this accident?" "What am I getting out of having had this accident?" "Am I avoiding something by having had an accident?" and so forth.

You then organize the questions into a card plan, drawing your layout and marking in the answer-position of each card, numbering the card positions on the plan. You decide how many cards to allot for each question, or for ramifications of the questions, and then choose a layout shape that appeals to both you and your readee.

As you order the questions and place the card positions in the plan, some questions will be dropped and more added. Include the readee in the entire process. You might, for example, want to add to the above list such questions as "What are the past influences that led to the accident?" and/or "How will this accident affect my future?" and so on.

The visual pattern of the spread can be varied according to your personal inclinations: some people work best with linear shapes, some with circular patterns, some with rectangles or star shapes. You can combine both your concept and your aesthetic sense in the layout, for this is what assures it will allow your intuition to "speak" through it.

Chapter 14

Doing Readings

Using the Tarot for readings is an extremely personal and individual matter. There are many reasons why a person picks up a deck of Tarot cards and begins the study of their interpretation. And no two people will have exactly the same motivation. For myself, as I mentioned before, my exposure to the Tarot originally was merely as part of my study of symbolic art. At the time, I had no knowledge of, nor was I particularly interested in, the Tarot as a tool for doing readings.

Coincidentally, when friends discovered that I had a deck of Tarot cards that I was studying, they began to ask me to read for them. I knew very little about the process—and absolutely *nothing* about the power they possessed. I found out about this later in a most dramatic manner.

When someone would ask me to "throw the cards," I always used the most common layout, the Celtic Cross, which was the only one I knew as the books I possessed regarding Tarot were not about doing readings but about the mystical significance of the Major Arcana and the numerological significance of the Minor Arcana. I was quite young, in my late twenties, and because I didn't take doing readings seriously, I made the mistake that many novices make—I used readings as a parlor game, to amuse my friends.

One day, however, a particularly good friend asked me to do a reading for her. She and her husband and a couple of other friends were visiting and while we weren't actually having a party, it was a congenial social occasion. At first I told her there was too much activity going on—mostly lively conversation along with classical music, but she insisted. To find some quiet and privacy, we retired to my bedroom and sat on a small couch there. I shuffled and laid out the cards, noticing that the atmosphere had taken on a tone of seriousness. I no longer remember what I said or what cards came up, but some time later, after she had divorced her husband, she said to me, "You know, you predicted my divorce."

I could not have been more stunned. In my opinion, I had done no such thing, but then I couldn't remember much about the reading. However, apparently whatever it was that I said had hit a nerve with her. I had no idea whatsoever that the marriage was unhappy, as her husband was my friend as well as she.

It was at this point that I realized with a shock that the Tarot cards were not merely interesting symbolic art work but that they possessed real, tangible power. This revelation frightened me as I knew quite well that I had no training or experience in the use of such potentially devastating power. I got rid of the set of cards and it was many years before I took up the study of Tarot again, as a mature woman with considerable experience of human psychology and the world in general. This time, with an attitude of humility and respect, I engaged in serious and long-term work with the cards and was rewarded by having them "speak" to me whenever I laid them out either for myself or for others. The success given to me (for I do not claim it as my own but as a gift from the invisible powers) encouraged me to begin to practice Tarot readings as a professional.

Therefore, I begin this chapter on doing readings with a cautionary note: recognize at the start that you are dealing with a power you do not understand fully. Respect that power absolutely and never, *never* fool around with the cards for mere amusement or frivolous entertainment purposes.

Readings help me confront myself in a spirit of optimism. They bring up points of view I had not considered and often surprise me with a profound response to a superficial question. They remove me from the echo chamber of my own circular thoughts and give me a way to focus on a particular issue, a way to dialogue with myself. Just as the progress and direction of science is determined by the question we ask, so is our personal growth. Our questions express our vision, lead us into the future, focus a light in the realm of the unknown. Zen masters do not teach by lecturing. They wait until the student asks a question; only then is the student ready to hear the answer and mature enough to use the knowledge.

—Biochemist L.J. Shepherd, *New Realities*, May/June 1990

Choosing a Deck

Whether you choose a standard deck, such as the Waite-Rider, which is the most common deck and the one in use the longest, or a modern deck of which there is an almost unlimited variety, is strictly up to you. The illustrations in this book are based on the Waite deck, but the symbolism of the Major Arcana is the same in all decks, even if it is depicted through different themes (e.g., feminist, Native American, naturalistic, etc.) As for the number, or pip cards, since the illumination is purely decorative, and even in some cases contradicts the meaning of the card's number symbology, you may want to choose a deck in which the Minor Arcana are not illustrated. These non-illuminated decks are usually decorative in some manner even if they only indicate the card's suit and number. In this instance, you have both a thematic and an aesthetic choice, a purely individual matter.

Much will depend upon whether you are primarily a visual person or not. For some people, the pictures on the Minor Arcana serve as memory aids to the card's meanings. In some decks it's difficult to tell immediately if the pip card is upright or reversed; in others it's obvious. My advice is to look at a number of decks and if one strikes your eye as "just right" for you, try it out. If you are less adventurous, just start with the Waite deck as most books

The major producer of Tarot decks in the United States is:

U.S. Games Systems, Inc.
170 Ludlow Street
Stamford, CT 06902
(203) 353-8400

Another producer is:

Llewellyn Worldwide
P.O. Box 64383
St. Paul, MN 55164
1-800-639-9753

Llewellyn also publishes books on Tarot; call to request a catalog.

about the Tarot are based on those illustrations. However, some of the newer decks often come in a package with a book that interprets that particular deck according to the designer's intent.

Another method of choosing a deck is intuitively. If you use a pendulum, you can utilize that method successfully. Or, you can hold different decks in your hands, one at a time, close your eyes, and see what vibrations come through to you about the deck. Different decks give off different vibrations—but different people receive different vibrations from the same deck. Again, it is an individual matter.

If after using a deck for a while you do not feel entirely comfortable with it and its symbols, get another deck. You need a deck that will resonate with your own inner symbology, that is compatible with your own belief system. Therefore, if the symbols used make you anxious or uncertain, you have chosen the wrong deck. If you like the symbolism used and it seems to suit your personal point of view—possibly crystals, animals, herbs and flowers, or some abstract configuration—fine. Use the deck. Feeling an affinity for the deck you are using is essential.

When choosing a deck, bear in mind that the Minor Arcana (pip cards) are not to be taken at face value when illustrated, and always remember that the Minor Arcana are *not* for meditation. Any symbols on the number cards are arbitrary. There is no historical precedent for illustrating the pip cards; they are not derived from any ancient mystical tradition so far as historians can tell. Therefore, the illustrations should not distract you from interpreting them according to their suit and numerical divinatory meanings.

Using More Than One Deck

Many people like to have two or more decks, sometimes for different purposes. Earlier I suggested that you might want to keep one deck for your own personal use, especially if you are using the Tarot for spiritual development, and use another deck for readings. These can be identical or of two different designs.

As so many decks exist these days, with new ones coming off the presses regularly, there is a vast choice available. However, I do not suggest that you start out with several decks as this can lead to confusion. Master one deck first, using it until you thoroughly understand the symbolism and can remember the meanings of the

Minor Arcana number cards. Mastery of a single deck will make mastery of secondary or additional decks much simpler.

If after meditating on the Major Arcana of one deck you then meditate on the Major Arcana of a second deck, you will begin to intuitively understand the differences between the decks. Follow the same process given above for choosing a single deck for selecting additional decks: if any one of them does not seem "just right" to you, either discard it (give it away) or lay it aside for a time and go back to it later on. During the interim, you may have changed, your intuition may have reached a different level, and the deck may work. If it still doesn't feel right, discard it.

Reading for Yourself

Reading for yourself is in my opinion the best way to learn the cards. This is because you can check the information you get for accuracy and make adjustments in your interpretations as you compare actual events or inner states with what the cards are saying to you.

Of course the first thing you must do in order to do readings for yourself is to learn the meaning of the cards. As many of the spreads call for a Significator card, you should choose a Significator card to represent yourself from among the Court cards, picking the one that most nearly matches your personality, Sun sign (or other planet if you know your astrological chart), or review the list of Major Arcana cards used as Significator cards (see page 000) and choose one of those. Usually, your Court card will remain constant–for example, if you are a fire sign woman who holds down an executive job, and/or have light or reddish coloring, you would choose the Queen of Wands to represent you–but a Major Arcana card used as a Significator can change with the circumstances of the moment. For example, if you are attempting to become pregnant, or dealing with issues about motherhood, you would choose the Empress. If you are about to go backpacking around the world with no particular goal in mind, you'd choose the Fool. And so on.

The best and easiest way to learn the meanings of the cards for beginners is to set aside some time each day to work with the cards. *Always*, before using your cards take the time to put yourself into a relaxed state, both mentally and physically.

Instant Mini-Relaxation

Once you have fully experienced relaxation and fixed this sensation firmly in mind as a mental picture, you can achieve instant relaxation simply by calling up the image you have created of your totally relaxed self. To do this, take a comfortable position and remember what it felt like to be completely relaxed. Your subconscious mind remembers everything. Tell it that you are now going to take ten deep breaths, and when you have finished you will be as completely relaxed as when you went through the entire relaxation process previously. Then, slowly and gently begin to breathe, counting to ten breaths.

Create a quiet and contemplative atmosphere. Ideally, have a special place in which you study and read the cards. If you have an altar in a corner, or a separate room that can be reserved for the purpose, so much the better, but any space you can make sacred will suffice. Some people like to enhance the space with candles, scent, such as an aromatherapy device or incense, flowers, or special objects such as crystals or pictures. It is always a good idea to silently ask for divine guidance before using the Tarot cards for a reading. Whatever ritual gestures you make, they should be devised to put you in a calm and open state of mind so that your intuition can flow easily into the meanings of the cards.

When in a relaxed state, and you have an expectation of success and a sense of optimism that the card or cards that appear will provide useful information regarding the matter at hand, begin shuffling your deck while stilling your mind to receive information. At the same time, formulate your question about the issue and hold it in your mind while you handle the cards. If any cards pop out of the deck while you are shuffling, consider them significant—a message that they are important. You can either lay them to one side as a comment on the reading to come, or insert them back into the deck after deliberating on them and seeing how they apply to your query. Ordinarily, unless you choose a fixed pattern of shuffling, there will come a point when it will *feel right* to stop. At this point, lay the entire deck in a single stack and cut three times, with the left hand in the direction of left. Then, restack the cards in the reverse order.

If you are totally unfamiliar with the Tarot deck, I suggest you begin by using a one-card spread. To do this, after shuffling and cutting, you can either draw a card from the top of the deck or fan out the cards and select one at random. *Always* keep a record of the date and the name of the card in your Tarot notebook or journal. Study the card on your own at first, seeing what the images present to your imagination, how they relate to your question. Then, look up the meaning in the book and compare your untutored impression to the interpretation given in the book. Remember that the interpretations given here or in any other book on Tarot are not carved in stone. You are free to engage your intuition and use your imagination.

At first, your reactions to the individual cards may vary from seemingly nonsensical to extremely profound, or anything in

Rhythmic Breathing

Most adults are shallow breathers. They sip the air the way a Victorian lady sipped her cup of tea, and for the same reason—not to appear coarse. Taking in generous amounts of air seems impolite to many people, especially those who feel socially restricted and insecure about how others will view them. A good belly breath, like a good belly laugh, seems not to belong in polite company.

Breath, like food, nourishes our every cell, and cleanses our blood. But, like anorexics, we insist on starving ourselves of this vital nutrient. The good news is that changing breathing patterns is easy. Anyone can do it. Changing your breathing starts with becoming aware of it.

This is a simple, basic exercise, a form of relaxing meditation, a way to harmonize body, mind, and spirit. Just relax and close your eyes. Observe your breath pattern but do not make any attempt to alter it. Merely pay attention to the breath going in and coming out. Now, begin to breathe slowly and deeply. Breath in through the nostrils and out through the mouth. Feel the coolness of the in-breath of fresh air coming in; feel the warmth of used air leaving your body. Imagine yourself being cleansed and energized by each breath.

Next, listen to any sounds you make while breathing. Do not judge, just listen. Also notice whether you breathe in shallow or deep breaths, where the air goes, into the diaphragm or into the belly. Does your chest rise and fall or does your abdomen rise and fall?

As you inhale each breath, be aware of the flow of air coming into and leaving your body. Follow the inhalation/exhalation cycle and see if you can find the point where they intersect. Actually, breath is one continuous movement, but we tend to separate the in-breath from the out-breath when we think about breathing. Continue doing this for several minutes. The object is to become aware of your own breath, to monitor its natural cycle of movement, nothing more. Imagine it filling up all the cells of your body like you would fill a balloon by blowing air into it. Let the sense of being filled with *prana*, the vital force of life, spread throughout your body. Do not force or strain.

Breathing with Color

What breathing consciously does is to develop a communications link between consciousness and the unconscious, between body and mind, between spirit and psyche. Adding the factor of imagination increases the benefit. The following is a yoga exercise known as "polarization."

To do this exercise, lie face up in a comfortable position, either on your bed or on a mat on the floor. Align your body with feet pointing south and head north, to the Earth's magnetic field. Let your palms rest face up with the arms stretched out alongside the body. Begin breathing slowly and rhythmically, and as you breathe, breathe in one *color* and exhale another. If you breathe in a warm color, breathe out a cool color, and vice versa. If you want to energize yourself, breathe in a warm color such as red, the strongest; orange, which enlivens; or yellow, which promotes optimism. Breathe out a cool color, such a blue or green. For a calming or relaxing effect, do the opposite—breathe in a cool color and breathe out a warm color. Think of the incoming breath as a positive current, the outgoing breath as a negative current. By breathing in these two polar opposites, you are balancing your energy state toward health. Imagine these polarized currents circulating through your body, one after the other, cleansing and purifying, healing and revivifying.

between. No matter what your response is, take note, for later on when you review your journal (as you should do periodically) new significance will be revealed.

If the card seems particularly apropos to your question, you may want to keep it out of the deck and look at it several times during the day, noting what new or different thoughts and feelings it stirs in you. Note these also in your record. Then, before retiring, review the card and your notes about it. If you chance to have a dream or fantasy derived from the images on the card, record those also. Very often dreams will comment on the daily work of study and reading.

Continue this one-card process until you have worked through all seventy-eight cards in the deck. By then, you will have a good sense of what all the cards mean and how they can be applied to a given situation, and your interpretive skills will be developing. As you continue this daily exercise, review your notebook frequently. Compare your interpretations of the same card on different dates to see if, and how, they have changed. It is your personal experience with the cards in this manner that will form your primary source of information about the meanings.

Once you have acquired a working familiarity with all of the cards in the deck, expand your daily readings to more cards—three or five, or alternate between those spreads using the same procedure as described above for the one-card spread. When you start using more cards in your daily spreads, you will of course be getting more detailed information, which will give your intuition a workout.

Reading for Others

If your primary reason for studying and using Tarot for readings is predictions, or what is generally called fortunetelling, then I advise you to be extremely careful about any pronouncements you make, especially for others. Bear in mind always that in the psychic world there are many variables, that there is always a lot you don't know, even about your own psyche and psychological structure, and that today's situation may well change in the future. This is especially true of any negative cards that come up. It is best to speak of trends and possibilities, rather than make absolute statements *that apply to the future*. There is great

Sequential Relaxation Technique

Lie comfortably on the floor or on a bed and breathe deeply several times, consciously inhaling fresh energy and consciously exhaling all negative tension. Then, starting with your toes, focus on each part of your body in turn: feet, ankles, calves, knees, thighs, hips, lower back, upper back, abdomen, chest, arms, hands, spine, neck, head. As you do this, mentally instruct each part to relax completely and linger until you feel your muscles loosen. Tell each set of muscles to go limp and feel yourself gradually sinking into an inert state of being. When you have finished with this sequence, do it in reverse, from head to toes.

danger of creating a self-fulfilling prophecy if you make a definite statement of future harm, ruin, disaster, or other ill fortune. It is much better to say something like, "It looks to me there might be a person around you who can't be trusted," or "The indication is that you are experiencing anxiety and pain." Let the client or readee give you feedback to either confirm or deny your interpretation. If he or she can't relate to what you are saying, don't push it. The querent may not be able to hear or accept the negative interpretation, even if it is correct—and you have no way of knowing it *is* correct without the readee's validation. Always be extremely careful with the words you choose when giving readings for others. You cannot know their inner state of mind, or their level of psychological savvy, or their ability to be open, especially if you are reading for strangers.

Practicing Readings

In the beginning, it is always best to do practice readings for yourself until you have mastered the interpretations of the cards and developed your own slant on how they "speak" to you. The best method for practicing readings is to choose a particular layout, preferably a simple one, like the five-card spread, and each morning lay out the cards and do an interpretation, following the method given above for formulating your question, relaxing, and being intuitively open to receive the correct information.

Practice with the same layout daily for several days (two to four weeks is recommended) until it becomes "second nature" for you to be able to put together a whole picture from the cards in their different positions. Keep a careful record of the spread, which cards appeared, what question you asked, and your interpretation. Makes notes also of your day—how you felt, what was going on, even the weather, and especially the emotional tone. Were you distressed about something, elated or happy, moody, confused?

If you get poor results, it may be because you are not in the proper frame of mind or spirit. If this is the case, practice mind-clearing and concentrate on your relaxation exercises beforehand. Sometimes, the channel just isn't clear because of your own inner state of being. Do not let this deter you; as with learning any new skill, you will stumble and make mistakes, like hitting a wrong note

Breathing Relaxation

This is a simple technique that takes only a little time. Sit or lie down in a safe and comfortable spot with no distractions. Loosen any tight clothing, unbutton or untie anything that is restrictive on your body. Begin to breathe *consciously*, following your breath in and out of your lungs. Breathe in through the nostrils, out through the mouth. Pay full attention to your breath, in and out, in and out. Listen to the sound and feel the rhythmic pulsing of it. Continue this until you begin to feel calm and relaxed, a state usually signaled by the breath becoming slow and even.

You can deepen your relaxation using breath by imagining that you are breathing in *prana*, or the vital force of life, and exhaling all tension and negative feeling or experience. One way to do this is to choose a color for both the prana and the negative energy and to see a stream of one color (positive) coming into your body as you inhale and to see a stream of the other color (negative) flowing out of you as you exhale. White and black are easy—white is the pure energy of light while black represents any dark thoughts. But feel free to use any color that represents positive energy and release of negative energy to you. Don't worry if distracting thoughts arise. Let them float off (you can tell them you will attend to their needs later) like soap bubbles in the air and return to attending your breathing.

while learning a new piano piece. Just keep practicing regularly—that's the important thing.

Once you have thoroughly familiarized yourself with a simple layout, pick a more complex one, such as the Celtic Cross or one with more cards, and practice with it until you feel comfortable you understand all of the different card positions and how they relate to each other as a whole. Don't switch around from spread to spread; be consistent using one spread until you have mastered it. Your intuition will tell you when it is time to move on to more complicated methods, and as you become more sure of yourself and your understanding of the multilevel meanings of the cards, you can do variations on a theme layouts by asking for clarification and then pulling out one or more cards at random from the deck.

Continue on in this manner until you have learned the either all the spreads or two or three that appeal to you. Personally, I rarely use the Tree of Life spread, but I almost always use the Horoscope Spread. Do at least a few practice sessions with each spread just to find out how it sits with you. Some will have more appeal than others. Which spreads to use is a matter of personal choice, but in order to choose wisely you need at least a working knowledge of all the spreads. Later, you can feel free to create your own spreads, as explained in Chapter 13. You can also develop your own variations such as laying the cards all face down or all face up, or a combination of both, using random drawing, setting aside a Significator, and so on.

When doing practice readings for others, in the beginning it is best to stick to people that you know well, such as family and friends. This gives you the advantage of having information about the situation the reading is addressing. In such cases, the cards can quickly confirm what was only suspected, provide guidance out of a difficult situation, or affirm what is positive.

When doing practice readings for others, conduct an interview to determine what the querent wants to achieve from the reading so that you know in advance the purpose and question to which you can direct the reading. Sometimes it happens (actually, quite often in my experience) that the surface question is a screen for what's really on the person's mind. In such cases, the Tarot will almost always reach down deep and bring up the real issue.

Lotus Meditation

Breathe slowly and deeply several times and allow your body to relax completely. Imagine yourself a seed at the bottom of a deep pool where all is dark and tranquil. Feel yourself begin to put out roots into the nourishing bottom and anchor yourself there. Next, feel a stem begin to grow up and out of you, reaching upwards for the light above. Feel it move through the abyssal water until it breaks the surface. Then, feel yourself putting out little new leaves on the surface of the water, stretching in all directions.

Say to yourself, *I open to the possibilities within myself. Spirit flows through me as I open to my authentic self. All obstacles to the experience of my inner truth are now permanently removed.*

As these leaves grow larger and stronger, feel yourself growing into the bud of a beautiful lotus. Let this bud rest on the surface in the light for a few minutes, and then—slowly—begin to open up your petals, one by one, until you have unfurled a glorious blossom, fully opened and gently floating on its undulant stem, but firmly rooted in the earth at the bottom of the pond. Feel the light on your petals, soak up the warmth of the sun, breathe in the coolness of the air.

Say, *I am open. I am open. I now open fully to all my possibilities. I open to my inner powers. I release and let go all constraints, restrictions, limits. Whatever comes, I welcome. My openness brings happiness, pleasure, reward. I remain open to the light at all times. My roots are strong so I have no fear of being open. My state of openness brings me all good things.*

Remain with this feeling of being totally, safely, and completely open for as long as the feeling lasts. When it begins to fade, *slowly* return to waking consciousness by breathing gently and easily, continuing to feel yourself as open to your inner possibilities. Write down what you felt and thought during the meditation so that you can recall it.

Rest quietly until you feel yourself retracting into the bud state. Now that your lotus self has blossomed fully, you know you can always open when you wish. You do not need to be fully open all of the time—you can rest in the bud state, or even return to the seed state to gather new force.

Be prepared for emotional responses, even tears. I always keep a box of tissues at hand when doing readings. And, if the readee's response is tearful, be sure to reassure her or him that crying is not only okay but healing. People try to repress their tears of sorrow or pain because they feel embarrassed, shy, or guilty. It's up to you to provide reassurance. By reading for others, you take on certain responsibilities, one of which is giving aid and comfort, another is of being totally honest insofar as your interpretative skills allow. That's why it's best never to make hard-and-fast predictions but always to allow some leeway for a possible misinterpretation on your part or for hope that, if a situation is difficult or painful, things will get better for the querent.

Sometimes, of course, you may want to do readings just for fun—that is to say on matters of trivial importance, such as whether someone should go on a blind date, or how a vacation trip will turn out. This does not violate the rule of being serious and respecting the power of the cards so long as you are sincere and not trying to get yourself an ego-boost. Be prepared, however, even with minor questions that more serious issues may lurk underneath that will be surprisingly revealed by the Tarot cards.

In the final analysis, after studying textbooks and practicing, we discover that the cards mean what our intuition and experience tell us they mean in any given reading for a particular person. There are no absolute or definite set meanings for any of the cards; the basic interpretations here are intended as a guide for your own eventual interpretations. At some point, you will find that your experience suggests meanings that aren't in the books. Go with them, for it means your intuition has been accessed at a deep level and is providing accurate information. In a successful reading, it's the inner voice that's activated. It has the capacity to offer nuances of meaning previously not considered. This kind of intuitive awareness of the deeper significance of the cards is a result of disciplined study and practice.

We have mentioned that ethics are essential to the reading process and this point cannot be overemphasized. By doing readings for other people, you voluntarily accept the responsibility for your judgment and if you are in any way unsure about how to interpret a card you must be honest about it saying something like, "It appears to me that such-and-such may happen, but I'm not quite sure I'm getting this clearly." Have no reluctance to admit that the information flow is murky, blocked, or unclear. Remember that you are *practicing*, and learning. You are a novice, not a professional, and therefore must take extreme care how you present information to others. Never assume that you know it all or that you can make absolute pronouncements. It's also important to choose your words carefully and keep interpretations as clear and simple as possible. Avoid esoteric references and metaphysical explanations; do not confuse the issue with the use of technical terms that might be unfamiliar to your readee. Stick to plain English and offer your insights with the other person in mind. What we and the cards communicate to a querent is only valid if they provide useful information or a new perspective. It's as possible to be off-target as it is to be "right on."

Even after nearly twenty years of being a practicing professional, I am still very careful to assess the client's state of mind and prepare my own before a reading. At times, I have invalidated a reading and given the client back the fee because I felt something was blocking the information–usually the client being closed off. To do successful readings for others, there must be a state of rapport between the reader and the readee. Not only must the querent be open and willing to receive the information but the reader must acknowledge that he or she is nothing more than a *channel* for the transmission of knowledge that is being transmitted from a Higher Source.

Without realizing it, man possesses immense powers. He is "engendered from the fount of wonder and the fount of desire and intelligence." And his most vital faculty is his imagination—imagination in the sense that Paracelsus used the word, the faculty for reaching beyond himself, beyond his everyday life...the doors are open.

—Colin Wilson, *The Occult*

INDEX

EVERYTHING

Trade paperback, 304 pages
1-55850-806-6, $12.95

The Everything Dreams Book

by Trish & Rob MacGregor

When you dream, your unconscious mind is sending discreet messages that hold the keys to your personal happiness. You can use dreams as tools for better understanding yourself, solving problems, or even increasing creativity and productivity. You can enhance relationships and gain insight into your well-being. In fact, if you learn to program your dreams correctly, you may be able to experience the ultimate whole body experience, and travel back–or forward–into time.

The Everything Astrology Book

by Trish MacGregor

The Everything Astrology Book is a primer to the mysterious, often surprising world of astrology. While most of us know what sign we are born under, we only see its relation to ourselves in the context of the pithy comments found in newspapers or magazines. But these brief remarks don't tell the whole story. Astrology enables us to fully understand who we are, and how to reach our full potential. In this book, Trish MacGregor explains in a light, informative style everything you need to know in order to understand your astrological chart.

Trade paperback, 320 pages
1-58062-062-0, $12.95

Available Wherever Books Are Sold

If you cannot find these titles at your favorite retail outlet, you may order them directly from the publisher. BY PHONE: Call 1-800-872-5627. We accept Visa, MasterCard, and American Express. $4.95 will be added to your total order for shipping and handling. BY MAIL: Write out the full titles of the books you'd like to order and send payment, including $4.95 for shipping and handling, to: Adams Media Corporation, 260 Center Street, Holbrook, MA 02343. 30-day money-back guarantee.